The Design of Rabelais's *Pantagruel*

THE DESIGN OF RABELAIS'S *PANTAGRUEL*

EDWIN M. DUVAL

YALE UNIVERSITY PRESS
New Haven & London

Published with assistance from the foundation established in memory of Amasa Stone Mather of the Class of 1907, Yale College.

Designed by Sonia L. Scanlon
Set in Galliard type by Keystone Typesetting, Inc., Orwigsburg, Pennsylvania.
Printed in the United States of America by BookCrafters, Inc., Chelsea, Michigan.

Library of Congress Cataloging-in-Publication Data
Duval, Edwin M.
The design of Rabelais's Pantagruel / Edwin M. Duval.
p. cm.
Includes bibliographical references (p.) and index.
ISBN 0–300–04803–3 (alk. paper)
1. Rabelais, François, ca. 1490–1553? Pantagruel.
2. Rabelais, François, ca. 1490–1553?—Technique.
3. Epic literature, French—History and criticism.
4. Christian literature, French—History and criticism.
5. Humanism in literature. 6. Utopias in literature.
I. Title.
PQ1694.P63D88 1991
843′.3—dc20 90-12960

The paper in this book meets the guidelines for permanence and durability of the Committee on Production Guidelines for Book Longevity of the Council on Library Resources.

10 9 8 7 6 5 4 3 2 1

Tuque ideo nisi mente prius, nisi pectore toto
Crebra agites quodcumque canis, tecumque premendo
Totum opus aedifices, iterumque, iterumque retractes,
Laudatum alterius frustra mirabere carmen.
Nec te fors inopina regat, casusque labantem.
Omnia consiliis provisa, animoque volenti
Certus age, ac semper nutu rationis eant res.

Marco Girolamo Vida
De arte poetica 2.156–62 (1527)

Eundem enim foetum conceperam, sed de editione angebar equidem animo atque intimis sensibus. Et si enim argumentum ipsum excogitationem non habebat difficilem, non facile tamen videbatur rudem et congestitiam molem enucleate, apte et concinne digerere.

Rabelais, dedicatory epistle to Jean Du Bellay
In Marliani, *Topographia antiquae Romae* (1534)

Il est impossible de renger les pieces, à qui n'a une forme du total en sa teste.

Montaigne, *Essais* 2.1 (1580)

CONTENTS

ACKNOWLEDGMENTS

The larger project of which this book is a part has received generous support from many sources over the past ten years, for which I am happy to have this occasion to express my gratitude at last. I am particularly grateful to the John Simon Guggenheim Foundation for a Research Fellowship in 1983–84 and to the University of California for a Regents' Junior Faculty Fellowship in 1979 and a Regents' Humanities Fellowship in 1983. I also wish to thank the University of California for academic leaves in 1980, 1983, and 1987 and Yale University for an academic leave in 1989. Without the liberality of these institutions this book would have remained a vague hunch.

Many students, colleagues, and friends have prodded this book into existence over the years with their questions, criticisms, and erudition. Terence Cave, Anthony Grafton, Michel Jeanneret, Raymond C. La Charité, George W. Pigman III, François Rigolot, Walter Stephens, and André Tournon, especially, offered not only models of what scholarship and criticism can be but the kind of informed resistance and generous debate that makes the academic life worth living. Most of all I am indebted to three friends whose example has been a constant inspiration to me, and whose advice, encouragement, and patience have helped me through many difficult passages and dark hours. To Gérard Defaux, to Richard Helgerson, and to David Quint this book owes its existence, and to them it is gratefully dedicated.

Two portions of this study have appeared elsewhere in a substantially different form. Chapter 2 recasts and expands the argument of "Pantagruel's Genealogy and the Redemptive Design of Rabelais's *Pantagruel*," *PMLA* 99 (1984), 162–78. Chapter 3 includes a few pages excerpted and modified from "The Medieval Curriculum, the Scholastic University, and Gargantua's Program of Studies (*Pantagruel,* 8)," in *Rabelais's Incomparable Book: Essays on His Art,* ed. R. La Charité (Lexington: French Forum, 1986), pp. 30–44. I wish to thank the Modern Language Association of America and Raymond C. La Charité of French Forum Monographs for their kind permission to use here the material contained in those articles.

A NOTE ON TEXTS AND ABBREVIATIONS

The text of Rabelais used here is that of the *Oeuvres complètes* edited by Pierre Jourda and published in two volumes by Garnier. Quotations from Rabelais's major works will be identified in the text by title, chapter, and page number in this edition (see list of abbreviations below). Quotations from minor works will be similarly identified by volume and page number in Jourda. I have occasionally modified Jourda's text (which for the *Pantagruel* is based on the "definitive" edition of 1542) to reflect readings from earlier editions. All such modifications are clearly identified as variants and, in the case of 1532 readings, accompanied by chapter and page numbers referring to V. L. Saulnier's edition of the *editio princeps.* In the rare instances where the Jourda or the Saulnier texts are faulty I have emended them to conform to the appropriate original edition. For variant readings I have relied on the unfinished critical edition of the *Oeuvres* begun in 1913 by Abel Lefranc and his team.

The text of Erasmus's works is that of the Clericus edition of the *Opera omnia.* Because the superb North-Holland edition, which is destined to supersede that eighteenth-century classic, is not yet complete, simplicity and the reader's convenience seemed to demand that all references be made to the Clericus edition and identified simply by volume and column number in the "*Opera.*"

Quotations from the Bible generally follow the text of the Revised Standard Version (RSV) but depart from it whenever necessary to reflect the meaning of the text Rabelais and his readers knew and used—most often that of the Latin Vulgate, occasionally that of the Greek New Testament and Septuagint, and in a few cases that of the Hebrew Bible. I have indicated all such departures from the RSV in brackets.

Unless otherwise indicated, quotations from Greek and Latin literature are from the editions of the Loeb Classical Library. Wherever textual detail is crucial to my argument I have quoted instead from sixteenth-century editions that would have been easily available to Rabelais and his readers, indicating my sources in the notes and bibliography. In the case of some Greek words this has meant quoting from a standard Renaissance

Latin translation. All translations from Greek and Latin into English are my own.

Principal abbreviations used throughout these pages are the following:

AP	*Ars poetica*
BHR	*Bibliothèque d'Humanisme et Renaissance*
CL	*Cinquiesme Livre*
ER	*Etudes Rabelaisiennes*
G	*Gargantua*
HN	*Historia naturalis*
Met	*Metamorphoses*
P	*Pantagruel*
PL	*Patrologia Latina*
PMLA	*Publications of the Modern Language Association of America*
QL	*Le Quart Livre*
RHLF	*Revue d'Histoire Littéraire de la France*
RQ	*Renaissance Quarterly*
STFM	Société des Textes Français Modernes
THR	Travaux d'Humanisme et Renaissance
TL	*Le Tiers Livre*
TLF	Textes Littéraires Français

INTRODUCTION

THE DESIGN OF RABELAIS'S CHRISTIAN HUMANIST EPICS

What literature has in common with painting, according to Horace, is that some poems, like some paintings, are best judged when examined attentively at close range, others when viewed more globally from a distance:

> Ut pictura poesis: erit quae, si propius stes,
> Te capiat magis, et quaedam, si longius abstes.
> [*AP* 361–62]

Horace's point is simply that in judging large works—whether paintings or poems—the critic must not focus myopically on the weakest parts but must broaden his view to consider the overall effect of the whole. If Homer occasionally nods, he may be excused by the vast, epic proportions of his poems (*AP* 347–60).

But the distinction between microscopy and macroscopy is useful for interpreters as well as for judges of literature. In coming to terms with large and complex works we are often tempted to stand too close, so to speak, and to scrutinize small details without stepping back to consider their place and function within the larger picture of the whole. The result can easily be an imperfect sense—or a partial sense, or even no sense at all—of what the work is all about.

The long narrative works of François Rabelais have suffered perhaps more than those of any major author from this kind of interpretive microscopy. Even the best of readers tend to focus on individual episodes and details isolated from their context and to arrive at a general view only indirectly and inductively by selecting, combining, and interpreting at will a limited number of smaller parts.

This tendency is perhaps understandable. Many superficial aspects of Rabelais's books—their apparent spontaneity and exuberance, their comic truculence, their inconsistencies and internal contradictions, their episodic structure, their radical open-endedness—conspire to suggest to postclassical readers not a coherent and ordered composition but something akin to those grotesque composite images described by Horace, which start as a beautiful woman and end as an ugly fish—ridiculous, incoherent forms like the dreams of a sick man in which neither the beginning nor the end corresponds to the middle:

> . . . cuius, velut aegri somnia, vanae
> Fingentur species, ut nec pes nec caput uni
> Reddatur formae.
>
> [*AP* 7–9]

From these appearances has been derived an implicit but almost universal assumption that Rabelais's books are not really works at all but rather miscellaneous "texts," Menippean grab bags of discrete, tenuously related episodes whose order and number could be modified without significantly altering the meaning of the whole.[1] Such a view would seem to justify and even to require a myopic focus on its individual parts.

The present study takes its point of departure in the conviction that this widely held assumption of formal incoherence is mistaken and that, superficial appearances and received ideas notwithstanding, each of Rabelais's books is a complete, whole, and meticulously ordered *work* in the fullest sense of the word. As such each belongs squarely in Horace's second category of paintings and poems that "te capia[n]t magis . . . si longius abstes" (*AP* 362). This is not to suggest that careful attention to the smallest details is not indispensable for an adequate understanding of Rabelais's books, but rather that every episode and virtually every detail is subordinated to a coherent, overarching design that must be clearly apprehended before any particular episode or detail may be properly understood.[2]

By *design* I mean not the kind of thematic unity or general coherence of vision that might be inferred from the sum of a work's several parts, but rather a master plan that appears to have preceded and governed the composition of each of Rabelais's books, that is meant to be discerned by the reader even before he has arrived at an understanding of any single episode, and that functions as a guide toward a proper understanding of not only the whole work but also its constituent parts. Consisting in an overall structure and not in the words that fill the structure out, it exists independently of the local, textual ambiguities that have elicited so many divergent interpretations and, transcending them, provides the stable perspective from which all such ambiguities may be properly understood.

Design in this sense is thus simultaneously an intention, a structure, and a built-in hermeneutic device. It is a sure and indispensable guide to correct interpretation that reveals, through form, the meaning and most profound intentions of the work.

In keeping with this fundamental conviction I have undertaken in this study to read the first of Rabelais's Pantagrueline books not as a mere text or collection of unrelated texts but as an integral, organic work informed by a clear and meaningful design. To this end, rather than proceed from a close examination of a few parts to a more general interpretation of the whole, I have deliberately begun with the Horatian long view, moving closer to examine problematic episodes and details only after their place and function within the overall design have been clearly understood.[3]

But design as I have found it to function in Rabelais's works is not simply a matter of pure, universal form that is immediately obvious and intelligible to all readers of all times. As the expression of an intention it involves a point of view and a complex of opinions and judgments relating to a specific historical moment, and an ideology unique to a culture very remote from our own. As a built-in hermeneutic device it is a culturally determined means of communication fashioned to be deciphered by a specific group of readers whose experience with literature and habits of reading were radically different from those of readers today. This being the case, the macroscopic perspective necessary to perceive an overarching design must constantly be supplemented by an even broader historical perspective, without which any such design would remain largely unintelligible. I have therefore made every effort to bring to the *Pantagruel* as much as I could of the knowledge, beliefs, experience, expectations, and habits of mind that it presupposes in its readers, so as to respond to its design in something approaching the way it was fashioned to make its readers respond.

I have found two general contexts to be particularly important in this regard. One is strictly literary and involves the traditions and the conventions that determine what we would today call its genre. Genre is of course intimately related to questions of design, for not only is the structure of a work determined in large part by its genre but, as Alastair Fowler has argued, genre is itself an "instrument of meaning" in that literary works actually produce meaning through deliberate "modulations or departures" from recognizable but constantly evolving generic norms (*Kinds of Literature,* esp. pp. 22–23). If this is so then it is obviously a matter of extreme importance not to mistake the generic pretensions of works whose overall design and meaning we wish to understand.

To read Rabelais's books as "novels," "comedies," "satires," or "chronicles," as modern readers have variously done, is to expect from them a design they do not or cannot possibly have. Worse yet, it is to force them to work within a framework of norms and conventions very different from those they are specifically designed to modulate, and consequently to overlook their specific literary meaning while reading into them an entirely inappropriate one. Even read as "romances" these books are bound to be seriously misunderstood. Their utter disregard for women and love, and especially their strict unity of hero and action, clearly set them apart from a genre whose most characteristic features are courtly eroticism and multiple plots and heroes.[4]

All of Rabelais's works identify themselves in one way or another—through various patterns, allusions, echoes, and what Fowler calls "generic signals"—as epics of a kind. This is most obviously true of the *Pantagruel*. From the very beginning this self-proclaimed sequel to a burlesque Arthurian epic constantly points to its own epic pretensions. Its subject is a single heroic action performed after due preparation by a single epic hero. And as we shall see the *Pantagruel* as a whole, like all of Rabelais's books, conforms not only to many of the most immutable characteristics of epic but even to a strict Aristotelian definition of ἐποποιία. Its story is constructed "dramatically around a single piece of action, whole and complete in itself, with a beginning, middle, and end, so that like a single living organism it may produce its own peculiar form of pleasure" (*Poetics* 1459a 23.1). And despite its episodic structure it is not so long, so complex, or so rich in the "reversals, discoveries, calamities," or "diverse episodes" permitted to epic that it cannot be "perceived as a whole in a glance, from beginning to end" (1459b 24.2, 5, 7).

In short, the *Pantagruel* demands to be read primarily as an epic, inscribed in the heroic tradition illustrated by the *Iliad*, the *Odyssey*, the *Aeneid*, and later *chansons de geste* like the chronicles of Turpinus and *Fierabras*. Only by doing so will we be able to discover the full implications of its design and the new meaning it generates by modulating, innovating, transforming, and subverting the norms and conventions of the genre.

The second context I have found to be indispensable for a proper understanding of the *Pantagruel*'s design is the more broadly cultural and intellectual one commonly referred to as Christian humanism. By qualifying Rabelais's epic as "Christian humanist" from the outset I mean to identify not so much the ideology that it is designed to express—for this is a matter to be proved, not taken as a point of departure—but simply the matrix of texts and attitudes within which the book is designed to function, to which it constantly alludes, and through which it signifies by a process we today would call intertextuality.

For although Rabelais obviously wrote his first book to be understood and enjoyed by virtually everyone, it is equally obvious to anyone who has read Rabelais with some degree of attention that he designed all his books to be understood and enjoyed most fully by the small community of readers who knew the languages of humanism and could recognize tags, allusions, and resonances from classical, biblical, and modern humanist texts. If we were to read the *Pantagruel* as aliens, ignorant of the languages it speaks and unfamiliar with the humanistic culture it shares with the readers to which it was principally addressed, then we would certainly misunderstand its nature as a work and misinterpret the most profound implications of its design, whatever else we might be able to make of the words on the page of the "text." Only to the degree that we are able to enter the community of intended readers by bringing to the *Pantagruel* the Christian humanist culture it presupposes in us will we be successful in making sense of its design.

Here a word of caution is perhaps in order. By setting aside the comic and "popular" aspects of the *Pantagruel* to focus almost exclusively on its humanistic erudition and its higher, serious meanings, the following pages are likely to give the impression of an arbitrary preference for high culture over low, or of an a priori judgment that the importance of the book lies more in its humanism than in its humor. This is not at all the case. It is rather an inevitable consequence of the fact that the fundamental, overarching design of the *Pantagruel* is revealed through elements whose humor is extraneous to their function of revealing design, that the design itself is by nature neither serious nor comic but rather a neutral structure and guide to interpretation, and that the primary meanings to which the design leads us turn out to be relatively serious meanings that can only be qualified as "Christian humanist." In short, the boisterous, ribald, good-natured humor so characteristic of Rabelais's first book proves on inspection to be essentially extrinsic to its fundamental design, and therefore to the focus of this study.

This is not to say that the comic, the low, the obscene are somehow extraneous or irrelevant to the work itself. On the contrary, since my thesis is precisely that Rabelais's books are true works in which *everything* is strictly subordinated to a single overarching design and integrated into a perfectly coherent whole, then this study can fairly be said to fail unless it can demonstrate that the *Pantagruel*'s most popular forms of expression and crudest forms of humor are not only compatible with the serious meanings to which its design leads us, but are necessary and integral to the work itself. Such a demonstration indeed forms a crucial part of my argument, but it cannot be undertaken until the design of the work and the meanings to which it points have been fully understood. For this reason and this reason alone I have put off consideration of the most obvious aspects of the *Pantagruel* until the end.

The reader's indulgence is therefore begged in advance for what may first seem a partial and tendentious treatment of the *Pantagruel,* or at best a backward approach to the most conspicuous aspects of the book. In the epilogue I have tried to show how the Christian humanism of the *Pantagruel,* far from residing only in serious meanings separable from and unrelated to the popular medium through which they are expressed, is an all-encompassing ideology that embraces both content and form, serious and comic, high and low, sacred and profane in a single coherent view, and that low style and coarse, popular humor are in fact crucial to its meaning in a way that shortcuts to such a conclusion would not have allowed us even to imagine.

My single aim throughout this book has been to determine as precisely, as accurately, and as completely as possible what the *Pantagruel* is about—what it is supposed to mean and how it means what it does. This is not the same thing as proposing to reduce an obviously complex work to a single valid meaning, or undertaking to exhaust all its possible meanings. My purpose has been rather to arrive at what I believe must be viewed as the primary meanings of the work—immanent, stable, fundamental meanings from which all others can be shown to derive and which establish clear limits within which further interpretation may legitimately operate. Having discovered these meanings I have not undertaken to explore the vast range of secondary meanings these generate and sanction. My conclusions about design and meaning are offered not as a last word on the *Pantagruel* but, on the contrary, as a first step toward a more complete and coherent understanding, and a foundation on which valid interpretation may continue to build. If design in Rabelais is everything I believe it is and have tried to show it is here, then there should be virtually nothing in this difficult and complex work whose presence cannot eventually be accounted for, whose relation to everything else cannot eventually be explained, and whose full range of possible meanings cannot eventually be understood and guaranteed, by its design.

1

THE *AENEID*, REVELATION, AND ALCOFRYBAS'S EPIC NEW TESTAMENT

More than any other of Rabelais's books, the *Pantagruel* strikes modern readers as a hodgepodge of semiautonomous satirical and parodic episodes thrown together with little regard for sequence, coherence, or unity—a Menippean satire, in short, or rather a "roman de verve."[1] Yet in spite of its episodic and apparently haphazard composition, the *Pantagruel* as a whole does conform to a certain linear plan whose broad lines are obvious to everyone. It has long been recognized that the *Pantagruel* follows the basic canonic structure of the medieval epic romance by tracing first the birth, then the education, and finally the heroic exploits of a single hero.

Less commonly recognized, perhaps, are the compelling relations among the three distinct parts of this sequence and the strong sense of direction they lend to the basic plan. Pantagruel is predestined from the very beginning of the book to perform a particular heroic exploit. At the moment of his birth Gargantua foresees, "en esperit de prophetie," that his newborn son will someday be a "dominateur des *alterez*" (emphasis mine), and his prophecy is immediately corroborated by a miraculous "signe plus evident" which the midwives, also "en esperit propheticque," interpret to mean that the infant "fera choses merveilleuses" (*P* 2:231). Pantagruel's heroic exploits at the end of the epic—his victory over the invading armies of Dipsodes and his subsequent conquest and colonization of Dipsodie—clearly mark the fulfillment of this initial prophecy, since "Dipsodes," as a native informant points out, "vault autant à dire comme gens *alterez*" (*P* 26:347–48, emphasis mine).

As for Pantagruel's education, it is specifically designed to prepare the hero for his predestined role. Gargantua concludes his famous letter to

Pantagruel by exhorting his son to become an "abysme de science: car," he explains in the crucial but generally unheeded justification of that famous phrase, "doresnavant que tu deviens homme et te fais grand, il te fauldra yssir de ceste tranquillité et repos d'estude et apprendre la chevalerie et les armes pour defendre ma maison, et nos amys secourir en tous leurs affaires contre les assaulx des mal faisans" (*P* 8:261). These "mal faisans" are none other than the Dipsodes, who will soon transgress their borders, invade Gargantua's realm, and besiege the Utopian city of the Amaurotes (*P* 23:335). Pantagruel's education is thus explicitly linked to the exploit to come. It is intended to prepare him to repel the Dipsodes and thereby to become "dominateur des alterez."

Clearly, the sequence of birth–education–exploit is not simply a convenient narrative formula serving only to accommodate the most heterogeneous episodes in a rambling and directionless Menippean satire. Rather it marks the crucial stages in an irresistible, forward-moving progression from promise, to preparation, to fulfillment of a preordained epic mission. The role of "dominateur des alterez" prophesied at the beginning is the predestined end toward which Pantagruel's career inexorably leads and the telos toward which the epic progresses.[2] With respect to its hero and action, then, the *Pantagruel* is a perfectly linear, powerfully teleological heroic narrative that is worlds removed from amorphic Menippean satire, and even from the multiple heroes, multiple actions, and complex chronologies of late medieval and Ariostan romance. In spite of its episodic elaboration and superficial appearance of spontaneity, it respects to an astonishing degree the not-yet-current Aristotelian requirement that an epic be the dramatic representation of a single, whole, and complete action with a clearly identifiable beginning, middle, and end (*Poetics* 1450b 7.1–7 and 1459a 23.1; compare Horace, *AP* 152).

In subject, moreover, the *Pantagruel* is manifestly heroic. The single exploit for which Pantagruel is predestined, and that marks the climax of his epic, is a military and political one very much like those of all epics in the tradition of the *Iliad,* from Homer down to Turpinus. But of all epics, the *Aeneid* seems to provide the most direct model for the *Pantagruel.* Both the *Pantagruel* and the *Aeneid* are imperial epics in which an elect hero, acting with divine sanction and assistance, accomplishes a predestined military victory over a predestined adversary that results in the colonization of an indigenous population and the implantation of a new, preordained, utopian order. Aeneas's predestined victory in single combat with Turnus and eventual conquest of the Lavinians is accomplished to prepare for the establishment of an empire to end all empires and a universal pax romana. Similarly, Pantagruel's predestined victory in single combat with Loup Garou and conquest of the Dipsodes result in the establishment of a colony in Dipsodie, a universal "liesse divine," and what is pointedly called a return of the Golden Age ("Ce feut un renouvellement du temps de Saturne, tant y fut faicte lors grande chere," *P* 31:374).

Pantagruel, future "roy des Dipsodes," is in fact compared to Aeneas at two crucial moments of his epic *gesta*. The first occurs in chapter 9, just as the hero is about to take on his requisite *comes,* or epic companion. At the conclusion of his first meeting with Panurge, Pantagruel casts himself in the role of Aeneas, and his future *comes* in the role of *fidus Achates:* "Vous et moy ferons un nouveau pair d'amitié," he explains, "telle que feut entre Enée et Achates" (*P* 9:269). The second moment occurs in chapter 24, when Pantagruel is about to set sail for Utopie where he will accomplish at last the specific epic exploit for which he has been chosen. In his haste to leave Paris and return to his native land, Pantagruel has neglected to take leave of a certain Parisian lady "laquelle il avoit entretenue bonne espace de temps" (*P* 23:337). Accused by her of disloyalty, he is tempted to return to make his peace with her. But because the slightest delay could spell disaster for Utopie, Epistemon persuades him to put *patria* before personal attachments. He does so by assimilating the hero to Aeneas, and the Parisian lady to the Carthaginian queen Dido: "Luy reduyt à memoire le departement de Eneas d'avecques Dido, et le dict le Heraclides, Tarentin, que, la navire restant à l'ancre, quand la necessité presse, il fault coupper la chorde plus tost que perdre temps à la deslier" (*P* 24:340).

Except for its comic low style, then, and the fact that it begins ab ovo, "au commencement du monde" (*P* 1:221), rather than in medias res, Rabelais's first work is, in its broadest outline, not only entirely coherent and teleological but generally faithful to the classical epic tradition from which it ultimately derives, and particularly to the single greatest model of the political epic, the *Aeneid.*

But knowledge of the underlying coherence and direction of the *Pantagruel* does not go very far in helping us understand what the book is actually *about*. How, exactly, are we to understand a popular, comical, and often ribald rewriting of Vergil's great epic in which Aeneas has been transformed into a giant drawn from popular theater, and in which style and tone have been downgraded accordingly? Is this merely burlesque or, as in the case of the *Aeneid,* is some higher purpose involved? And what are we to make of the abundant satirical episodes that are inserted into the broad outline of the epic? Are they mere filler or, on the contrary, are they the real meat of the book? Are they essentially independent from the overall structure that contains them or subordinated to it in some meaningful way? To answer these fundamental questions we need some further indication of the direction and intention of the book. We need to look for an overarching design that is more comprehensive and specific than the epic pattern governing its broad lines, one that will direct our interpretation of it.

Rabelais offers an important glimpse at such a design in the opening pages of the volume where his fictional narrator, Alcofrybas, speaking to us directly from the prologue and addressing us as "très illustres et très chevaleureux champions" (*P* prol:215), prepares us, his heroic readers, to receive in the appropriate manner the heroic narrative that follows.

The ostensible purpose of the prologue is merely to present the *Pantagruel* as a thing of great value from which readers will derive incalculable profit. Alcofrybas develops this single idea through a sustained comparison between his own book and the runaway best-seller of 1532, the *Grandes et inestimables Chronicques de l'enorme geant Gargantua*. The *Pantagruel*, he claims, is both a sequel—a "livre de mesme billon"—and superseder to the *Chronicques,* which will prove to be even truer and more useful than the earlier book: "un peu plus equitable et digne de foy que n'estoit l'aultre" (218). The first two-thirds of the text simply establish the *Grandes Chronicques* as a fixed point of comparison, a veritable paragon of veracity and utility, in relation to which the *Pantagruel* can then be said, in the second part of the prologue, to be even more true and more profitable.

In the first part of the prologue Alcofrybas makes his absurd case for the *Chronicques* through an extended use of the *utile dulci* topos. His basic thesis, stated at the end of the second paragraph, is simply that in this funny little book "il y a plus de fruict [*utile*] que par adventure ne pensent un tas de gros talvassiers tous croustelevez, qui entendent beaucoup moins en ces petites joyeusetés [*dulce*] que ne faict Raclet en l'*Institute*" (*P* prol:216). He goes on to support this claim by citing three specific circumstances in which the *Chronicques* have proved to be particularly beneficial: they have provided (1) a "refuge de reconfort" against the chagrin of a disappointed hunter; (2) a "remede plus expedient" than medicine for the physical affliction of a toothache; and (3) "consolation" and "allegement manifeste" for patients undergoing the excruciating sixteenth-century cure for venereal disease.

All three of these examples describe a perfectly natural phenomenon, of course—the well-attested capacity of pleasure caused by "petites joyeusetés" to bear "fruict" by lifting spirits or distracting the mind from physical pain. But Alcofrybas transforms these examples through comic and increasingly hyperbolic language into examples of quasi-supernatural phenomena: occult cures and miracles wrought by the physical application of a volume to the source of pain, or the incantational recitation of a magical text like the life of Saint Margaret. This comic transformation then allows Alcofrybas to conclude the first part of his prologue by restating his original thesis in even stronger terms, claiming that there exists *no* book, "en quelque langue, en quelque faculté et science que ce soit" that possesses "telles vertus, proprietés et prerogatives" as the *Grandes Chronicques* (217), and that although some books do have "certaines proprietés occultes," these properties are in no way comparable to the "grand emolument et utilité" that everyone knows from infallible personal experience to reside in the *Chronicque Gargantuine* (218). Such, then, is the miraculous and heretofore literally incomparable book that the *Pantagruel* will supersede, as a "livre de mesme billon" but "un peu plus equitable et digne de foy que n'estoit l'aultre."

This simple comparison, which mocks the success of a ridiculous and rather inconsequential little burlesque epic by praising it as a paragon of veracity and utility, was undoubtedly very amusing to the first readers of the *Pantagruel*, who most likely bought their copy of Rabelais's chapbook at the same Lyon fair where they had bought the *Chronicque Gargantuine* some six months earlier. And it undoubtedly succeeded very well in its stated purpose of establishing this new book as a worthy, and in fact much funnier, sequel to the earlier chronicles. But in that same comparison we may perhaps discern a more important purpose as well.

In the process of exaggerating the veracity and utility of the *Chronicques* and mocking their huge success, Alcofrybas draws a deliberate and consistent parallel between them and sacred texts. We chivalrous readers, he reminds us, have believed those chronicles as "vrays fideles . . . tout ainsi que texte de Bible ou du sainct Evangile" (215 var.; Saulnier, p. 3).[3] He praises us for doing so and goes on to exhort us to put aside all other occupations in order to devote ourselves entirely and exclusively to studying the precious chronicles. He even asks us to learn them by heart so that the hidden "fruict" they contain might not perish with the perishable volumes in which they are recorded but be kept alive forever in the hearts of those who have learned them, and be passed down orally from one generation to the next, to all future generations. This implicit allusion to the traditional oral law of Mishnah, or even to the rabbinic Tradition itself (Cabala = *traditio*), was made explicit in a later (1537) addition to the original text: "affin que . . . un chascun les peust bien au net enseigner à ses enfans, [1537: et à ses successeurs et survivens bailler comme de main en main, ainsy que une religieuse Caballe]" (215–16). And finally, he informs us that thanks to the widespread recognition of the "emolument et utilité" of the *Chronicques,* more copies of that miraculous book have been sold in two months "qu'il ne sera acheté de Bibles en neuf ans" (218).

This hyperbolic assimilation of the *Chronicques* to sacred literature is typical of a certain strain of late medieval humor. As such it might easily be dismissed as entirely inconsequential if the second part of the prologue did not contain specific echoes and quotations from the Bible, whose sole purpose, it would seem, is to develop the consequences of that assimilation in a rather unexpected way.

In support of his contention that the *Pantagruel* is even more "equitable et digne de foy" than the *Chronicques,* Alcofrybas maintains his absolute truthfulness as a narrator by claiming to speak "comme sainct Jehan de l'Apocalypse: *quod vidimus testamur*" (218 var.; Saulnier, p. 7).[4] The emphasis here is on complete and direct "revelation" (ἀποκάλυψις) of revealed truth. Alcofrybas's account, like John's, will be a full, firsthand account of things vouchsafed to him and actually *seen* by him as an eyewitness. And indeed his claim echoes closely the words with which the Revelation of "sainct Jehan" begins: "The revelation [ἀποκάλυψις] of Jesus Christ, which God gave him to show to his servants what must soon take place; and he made it known by sending his angel to his servant John, who bore witness [*testimonium*] to the word of God and [. . .] of Jesus Christ, even to all that he saw [*quaecumque vidit*]. . . . I heard behind me a loud voice like a trumpet saying, 'Write what you see in a book' [*quod vides, scribe in libro*]" (Rev 1.1–2, 10–11).

But this simple, burlesque claim to authority, authenticity, and absolute veracity takes on its full significance only when it is read in its complete context: "Car," explains Alcofrybas, "ne croyez pas . . . que j'en parle comme les Juifz de la Loy. . . . J'en parle comme sainct Jehan de l'Apocalypse: *quod vidimus testamur*" (218 var.; Saulnier, pp. 6–7). The obvious parallelism between these two sentences establishes a clear and deliberate opposition between the Law and Revelation—that is, between the Old Testament, in which truth and divine intention were revealed only imperfectly, indirectly, and figuratively, and the New Testament, in which the partial revelations of the Old are completed and its veiled meanings unveiled in a complete, direct revelation of the Truth.

This general opposition is confirmed and focused by a specific biblical reference contained in each of these corresponding allusions to the Law and Revelation. It has long been recognized that in quoting "sainct Jehan," Alcofrybas is quoting not from the book of Revelation but from the Gospel of John. In that book the words "quod vidimus testamur" are spoken by Jesus who, like John in Revelation, is claiming that his teaching is a direct revelation from God: "Truly, truly, I say to you, we speak of what we know, and *bear witness to what we have seen*" (Jn 3.11, emphasis mine). But the larger context in which these words were originally pronounced lends an unexpected force to their new context in Alcofrybas's prologue. Throughout John 3.1–15 Jesus is shown speaking to Nicodemus, a "Pharisee" and a "leader of the Jews," who has come to him as to a "Rabbi" and "a teacher come from God" (3.1–2). Jesus answers him with a metaphor that sets forth the precondition for "*seeing* the kingdom of God": "Truly, truly, I say to you, unless one is born anew, he cannot *see* the kingdom of God" (3.3, emphasis mine). The chief purpose of this famous metaphor is of course to distinguish between the physicality and literalness of the Old Law of the Jews, on the one hand, and the spirituality of the New Law that is to be that of the Christians, on the other. But Nicodemus, precisely because he is a Jew and remains under the veil of the Old Law, interprets the phrase "born anew" in an entirely physical sense, and thus as an absurdity. Jesus then explains the metaphor more fully and, in the process, states explicitly the distinction between the corporeal and the spiritual that was only implicit in the original image, explaining that "that which is born of the flesh is flesh, and that which is born of the Spirit is spirit" (3.6). When Nicodemus still fails to understand his meaning, Jesus utters the words quoted by John and, in turn, by Alcofrybas. "Are you a teacher of Israel, and yet you do not understand this? Truly, truly, I say to you, *quod scimus loquimur, et quod vidimus testamur;* but you do not receive our testimony. If I have told you earthly things and you do not believe, how can you believe if I tell you heavenly things?" (3.10–12).

Considered within the larger context of this narration, and especially within the immediate context of Jesus' last full reply to Nicodemus, the words quoted by Alcofrybas in support of the truthfulness of his chronicles—"quod vidimus testamur"—bring with them much more than a simple assurance of faithful and accurate eyewitness reporting. Their implicit, contextual function is to establish a fundamental distinction between Jews and Christians according to antithetical modes of both *seeing* and *understanding*. On the one hand there are the "teachers of Israel" who, like Nicodemus, are blinded to direct revelation and spiritual truth by the physicality and literalness of the written code of their Law. On the other hand there are those who will follow Jesus and adopt the new, spiritual mode of understanding offered by Jesus who has *seen* heavenly things face to face and bears witness to them "in the spirit."

Christians will understand and accept the direct testimony of things actually seen; Jews will neither see nor understand nor "receive our testimony." Such is the force of the words "about Christian revelation"—"de l'Apocalypse"—that Alcofrybas so deliberately quotes from the evangelist John.[5]

Like his allusion to what "John says about revelation," Alcofrybas's parallel allusion to what "the Jews say about the Law" contains a clear, though less explicit, reference to a specific biblical text. This is a passage from the beginning of the second Epistle to the Corinthians, in which Paul elaborates the same distinction between the Law of the Jews and the Revelation of the Christians that we find developed in the Gospel of John. In these well-known lines he points out that the old covenant (*testamentum*) is engraved on tablets of stone in letters that kill, whereas the new is engraved on human hearts by the Spirit, which gives life (2 Cor 3.2–6).

In the context of this crucial definition of the New and Old Laws Paul offers a famous allegorical interpretation of the passage in Exodus which says that when Moses descended from the summit of Mount Sinai with the two tables of the Law "his face shown because he had been talking with God," and that after transmitting the Law to his people he put a veil over his face, which he would take off whenever he went up to speak to God but would put on again whenever he came back down to speak to the people of Israel (Ex 34.29–35). "We are not like Moses," says Paul,

> who put a veil over his face so that the Israelites might not see the end of the fading splendor. But their minds were hardened; for to this day, when they read the old covenant, that same veil remains unlifted, because only through Christ is it taken away. Yes, to this day whenever Moses is read a veil lies over their minds; but when a man turns to the Lord the veil is removed. . . . We all, with unveiled face, beholding the glory of the Lord, are being changed into his likeness from one degree of glory to another; for this comes from the Lord who is the Spirit. [2 Cor 3.13–16, 18]

It would seem that this well-known representation of the way the Jews read and interpret the Law is precisely what lies behind Alcofrybas's pointed allusion to the way the Jews "speak about the Law." Even the diction of the prologue points to the similarity: "Car ne croyez . . . comme les Juifz de la Loy," says Alcofrybas (218); "et non sicut Moyses," said Paul (2 Cor 3.13).

This passage from Second Corinthians is intimately related not only to the general opposition between Revelation and Law around which the prologue turns but to the specific passage from the Gospel of John to which the prologue explicitly refers. Paul's systematic opposition between the "veiled," corporeal Law mediated by a veiled Moses to the "veiled" interpretations of the Jews and the unmediated vision afforded to the Christians by Christ, who removes the "veil" from their hearts, clearly parallels and complements Jesus' own remarks about Jewish misunderstanding and rejection of a firsthand, spiritual "testimony of things seen." But the relation between these passages is even more striking in the Latin version of the Vulgate, which Rabelais's readers would have known best, and which Rabelais quotes textually in this very passage. Unlike the Greek original, the Vulgate translation contains an elaborate play on the etymological meaning of *revelation* as an unveiling (*re-velare* meaning literally to take away a *velamen,* or veil). This fortuitous Latin pun suggests not only a contrast but an actual converse relation between Moses' giving (and veiling) of the Law to the Jews and Jesus' revelation (that is, unveiling) of the Gospel to Christians. The former is a velatio, the latter a re-velatio. "Moyses ponebat velamen super faciem suam" so that the Jews might not see it, and "idipsum velamen in lectione veteris testamenti manet non re-velatum." But after conversion to the Lord "auferetur velamen," so that Christians are able to see the glory of God "re-velata facie."[6]

In sum, then, the general idea of a complete and direct revelation of the truth first suggested by Alcofrybas's apparently comical reference to how "saint John talks about Revelation" is confirmed, refined, and focused by a perfectly coherent opposition that may be read on two distinct but mutually reinforcing levels: that of its own context in the prologue (the parallelism that opposes the way "sainct Jehan [parle] de l'Apocalypse" to the way "les Juifz [parlent] de la Loy") and that of the respective contexts to which the biblical tags and echoes of these parallel sentences refer (Jesus' words to Nicodemus, a "teacher of Israel," about not understanding and receiving a "testimony" [*testimonium*] of things seen, and Paul's words about the "veil" that lies over the hearts of Jews and has prevented them from seeing as they read the veiled "testimony" [*testamentum*] of Moses). All the various contextual and intertextual elements of this dense and highly allusive passage work in concert to alert the attentive Christian humanist reader to a single idea: the fundamental distinction between the Old Testament and the New as one of veiled, imperfect revelation of a partial, mediated truth, on the one hand, and a complete unveiling—that is, a "re-velatio," or "apocalypse"—of a perfect, seen truth, on the other.

Considered in the larger context of the whole prologue this carefully drawn distinction between Jews and Christians, Law and Revelation, clearly has little to do with Renaissance anti-Semitism or with the theology of revelation. Alcofrybas's purpose, it will be recalled, is simply to present the *Pantagruel* as a "livre de mesme billon" as the *Chronicque Gargantuine,* "sinon qu'il est un peu plus equitable et digne de foy que n'estoit l'aultre." Given this fact, and the deliberate assimilation of that same *Chronicque* to the Bible (and particularly to the Tradition or "Caballe" of the Jews) throughout the first part of the prologue, the intent of this crucial passage seems plain: to establish an exact analogy between the *Pantagruel* and the *Chronicque Gargantuine,* and the New Testament and the Old.

Like the Old Testament, the *Chronicques* are a miraculous and absolutely true book that provided more "emolument et utilité" than any other known to man. Like the New, the *Pantagruel* will provide a more direct, more authentic, more complete "re-velation" of the full truth and will prove to be even more useful. The truth we have found in the *Chronicques*, in other words, is a veiled truth which we have perceived as through a glass darkly. The truth we shall be shown in the *Pantagruel* is a revealed truth seen face to face and reported directly by the faithful scribe Alcofrybas. In essence, then, the analogy of the prologue can be reduced to the following simple equation:

Pantagruel : *Chronicques* = New Testament : Old Testament

But this equation can be understood in two different ways. If we choose to keep its two terms distinct and separate, then the analogy indicates nothing more than the precise relationship of the present chronicles to the *Grandes Chronicques*. The *Pantagruel* will continue, complete, and supersede the *Chronicques* in a manner analogous to the way the New Testament continues, completes, and supersedes the Old. Because the *Grandes Chronicques* are themselves a burlesque epic romance, the equation thus construed serves merely to confirm, through comic hyperbole, the epic pretensions of the *Pantagruel*. As a comic epic—"un aultre livre de mesme billon"—it will be more complete, more true, and more profitable than its predecessor, outdoing and surpassing it to the same degree that the New Testament outdoes and surpasses the Old.

But if we choose to understand the two terms of Alcofrybas's implicit equation as being to some degree interchangeable, as indeed their interpenetration throughout the prologue seems to invite us to do, then the analogy would suggest something more consequential: the *Pantagruel* is *like* the New Testament, not only in its relation to the book that has come before but in its own right as well. According to this understanding of the analogy, Alcofrybas's new chronicles are more than a true and useful account of things seen; they are actually a kind of Gospel and Revelation.

Beyond a useful "passetemps" they contain some kind of "Good News." And Alcofrybas himself, in addition to being a truthful eyewitness narrator, is a disciple and an evangelist "comme sainct Jehan."[7]

One understanding of the analogy, then, suggests that the *Pantagruel* is the ultimate comic epic. The other suggests that the *Pantagruel* is a comic New Testament, both Gospel and Revelation. Together they suggest something even richer: that the *Pantagruel* somehow fuses epic and Gospel, the *Aeneid* and Revelation, into some brave new hybrid genre that is simultaneously heroic and evangelical—a heroic gospel, or an evangelical epic. As the New Testament to the *Grandes Chronicques*'s Old Testament, the *Pantagruel* is presented from the outset as nothing less than an "epic New Testament," in all senses of the term.

True to the promise of the prologue, the *Pantagruel* does in fact bear a certain formal resemblance to a gospel narrative. Like the first of the four Gospels, it opens with a long genealogy of the hero and ends with a universal liberation and a return to an original, lost era of joy and peace, a "renouvellement du temps de Saturne" (*P* 31:374). In the original version the book even concluded, as does the entire New Testament, with a hint of events soon to come to light, including a burlesque harrowing of Hell and Ascension ("comment [Pantagruel] combatit contre les diables, et feist brusler cinq chambres d'enfer, et rompit IIII. dentz à Lucifer et une corne au cul. Comment il visita les regions de la lune"), all of which are to be so veracious as to constitute "beaux textes d'evangilles en françoys" (*P* 34:385 var.; Saulnier 23:177).[8]

Even more striking is a sustained assimilation of the Aeneas-like hero of the *Pantagruel* to the messiah of the New Testament. Throughout his epic narrative Alcofrybas consistently applies to Pantagruel the metaphors used to describe Christ in the various gospel narratives. Like Christ Pantagruel is "*plus quam Salomon*" (*P* 20:324 and Mt 12.42); like Christ he has his "apostoles" (*P* 28:355); like Christ he covers his disciples "comme une geline faict ses poulletz" (*P* 32:378 and Mt 23.37). And when Pantagruel sets out to establish his new reign in the land of the thirsty, he is pointedly compared to Christ's Old Testament prototype, Moses, crossing the Red Sea on his way to freedom and the Promised Land (*P* 31:375 and 1 Cor 10.1–5; Jn 3.14–15 and 6.48–51), as if to suggest that the establishment of a colony in Dipsodie somehow fulfilled the typological prophecy of the Old Testament in the same way that Christ's Crucifixion did.

Pantagruel's father, Gargantua, meanwhile—the hero of the "Old Testament" *Grandes Chronicques*—is clearly presented in the *Pantagruel* as a patriarch of the Old Testament. Like the earliest patriarchs he engenders his son at the Methuselan age of 524, "en son eage de quatre cens quatre vingtz quarante et quatre ans" (*P* 2.228). And in chapter 23 his death is comically assimilated to the ascension of the just patriarch Enoch, who "walked with God" (Gen 5.22 and 24), and of the saintly prophet Elijah, who "went up in a whirlwind to heaven" in a chariot of fire (2 Kgs 2.11). Even Alcofrybas's diction links Gargantua with the Old Testament at this point, his words being transposed directly from the Latin of the Vulgate: "Gargantua avoit esté translaté au pays des Phées par Morgue, comme fut jadis Enoch et Helye" (*P* 23:335 var.; Saulnier 15:125); "Enoch placuit Deo, et translatus est in paradisum" (Ecclesiasticus 44.16; compare Heb 11.5).

These and similar details would seem to confirm the implied claim of the prologue that the *Pantagruel* is indeed a kind of New Testament, not only in its relation to the earlier *Grandes Chronicques* but in some intrinsic way as well. But what of the more important and suggestive notion of an "*epic* New Testament" to which the prologue has led us? For confirmation we need only return to the two passages with which we began, in which we found Pantagruel assimilated to his epic prototype Aeneas. In the light of the prologue it is interesting to observe that each of these passages combines the explicit reference to Aeneas with an implicit but equally pointed reference to Christ.

In the first, we recall, Pantagruel invites Panurge to become his epic companion by enjoining him to play Achates to Pantagruel's Aeneas. Panurge responds not with an epic allusion but with a gospel tag. "Je accepte voluntiers l'offre," he answers, "protestant jamais ne vous laisser; et alissiez vous à tous les diables" (*P* 9:270). These words are a burlesque paraphrase of a scribe's words to Jesus as he volunteers, in the Gospels of Matthew and Luke, to become a disciple of Christ: "Teacher, I will follow you wherever you go"—"Magister, sequar te, quocumque ieris" (Mt 8.19 and Lk 9.57). It would seem that Panurge is being presented at this crucial juncture as both an Achates and a disciple, and Pantagruel simultaneously as Aeneas and Christ.

The second passage is even more interesting in this regard. As noted above, Pantagruel, in leaving his Parisian lady for Utopie, is cast in the role of Aeneas leaving his Carthaginian queen Dido for Rome. This assimilation is immediately preceded by an apparently irrelevant digression having to do with the decipherment of a hidden message. The lady has sent to Pantagruel a diamond ring inscribed with the words "lamah hazabthani," which Epistemon translates as "Pourquoy me as tu laissé?" The diamond proves on inspection to be a fake—a "dyamant faulx"—and the ring is finally understood to be a rebus whose meaning is: "Dy, amant faulx, pourquoy me as tu laissée?" (*P* 24:339).

The entire anecdote, which Rabelais merely transposed from the *Novellino* of Masuccio Salernitano (novella 41), would seem to be extraneous were it not for certain details that lend it a rather unexpected force. First, the ring is sent in an envelope addressed to "PNTGRL" (*P* 23:337). The absence of vowels is clearly meant to recall Hebrew writing. This suggestion is borne out by the inscription, which is written "en Hebrieu" with "motz Hebraicques" (*P* 24:339). Second, contrary to what all modern editors of Rabelais have asserted, these words are *not* Christ's dying words on the cross. Christ had said not "lamah hazabthani" but "*λαμὰ σαβαχϑανί*"—"lama sabachthani?" (Mt 27.46; Mk 15.34). The difference is crucial, for in uttering his famous last words Christ was speaking not Hebrew but his own native Aramaic. In doing so, moreover, he was not speaking spontaneously and from the heart but was deliberately quoting, in his own dialect, a well-known verse from the Hebrew Bible—the first line of Psalm 22 [21]: "לָמָה עֲזַבְתָּנִי." Rabelais was a good enough Christian humanist, and a good enough student of Semitic languages, to know the difference between the original Hebrew text and the dialectical form in which Christ quoted it. The "motz Hebraicques" inscribed "en Hebrieu" inside the lady's ring and sent to her false lover "PNTGRL" are the words of the original Hebrew psalm, transliterated exactly, according to the conventions of the sixteenth century, into Roman script.[9]

The particular psalm quoted by the Parisian lady sings the tribulations of David and of Israel and the expectation of a future deliverance. It is a manifestly *messianic* psalm and, as such, was associated from the beginnings of Christianity with the Passion of the Christian messiah, Jesus. Not only did Mark and Matthew make Jesus quote its first line on the cross, thus indicating that David's messianic prophecy was at that moment being fulfilled, but pseudo-Paul in the Epistle to the Hebrews attributed another of its lines to Christ as well (compare Heb 2.12 and Ps 22.22 [21.23]). In addition, a well-known episode of the Passion—the casting of lots for Jesus' seamless cloak—was drawn directly from yet another line, as from a prophecy of the crucifixion (compare Jn 19.23–24 [Mt 27.35; Mk 15.24; Lk 23.34] and Ps 22.18 [21.19]). The significance of such a psalm for a Christian humanist reader of Rabelais's generation would be easy enough to surmise. But there is no need to surmise, because we find it succinctly stated in a most accessible place. Marot's French translation of the psalm is preceded by an "argument," which observes matter of factly that this is a "Prophetie de Jesuchrist . . . propre pour chanter à la passion du redempteur" (Marot, *Oeuvres complètes* 6.374). The crucial point in all this is that Pantagruel's Parisian lady is made to quote not the messiah of the New Testament at the moment of his redemptive act but rather David's messianic prophecy of that redemptive act from within the Old Testament and under the veil of the Old Law.

Bearing all this in mind we may begin to see that Pantagruel's Hebrew-speaking lady friend is being deliberately cast in the role of the *sponsa* of the Old Testament—that is, in the role of the Synagogue, the chosen people whom God loved, according to the metaphor of the Song of Solomon, as a bridegroom loves his bride.[10] Pantagruel, for his part, is cast in the role of the messianic *sponsus* of the New Testament, the Christ whose advent and redemption was prophesied in Old Testament texts like the very one quoted by the Parisian lady.

But let us recall once again the context of this passage. Pantagruel, having been born to become "dominateur des alterez," and having been prepared for that role by his education at Paris, is about to undertake the heroic exploit that will fulfill his destiny and complete the teleological design of the book. It is at this crucial moment that the abandoned Parisian lady is identified simultaneously as Dido and the Hebrew-speaking Synagogue, and that the hero Pantagruel is cast in the simultaneous roles of Aeneas and the prophesied messiah. The Parisian lady is abandoned by Pantagruel as he sets off to perform his predestined exploit in Utopie both in the way that Dido was abandoned when Aeneas set off to fulfill his epic destiny in Latium and in the way that the Synagogue was abandoned by God when the Christian messiah fulfilled her own prophecies of redemption. Once again, as in the case of Pantagruel's first meeting with Panurge, but in a far more suggestive way, the hero of the *Pantagruel* is deliberately presented as both an epic and a gospel hero, and the book maintains its double identity as an *Aeneid* and a Revelation or, to return to the phrase suggested by the prologue, an "epic New Testament."

While these two passages neatly bear out the implications of the prologue, they remain for the moment little more than isolated illustrations of what appears to be an important aspect of the *Pantagruel*. As such they are suggestive enough in themselves but remain virtually impossible to interpret in any convincing, verifiable way. To progress beyond this point we must look for indications of a more consistent and coherent design in what the prologue has prepared us to read not only as an epic but as a kind of gospel narrative. Only such a design will allow us to interpret odd details like those considered here, and more important, to arrive at a clearer sense of what this curious, burlesque, epic New Testament is about and what it is supposed to mean.

2

THE REDEMPTIVE DESIGN OF THE *PANTAGRUEL*

Having prepared us in the prologue to view his book in a particular way and having shown us what to look for in it, Rabelais provides us in the first pages of the narrative with all the information necessary to discover the direction and the intent behind the ostensibly spontaneous and disjointed narration that follows.

Several details in the first two chapters immediately confirm the intimations in the prologue of an "epic New Testament" and the implicit assimilation of the epic hero Pantagruel to Christ. The first and most obvious of these is, of course, the famous genealogy that occupies such a conspicuous place in the opening pages of the book. The long sequence of "begat"s ("Qui engendra") leading up to "le noble Pantagruel, mon maistre" in the first chapter of the *Pantagruel* (*P* 1:224–27) is clearly meant to recall the long sequence of "begat"s ("genuit") leading up to "Iesus, qui vocatur Christus" in the first chapter of the first book of the Gospels (Mt 1.2–16). As if the parallel were not sufficiently obvious, Alcofrybas points to it explicitly in the first sentence of his epic. In tracing his hero's lineage to its "premiere source et origine" he claims to be imitating all good historiographers, "non seulement des Grecz, des Arabes et Ethnicques, mais aussi les auteurs de la Saincte Escripture, comme monseigneur sainct Luc mesmement, et sainct Matthieu" (*P* 1:221 var.; Saulnier 1:9). Two years later he would confirm the parallel by means of a *praeteritio* in the opening chapter of *Gargantua:* "Je vous diz que par un don souverain de Dieu nous a esté reservée l'antiquité et genealogie de Gargantua plus entiere que nulle aultre,—de Dieu je ne parle, car il ne me appartient, aussy les diables (ce sont les caffars) se y opposent" (*G* 1:12 var.; Screech 1:21–22).[1] The genealogy is unambiguous in casting the hero of the *Pantagruel* in the messianic role of Christ.

The following chapter offers further confirmation of the promise of the prologue while reinforcing the decidedly messianic implications of the genealogy. Pantagruel's birth, like Christ's, is accompanied by natural disorders and strange "signes." One of these would have been immediately recognizable in the sixteenth century as a specifically messianic sign. On the day Pantagruel is born the drought-parched earth exudes enormous drops of salt water: "Visiblement furent veues de terre sortir grosses gouttes d'eaue, comme quand quelque personne sue copieusement" (*P* 2:230). This curious image of a sweating earth recalls and fulfills one of the best-known Sibylline prophecies of the advent of Christ. Attributed by Lactantius and Augustine to the Erythraean Sibyl, reprinted in sixteenth-century editions of the *Oracula Sibyllina,* and even incorporated into the liturgical chant for Christmas eve in some parts of Christendom, that familiar prophecy begins:

> A *sign* of judgment: *the earth will be drenched with sweat.*
> From heaven a king will come to rule forever,
> To judge in person all flesh, the whole world,
> So that doubter and faithful alike shall see God
> Above with the saints, now at the very end of an age.
> [emphasis mine][2]

Thanks to the currency of this text, the miracle of the earth's sweating on the day of Pantagruel's birth—"tellus sudore madescet"—is a clear *signum* that the newborn hero is indeed a king come from heaven and a Christ.

A similar confirmation is contained in the lines immediately following these, in which Gargantua names his newborn son: "Et parce que en ce propre jour nasquit Pantagruel, son pere luy imposa tel nom: car *panta,* en grec, vault autant à dire comme *tout,* et *gruel* en langue Hagarene, vault autant comme *alteré,* voulent inferer que à l'heure de sa nativité, le monde estoit tout alteré, et voyant, en esperit de prophetie, qu'il seroit quelque jour dominateur des alterez" (*P* 2:231). Unlike the names given to Old Testament characters, which are merely commemorative, being inspired by the circumstances of a birth or a parent's first words on seeing a newborn child,[3] the name given to the messiah of the New Testament is actually prophetic and contains a clear indication of the bearer's future role as Savior (Jesus < יֵשׁוּ < יְהוֹשֻׁעַ = "God saves" or "God will save"). The naming of Pantagruel combines elements of both Old and New Testament traditions. As a name commemorative of the drought into which he is born, "Pantagruel" links the hero to his Old Testament forebears. But as a prophetic and providential "signe" of his entelechial victory over the Dipsodes—that is, over the "gens alterez" (*P* 26:348)—

that same name uniquely links him to the messiah named "Jesus" in the New Testament.

Indeed Alcofrybas's last word on the naming of Pantagruel—"voyant, en esperit de prophetie, qu'il seroit quelque jour dominateur des alterez"—recalls the precise terms of Matthew's passage on the naming of Jesus: "An angel of the Lord appeared to [Joseph] in a dream, saying . . . '[Mary] will bear a son, and you shall call his name Jesus: for he will save his people from their sins'" (Mt 1.20–21). Considered in this light "Pantagruel" might reasonably be understood as an echo of the prophetic and messianic "Emmanuel" (עִמָּנוּ אֵל = "God with us"), which Matthew goes on to apply to Jesus in this same passage (Mt 1.22–23; compare Is 7.14). In any case, the manner in which the hero is named, if not his actual name, clearly identifies him as a kind of Christ, and his future exploit as a messianic one.[4]

Yet while these details confirm and focus the evangelical implications of the prologue, they do not suffice to reveal a clear intention behind them. For the larger picture that will allow us to make sense of these messianic details we must return to the opening chapter of the *Pantagruel*, considering it not for the genealogy alone but as an organic whole. In its dense network of biblical quotations, echoes, and allusions we will easily perceive a comic but perfectly coherent reduction of sacred history from Genesis ("au commencement du monde") to the beginning of the Gospels (the genealogy)—that is, a kind of rudimentary Old Testament in brief, which recapitulates the crucial events against which the heroic gesta of Alcofrybas's "New Testament" are to be understood. By considering the place and function of Pantagruel's genealogy within this parodic scheme of sacred history we shall discover its purpose and easily discern the overarching design that we are looking for.

Alcofrybas begins his story by tracing Pantagruel's ancestry back to its "premiere source et origine" (*P* 1:221)—not to the sixth day of Creation but to a time shortly thereafter when Pantagruel's line became distinct from all others as a separate race of giants. The first ancestor of that race, from whom Pantagruel descends linearly, is Chalbroth. His transformation from an ordinary man into a giant is an event that Rabelais takes considerable pains to assimilate to the biblical account of the Fall.

In the beginning Chalbroth, along with many other men and women of his time, ate with great pleasure the fruit of a medlar tree (*P* 1:222).

These medlars caused everyone who ate them to grow excessively large in some bodily part, but they affected Chalbroth's entire body, "en long du corps" (*P* 1:224). As an explicitly original act, the eating of a "beau et gros fruict" cannot help but recall Adam and Eve's original act of eating the forbidden fruit of the Tree of Knowledge of Good and Evil. Nearly every detail in Alcofrybas's account reinforces this obvious parallel. Like the narrative in Genesis, this narrative begins *in principio* (Gen 1.1), "au commencement du monde" (*P* 1:221). Like the forbidden fruit of the Fall, the medlars are only one of many delightful fruits produced spontaneously and in great abundance by nature: "La terre . . . fut certaine année si très fertile en tous fruictz qui de ses flans nous sont produytz, et singulierement en mesles" (compare "Produxitque Dominus Deus de humo omne lignum pulchrum visu, et ad vescendum suave: lignum etiam vitae in medio paradisi, lignumque scientiae boni et mali" [Gen 2.9]). Most important, the medlars are identical to the forbidden fruit of Eden, both in appearance and in their effect on those who see them. Of the medlars Alcofrybas says: "Le monde voluntiers mangeoit desdictes mesles, car elles estoient belles à l'oeil et delicieuses au goust. . . . Les hommes et femmes de celluy temps mangeoyent en grand plaisir de ce beau et gros fruict" (*P* 1:222). These are precisely the terms used in Genesis to describe the forbidden fruit of the Fall: "Vidit igitur mulier quod bonum esset lignum ad vescendum, et pulchrum oculis, aspectuque delectabile: et tulit de fructu illius, et comedit deditque viro suo, qui comedit" (Gen 3.6). And finally, just as Adam and Eve are subject to toil, travail, and death as a consequence of having eaten the forbidden fruit, so the eaters of medlars pay a price for their consumption: "Accidens bien divers leurs en advindrent" (*P* 1:222). The fruit eaten by Chalbroth and his contemporaries is clearly meant to be recognized as a burlesque counterpart to the one eaten by Adam and Eve.

This intention becomes even more evident when we recall that the forbidden fruit of Eden is traditionally identified as an apple, for a "mesle" is in fact a kind of miniature apple and is explicitly described as such by classical and medieval naturalists. Pliny, Isidore of Seville, and Vincent de Beauvais, for example, all agree that "the medlar is a thorny tree whose fruit is similar to that of the apple, but somewhat smaller. Hence its name [*mespila*], which derives from the fact that its fruit have the shape of a little ball [*pilula*]."[5] The "grosses mesles" are thus a burlesque element identical in nature and function to Pantagruel himself. Just as a diminutive devil of late medieval mystery plays is comically enlarged to gigantic proportions and cast in the role of Christ, so puny apples normally no larger than little balls are comically enlarged to the point that a bushel basket can contain only three ("les troys en faisoyent le boysseau") and cast in the role of the forbidden fruit of the Fall.

In light of these deliberate parallels with the biblical account of the Fall it is not difficult to discover in the "enfleure très horrible" that afflicts various eaters in various parts of their bodies a physical metaphor for a kind of fall from grace—the visible deformation of the protoplasmati created "ad imaginem Dei" (Gen 1:27). Modern readers are often tempted to interpret this "enfleure" positively as a sign of grace or superabundant life, and the resulting giants as good, larger-than-life heroes who embody the limitless aspirations of Renaissance man. But Rabelais's text is unambiguous in presenting the original swelling as something catastrophic,[6] and the races that result from it as horribly deformed and freakish. Through the truculent good humor of the narrative come images of grotesque disproportion: hydropic bellies, horrible hunchbacks, various members inflated by acute elephantiasis. At least one of these races (consisting of those who "enfloyent en longueur par le membre") was so miserable as to have perished from the earth. Such swellings can hardly be viewed as signs of either grace or vigor.

As for the race from which Pantagruel descends, it may first appear to be less fallen than the others in that only its size, not its relative proportions, is affected by the dreadful swelling. But giants, as every Renaissance reader knew, are by their very nature the most evil and wicked of all rational creatures. This is a point on which all levels and phases of the Western tradition agree—elite and popular, biblical, Greco-Roman, and medieval.[7] Giants are by definition criminally impious, the enemies of God and of God's people (witness Nimrod, Goliath, the revolt of the Giants against the Olympians). They are a lawless and seditious race (see *Odyssey* 9.105–15, 259–78; Plato, *Laws* 3.701b–c; Cicero, *Laws* 3.2.5). They are the archetypal oppressors of humanity whom heroes like Hercules and Odysseus, Rolandus and Olivier, Geoffroy la Grand Dent and Astolfo must maim, slay, or enslave if the human race is to survive (witness Cacus and Polyphemus, Ferracutus and Fierabras, Caligorante and Grimaud). Lest any doubt remain as to whose side the giants are on, their most familiar epic representatives—Polyphemus, Cacus, and Caligorante—are notorious anthropophagi whom poets invariably depict engorging the still-palpitating flesh and drinking the still-warm blood of their innocent human victims.[8]

Such indeed are the giants we find mentioned by name in Pantagruel's own genealogy: Nimrod and Goliath; Polyphemus, Cacus, Typhoeus, Briareus, and Antaeus; Fierabras and Ferragus. These are not "good giants" or members of an elect race of the saved, but the most abominable, unredeemed enemies of God and man to be found in biblical, classical, and popular legend. In spite of what a modern reader might like to believe, the race of giants originating with Chalbroth and culminating in Pantagruel is a decidedly fallen race. Its gigantism is the visible effect and the irrefragable proof of an "original sin" committed by a first ancestor and transmitted in the flesh—quite literally—to successive generations of savage sinners.

But what, precisely, is the nature of Chalbroth's original sin in this farcical rewriting of the Fall? The answer is clearly not "scientia boni et mali" as it is in Genesis (Gen 2.17), since the hero of this epic New Testament, the Christ-like Pantagruel himself, will soon become an "abysme de science" (*P* 8:261) and the very "imaige de science et de sapience" (*P* 18:313) whose divine wisdom surpasses even that of wise Solomon (*P* 14:288, 18:313, 20:324). "Bonne doctrine" and "honneste sçavoir" are in fact characterized throughout the *Pantagruel* not as presumptuous and sinful but as a saving grace from God, as "manne celeste" (*P* 8:260, 18:315), while the cursed kings of the world—"ces diables de roys"—are damned to hell because they "ne sçavent ny ne valent rien" (*P* 31:376).

Nor is the original sin of the *Pantagruel* the sin of pride that prompted a desire for knowledge in the biblical account of the Fall ("aperientur oculi vestri et eritis sicut dii, scientes bonum et malum" [Gen 3.5]). The one thing that distinguishes the mesles of the *Pantagruel* from the fruit of Genesis is precisely that the mesles are not forbidden. Alcofrybas states specifically that the eaters of medlars were not conscious transgressors of a known interdict but innocent victims of involuntary self-contamination: "Mais tout ainsi comme Noe, le sainct homme . . . fut trompé en le beuvant [le piot], car il ignoroit la grande vertu et puissance d'icelluy, semblablement les hommes et femmes de celluy temps mangeoyent en grand plaisir de ce beau et gros fruict" (*P* 1:222). The original transgression of the *Pantagruel* therefore resides not in the *act* of eating the medlars but in some essence concealed within the calamitous medlars themselves. All who partake of them are contaminated unawares, deformed for having ingested a poison they did not know was there.

That poison is identified in unmistakable terms at the beginning of the narrative, in the first, most conspicuous, and most concrete biblical allusion of the chapter: "Il vous convient doncques noter que, au commencement du monde, . . . peu après que Abel fust occis par son frere Caïn, la terre embue du sang du juste fut certaine année si très fertile en tous fruictz qui de ses flans nous sont produytz, et singulierement en mesles, que on l'appella de toute memoire l'année des grosses mesles. . . . Faictes vostre compte que le monde voluntiers mangeoit desdictes mesles, car elles estoient belles à l'oeil et delicieuses au goust" (*P* 1:221–22). The abundance of proverbial expressions meaning "never" interpolated into this account in the definitive edition of the *Pantagruel* has tended to distract readers from what is clearly the most specific and significant detail of this highly charged opening—namely, that the "grosses mesles" of Utopie are "grosses" precisely because they are bloated with the blood of Abel the just, spilled by his brother Cain and absorbed through the rich soil into the fruit whose effect on the Utopians will be so catastrophic.[9] The medlars, in short, are the fruit of the first fratricide. By eating that baleful fruit the Utopians have in effect become unwitting participants in Cain's original crime by drinking, like the cannibal giants they are about to become, the blood of Cain's innocent victim. The "enfleure très horrible" that afflicts all partakers of the tainted medlars is merely the effect and the sign of their participation in that original murder, their communion in Cain's original crime against his brother.[10]

It may be noted in passing that although the opening pages of the *Pantagruel* may appear novel as a systematic rewriting of the Fall, they depart very little from either the Judeo-Christian or the Greco-Roman tradition as an account of the origin of Pantagruel's race. The standard explanation for the sudden and unaccountable appearance of giants in early sacred history (for example, in the Vulgate, Num 13.34; Deut 2.11 and 20, 3.11; and so on) was based on a passage in Genesis (6.4), which in the Vulgate reads: "The [giants] were on the earth in those days, [for after] the sons of God came in to the daughters of men, and they bore children, these were the mighty men that were of old, the men of renown" ("Gigantes autem erant super terram in diebus illis: postquam enim ingressi sunt filii Dei ad filias hominum, illaeque genuerunt, isti sunt potentes a saeculo viri famosi"). Throughout the Middle Ages and Renaissance the enigmatic phrase "sons of God" was interpreted to mean the descendants of Abel's replacement Seth, and "daughters of men" to mean the descendants of the proscribed Cain. (See, for example, Augustine, *De civ. dei* 15.23.) According to this canonical explanation giants formed a separate race that resulted from the illicit miscegenation between the godly progeny of Seth and the wicked progeny of Cain.[11] By relating the origin of Pantagruel's race directly to Cain's murder of Abel, Rabelais remains remarkably faithful to an essential aspect of this universally accepted explanation. His version merely emphasizes and focuses the traditional notion that giants are somehow the children and the inheritors of the fratricide Cain.

In the classical version of the Fall as it is narrated in Ovid's *Metamorphoses,* the origin of the impious giants is equally vague but similarly linked to violence among men. Giants first appear in the Iron Age as a sign of unbounded iniquity in the world. They storm the heavens in their revolt against the Olympians, while on earth *pietas* lies vanquished as kinsmen murder one another and "even love between brothers is rare" (*Met* 1.144–55). As a last step in the gradual process of degeneration, the earth, imbued with the blood of the defeated giants, produces a new race of hominids whose contempt for the gods and whose lust for slaughter bear witness to the blood from which they are born:

> Perfusam multo natorum sanguine Terram
> Immaduisse ferunt calidumque animasse cruorem
> Et, ne nulla suae stirpis monimenta manerent,
> In faciem vertisse hominum; sed et illa propago
> Contemptrix superum saevaeque avidissima caedis
> Et violenta fuit; scires e sanguine natos.
> [*Met* 1.157–62]

Although the relation between fratricide and giants in this account is quite different from that of the biblical account, the two are linked in a way that further illuminates the burlesque Fall narrated by Alcofrybas. In particular, the idea of a wicked race born of spilled blood and a fertile earth ("perfusam multo natorum sanguine Terram / Immaduisse ferunt") resonates in Rabelais's text ("la terre embue du sang du juste fut . . . si très fertile") and lends to it a special force. The savage line from which Pantagruel descends is indeed like that of the cruelest, giant-born line of Iron Age mortals, both in its origin and its nature.[12]

From all this it is evident that Rabelais has deliberately rewritten Genesis in such a way as to substitute fratricide for pride as the Original Sin and occasion of the Fall and to substitute giants for men as the inheritors of that sin. Adapting to his own purposes the traditional associations of giants with impiety, violence, cannibalism, fratricide, and even with Cain himself, Rabelais has made of Chalbroth's descendancy a fallen race exactly analogous to that of postlapsarian man—one whose calamity was caused not by the first sin of man against the God who created him but by the first sin of a man against his fellow creature.

To understand the significance of this substitution one must consider the transgressions of Adam and Cain from the perspective of Christian ethics, and more specifically in terms of the single law of the New Testament, the Great Commandment, which Christ himself defined as the first and greatest and on which "all the law and the prophets" depend:

> Diliges Dominum Deum tuum ex toto corde tuo, et in tota anima tua, et in tota mente tua. Hoc est maximum, et primum mandatum. Secundum autem simile est huic: Diliges proximum tuum, sicut teipsum. In his duobus mandatis universa lex pendet, et prophetae.
>
> You shall love the Lord your God with all your heart, and with all your soul, and with all your mind. This is the great and first commandment. And a second is like it, You shall love your neighbor as yourself. On these two commandments depend all the law and the prophets. [Mt 22.37–40; Mk 12.29–31; Lk 10.27]

The sin of the first created man was a transgression of the first article of this Great Commandment. Instead of loving God unconditionally, Adam disobeyed God and presumed to become his equal. The sin of the first *born* man, on the other hand, was a transgression of the second article of the Great Commandment, otherwise known as Christ's own New Commandment of *caritas* (Jn 13.34), the single law that sums up and fulfills every law of the Old Testament, and on which the entire edifice of Christian ethics is built (Rom 13.9; Gal 5.14; Jas 2.8). Instead of loving his brother as himself, Cain murdered his brother out of hatred and envy.

Seen in these basic terms, fratricide must be understood as the opposite of brotherly love, and Cain as a moral type opposed to the law of caritas. This is, in fact, precisely the value attached to murder in general, and to Cain in particular, in the New Testament. In the first epistle of John, which is devoted almost exclusively to the New Commandment of brotherly love, Cain is mentioned explicitly as a counterexample of Christ's law of caritas:

> Whoever does not do right is not of God, nor he who does not love his brother [*diligit fratrem suum*]. For this is the message which you have heard from the beginning, that we should love one another, and not be like Cain who was of the evil one and murdered his brother [*occidit fratrem suum*]. . . . We know that we have passed out of death into life, because we love [our brothers] [*diligimus fratres*]. He who does not love remains in death. Any one who hates his brother is a murderer [*omnis qui odit fratrem suum, homicida est*]. [1 Jn 3.10–12, 14–15]

For John, killing one's brother ("occidere fratrem suum") is diametrically opposed to loving one's brother ("diligere fratrem suum"), and fratricide is the antithesis of caritas. Cain is thus the antitype of Christ, who is caritas incarnate. Instead of loving his brother, he hated his brother; instead of laying down his life for his brother, he took his brother's life. Anyone who does not obey Christ's commandment to love his brother, moreover, *is* a Cain, a *homicida*.

This moral interpretation of Cain's act was largely ignored by patristic and medieval exegesis, which favored a racial interpretation according to which Cain's murder of Abel figured the Jews' crucifixion of Christ or persecution of the Christians. But in the early Renaissance Christian humanists abandoned the medieval tradition to return with great vigor to the moral interpretation proposed in the Bible by John. Thus Erasmus, in his paraphrase of 1 John 3.12, insisted that although Cain and Abel were brothers by blood, they belonged by their behavior to two separate families: Abel, the innocent son of God, was inflamed with the desire to perform acts of kindness; Cain, the invidious and loathing son of the devil, strove to slaughter his more charitable brother rather than to mend his own ways.[13] Two decades later Clément Marot, in *L'Enfer,*[14] played even more explicitly on the opposition between Cain and caritas by attacking the legal system of France as both a symptom and a source of discord among neighbors. Lawsuits, he says, are serpents descended from the Hydra

> . . . qui au profond de Thrace,
> Où il n'y a que guerres et contens,
> Les engendra dès l'aage et dès le temps
> Du *faulx Cayn*.
> [*L'Enfer* 184–87, emphasis mine]

And the reason for the proliferation of lawsuits today is "faulte de charité / Entre Chrestiens" (189–90):

> A escouter voz Prescheurs, bien souvent
> *Charité* n'est que donner au Couvent.
> Pas ne diront combien Proces differe
> Au vray Chrestien, qui de touts se dict *frere*.
> [*L'Enfer* 193–96, emphasis mine]

Maurice Scève hinted at something similar, though in less explicitly evangelical terms, in a political poem written some ten years after Marot's. Scève denounces the presumed role of Charles V in the alleged murder of the dauphin François by decrying the "appetit de l'homme" that "pour sa commodité / Viole foy, honneur, et innocence," and then equating the supposed murder and the violation of social principles it entails with Cain's fratricide:

Ne pleure plus, France: Car la presence
Du sang d'Abel devant Dieu criera
Si haultement que pour si grande offence
L'aisné Cain devant toy tremblera.

[*Délie* 116]

In all these widely diverse contexts, Cain functions in the same ahistorical, nonanagogical manner as a moral type, the figure of a man who behaves in a manner directly contrary to that prescribed by the New Commandment.[15]

Appearing as it does in the context of this humanistic, Johannine tradition, Rabelais's new version of the Fall must be understood as a deliberate, systematic transposition of the great scheme of salvational history from a divine to a strictly human plane. In place of the first sin committed against God Rabelais substitutes the first sin committed against man; in place of a transgression of the first article of what will become Christ's Great Commandment he substitutes a transgression of the second article elevated by John, Paul, and all Erasmian Christian humanists to the status of the single New Law of the Christians; in place of defective love for the Creator in heaven he substitutes defective love between fellow creatures here below. The giants who descend from their first ancestor, Chalbroth, are a fallen race not because they have become alienated from God but because they have become alienated from one another. Inheritors in the flesh of the first sin of brother against brother, polluted by the blood of the original fratricide, they are the cruel and violent progeny of Cain, agents and literally incarnations of anticaritas.

Considered as part of the larger scheme implied by this new version of the Fall, Pantagruel's genealogy takes on a meaning at once more specific and more consequential than any we might first have supposed. The genealogy indeed casts Pantagruel in the role of Christ, the Christian messiah. But Christ's messianic role, we must recall, was precisely to redeem fallen man by reversing the effects of Original Sin and reconciling man to God. Because in Alcofrybas's version Cain's transgression replaces Adam's as the Original Sin and Pantagruel replaces Christ as messianic redeemer, the two scriptural parodies work together to establish a single fundamental analogy:

Pantagruel : Chalbroth-Cain = Christ : Adam

According to this analogy Pantagruel stands in the same relation to the eating of medlars and the resulting swelling of his race that Christ stands in relation to the eating of the forbidden fruit and man's resulting fall from grace. Just as the messianic function of Christ is to redeem his race by taking away Adam's Original Sin against God, so the messianic role of Pantagruel must be to redeem his race by taking away the harm of Cain's "original sin" against Abel. Just as Christ is an anti-Adam, so Pantagruel must be an anti-Cain.[16] Keeping in mind the particular significance attached to Cain's fratricide by sixteenth-century humanists, we may begin to understand that Alcofrybas's parody of Christ's genealogy, coupled with his parody of the Fall, serves to define for the improbable hero of this burlesque epic a serious and specific messianic role: that of a secularized *type* of the Christian messiah, a redeemer of the original sin of anticaritas in a fallen world of hating brothers.[17]

In addition to defining the precise nature of Pantagruel's messianic role, the genealogy establishes an unbroken chain of generations through which the messiah inherits the original sin he is born to abolish. Being descended directly from the first giant Chalbroth, the giant Pantagruel assumes at birth, with his physically deformed flesh, the visible effects (the "enfleure très horrible") of Cain's original sin against Abel, just as the messiah Christ, being descended directly from the first sinner Adam, assumed at the moment of incarnation the flesh tainted by Adam's Original Sin against God. In each case, the continuity of generations is the guarantor of the continuity of sin, and corrupted flesh the medium through which sin is transmitted from the first sinner to the messiah who will eventually redeem it.

Given the combined force of Rabelais's parodies of the Fall and the genealogy of Christ, we may now understand the relevance of yet a third biblical parody included in the first chapter of the *Pantagruel*—that of Noah's flood. The flood was of course an effect of God's wrath at the utter depravity of fallen man. In the narratives of both Genesis and the *Metamorphoses* it is linked sequentially, and perhaps even causally, to the origin of giants in the world. In the Bible the mention of "giants" born of the "sons of God" and the "daughters of Cain" is followed immediately by God's dismay at the wickedness of man and his resolve to destroy all living creatures by a great flood (Gen 6.5–7). In the *Metamorphoses*, similarly, the wickedness of the new race sprung from the blood of the giants is the immediate cause of Jupiter's wrath. Recalling the recent crime of Lycaon, which merely illustrates his race's impiety and "lust for slaughter," Jupiter, like God, resolves to destroy the entire race by means of the universal flood (*Met* 1.162–261). Seen in the light of this traditional association of giants, depravity, and the flood, the inclusion of a long digression on Noah's ark in Alcofrybas's narrative appears perfectly natural.

Far more important, however, is the fact that the flood, according to both the biblical and classical traditions, was originally intended to eliminate the race of fallen men from the face of the earth altogether. The crucial importance of Noah in terms of salvational history (and of Deucalion in its classical counterpart) is that without him there would have been no messiah, nor indeed any need of one, since the messiah's line would have died out long before his advent, and in any case none of Adam's descendants would have remained to be saved. Only Noah's survival assures that between Adam's sin and Christ's redemption the line goes on and the story of salvation continues.

This is clearly the point that concerns Alcofrybas in his burlesque rewriting of the Flood. Having traced his hero's ancestry continuously from a first ancestor and original sinner all the way down to a messiah and redeemer of original sin, he must address his readers' well-founded objection that Chalbroth's race could not possibly have survived the flood for the simple reason that no giant was in the ark with Noah: "J'entens bien que, lysans ce passaige, vous faictez en vous mesmes un doubte bien raisonnable et demandez comment est il possible que ainsi soit, veu que au temps du deluge tout le monde perit, fors Noë et sept personnes avecques lui dedans l'Arche, au nombre desquelz n'est mis ledict Hurtaly?" (*P* 1:227). Pantagruel's line must certainly have perished in the universal catastrophe of Genesis 7.11–24 and *Metamorphoses* 1.262–312—all the more so because the iniquity of the giants is what provoked the flood in the first place and because the flood was presumably intended to destroy that race.

Alcofrybas answers this challenge to the veracity of his chronicle by claiming with comic casuistry that Pantagruel's ancestor Hurtaly, "qui . . . regna au temps du deluge" (224), was not *in* the ark with Noah but *on* the ark, which he straddled as a child does a stick horse.[18] Thus the continuous line of giants from first ancestor to messiah was able to survive the universal flood that was sent to destroy them, without compromising the literal truth of biblical narrative. Hurtaly saves the fallen race of giants for the messiah Pantagruel, just as Noah saves the race of fallen men for the messiah Christ.

We may now see that the sacred history traced in the first chapter of the *Pantagruel* is in fact a strictly *salvational* history, reduced to three of its four most essential elements: a Fall, a Flood, and the complete ancestry of a Messiah. Though parodic and burlesque, this salvational history is both parallel to the canonical biblical version and consistent with the letter of Scripture. And like the canonical biblical version it parodies, it lays the groundwork for a coherent redemptive scheme in which a promised messiah will inherit an original sin in order to abolish it. In this simple redemptive scheme lies the design we have been looking for—the larger, governing pattern that will allow us to interpret Pantagruel's double identity as both an Aeneas and a Christ, as well as many other perplexing aspects of Alcofrybas's epic New Testament.

Before leaving the first chapter ot the *Pantagruel* to consider how this larger design is brought to completion at the end, it will be useful to consider one last detail that may serve to dispel any lingering doubts about the reality of the redemptive scheme we have discerned here. Proof that this scheme is both intended and consistent is to be found in an unnoticed but significant difference between the messianic genealogies of Pantagruel and Christ.

Unlike Alcofrybas, Matthew does not trace Christ's ancestry back to his first ancestor, for he is less concerned with the self-evident fact that Jesus, as born a man, is an inheritor of Original Sin than with the far more crucial point that Jesus is the messiah foretold by the prophets of the Old Testament. He must prove this by demonstrating that Jesus, in accordance with messianic prophecy, is descended directly from King David. To this end he needs to set forth only the most controversial part of Christ's ancestry,[19] starting with Abraham, the father of the chosen people to whom God first made his promise of election, and continuing through David, the father of the messianic line. The title of Matthew's first chapter is explicit in stating this purpose: this is the "book of the genealogy of Jesus Christ, the *son of David,* the *son of Abraham*" (Mt 1.1, emphasis mine). For the earlier part of Jesus' ancestry he relies on the reader, who is familiar with Genesis and Chronicles, to supplement his partial genealogy with the well-known genealogy of Abraham. To obtain the complete genealogy of Christ one must string together three separate biblical texts: the "Liber generationis Adam" (Gen 5.1), which extends from Adam to Noah, the "generationes filiorum Noe" (Gen 10.1)—and specifically that part entitled the "generationes Sem" (Gen 11.10), which extends from Noah to Abraham—and the "Liber generationis Jesu Christi filii David, filii Abraham" (Mt 1.1), which extends from Abraham to Christ.

This, in effect, is precisely what Alcofrybas does in tracing Pantagruel's line all the way back to his first ancestor, Chalbroth, and the "premiere source et origine" of his entire race. The first chapter of the gospel according to Alcofrybas, unlike that of Matthew, *includes* Genesis in its messianic genealogy. This inclusion explains why Alcofrybas's genealogy, while deliberately recalling Matthew's, nevertheless incorporates Old Testament–style epithets like "Eryx, lequel fut inventeur du jeu des gobeletz" and "Etion, lequel premier eut la verolle pour n'avoir beu frayz en esté, comme tesmoigne Bartachim" (*P* 1.225). The reason for these epithets is clearly not that Rabelais wished to mock only Old Testament genealogies while respecting the sacrosanct genealogy of Christ,[20] but rather that he has combined elements from both the Old *and* New Testaments to form one complete messianic genealogy tracing Pantagruel's ancestry from the beginning to the end of a fallen line.

But the most crucial importance of this difference has to do with the number of generations that separate messiah from first sinner in each of the genealogies. The exact number of generations in Christ's genealogy was a matter of common knowledge throughout the Middle Ages and Renaissance, in part because Matthew speaks so portentously of numbers at the end of his own genealogy. "So," he concludes, having arrived at last at "Jesus, who is called Christ"—"all the generations from Abraham to David were fourteen generations, and from David to the deportation to Babylon fourteen generations, and from the deportation to Babylon to the Christ fourteen generations" (Mt 1.17). Matthew's primary purpose in pointing so deliberately to the hidden order of his genealogy is to suggest a rational, preconceived design or intention governing the ancestry of his messiah.[21] In so doing, however, he was merely following a precedent set by the Old Testament genealogies, which his own was intended to complete. Both the "Book of generations of Adam" and the "Book of generations of Shem" contain exactly ten names, so that the history of the chosen people up to and including Abraham appeared to be divided into two parts of equal numbers of generations (Adam to Noah, Shem to Abraham), punctuated by the principal events and patriarchs (Fall of Adam, Flood and first covenant with Noah, second covenant with Abraham, the father of the chosen people). Matthew's forced order merely prolongs this pattern by dividing the rest of sacred history into three groups of equal numbers of generations, punctuated by the combined kingship, the fall of the kingdom of Judah and exile from the Promised Land, and the advent of the messiah and redemption of Original Sin. Thus all of history from Fall to Salvation appeared to unfold in such a way as to reveal an infused, premeditated order, and all the generations from Adam to Christ, the two sons of God, were grouped by the most important patriarchs and events that determined its course (Adam–Noah–Abraham–David–captivity–Christ) into numerically rational groups (10–10–14–14–14).

This pattern and these figures were by no means arcane knowledge in the Renaissance, for they had been commonly reproduced by precisely the kind of chroniclers, cited as precedents by Alcofrybas, who trace their history to its "premiere source et origine." A typical example well known to Rabelais and his contemporaries was Gregory of Tours, who began his *Historia Francorum,* as Alcofrybas does his chronicle, from the "commencement du monde" (*P* 1:221) and counted, like Matthew, the generations in the genealogy of Christ: "From Adam to Noah there are ten generations. . . . The first son of Noah was called Shem, and from him, in the tenth generation, was born Abraham. . . . From Abraham to David there are fourteen generations. . . . From David to the destruction of the Temple and the Babylonian captivity there are fourteen generations. . . . From the beginning of the Captivity until the birth of Christ there are fourteen generations."[22] The number of generations in the complete genealogy of Christ was thus common knowledge in Rabelais's day. Anyone who could read in the early sixteenth century knew as a matter of course that Matthew's genealogy contained forty-two generations (14 + 14 + 14 = 42), that the genealogy of Abraham contained twenty generations (10 + 10 = 20), and that the total number of generations from Adam to Christ was therefore *sixty-two* generations.[23]

Alcofrybas does not divide his genealogy into neat groups in the manner of Old Testament, New Testament, and medieval French chroniclers, but he seems to have been equally preoccupied with numbers. Of all the lists, catalogs, and "kyrielles" in the *Pantagruel,* the catalog of giants with which it begins is the only one that Rabelais never expanded in later editions of the book. Between the first (1532) and definitive (1542) editions of the *Pantagruel* the number of different "races" originating with the swelling of a particular part of the body (*P* 1) increased from six to eight; the number of books in the library of Saint Victor (*P* 7), from forty-two to 139; the number of languages spoken by Panurge during his first meeting with Pantagruel (*P* 9), from nine to thirteen; the number of replies in the silent debate between Panurge and Thaumaste (*P* 19), from fifteen to twenty-two; and the number of damned souls in hell (*P* 30), from forty-two to eighty-one, to mention only the most notable examples. But the number of generations in Pantagruel's genealogy remained constant, in spite of the addition of eight more Old Testament–style epithets and attributes appended to names already on the list. The number was obviously a matter of some importance, since Rabelais apparently had to resist his usual penchant for verbal proliferation to maintain it. That number is *sixty-one* generations.

The number of generations from Chalbroth to Pantagruel (sixty-one) is thus one short of the familiar number of generations from Adam to Christ (sixty-two). The reason for this curious discrepancy will be self-evident to the careful reader of Alcofrybas's opening chapter. Chalbroth is identified on the first page of the book as a contemporary not of Adam but of Adam's sons, Cain and Abel: his accidental transformation into a giant takes place "peu après que Abel fust occis par son frere Caïn" (*P* 1:221). Whereas Christ's generations are counted from the first generation of humankind, Pantagruel's are counted from the second. Thus the genealogy deliberately places Pantagruel in the same generation as Christ: the sixty-first counting from Cain and Chalbroth, the sixty-second counting from Adam. Not only is Pantagruel cast in a role exactly analogous to Christ's, he is also presented as an exact contemporary of Christ.

This astonishing correlation proves that the correspondence between the two genealogies is deliberate and that it was conceived and executed with a meticulousness entirely alien to what is generally thought of as "Rabelaisian" spontaneity and the "verve" of the *Pantagruel*. More important, it sanctions and guarantees the redemptive scheme on which the entire chapter is predicated and offers incontrovertible proof that Pantagruel is the kind of messiah the scheme suggests. As both a type and a contemporary of Christ removed by sixty-one (as opposed to sixty-two) generations from an original sinner, Pantagruel is a messiah born to redeem a sin committed in the second (as opposed to the first) generation of men, that sin being Cain's transgression of the second article (as opposed to Adam's transgression of the first article) of Christ's Great Commandment, the New Commandment of brotherly love.

Thus all the allusions and echoes of Rabelais's first chapter, even down to its smallest details, conspire to suggest a typological design whose messianic implications are entirely coherent and clear: just as Christ, the linear descendant of Adam, was born to redeem the Original Sin of Adam and Eve in eating the forbidden fruit of Eden, so Pantagruel, the linear descendant of Cain's contemporary, Chalbroth, is born to redeem the original sin of Cain, which infected Chalbroth when he unwittingly ate the medlars swollen with the blood of the just and which has afflicted every subsequent generation down to Pantagruel's. If "Christus Iesus Dominus" is an anti-Adam, then "Pantagruel, mon maistre" is an anti-Cain. He is unequivocally presented at the outset of this strange epic as a kind of secular messiah who will abolish Cain's sin, redeem the original fratricide, reconcile brother to brother, and reestablish caritas in a fallen world of hatred among fellow creatures. The hero of the *Pantagruel* is none other than the long-awaited savior of the brotherhood of man.[24]

The identity of Pantagruel as a type of Christ, once firmly established at the beginning, is maintained throughout the epic, as we have already seen. The Christian law of caritas, too—"Diliges proximum tuum, sicut teipsum"—once established in the first chapter as the foundation on which the *Pantagruel* is to be built, reappears constantly throughout the rest of the epic, sometimes together with the first article of the Great Commandment, sometimes alone as Christ's New Commandment. As part of the Great Commandment it is deformed and misused by the affected and self-loving Limousin schoolboy: "Je venere latrialement le supernel Astripotent. Je dilige et redame mes proximes" (*P* 6:245). It is expounded by Gargantua near the end of his letter to Pantagruel: "Il te convient servir, aymer et craindre Dieu, et en luy mettre toutes tes pensées et tout ton espoir; et par foy formée de charité, estre à luy adjoinct, en sorte que jamais n'en soys desamparé par peché. . . . Soys serviable à tous tes prochains, et les ayme comme toymesmes" (*P* 8:262). And it is quoted as part of a philological demonstration in a specious and self-serving argument by Panurge: "Car *accipies* est dit selon la maniere des Hebrieux, qui usent du futur en lieu de l'imperatif, comme vous avez en la Loy: *Dominum deum tuum adorabis, et illi soli servies; diliges proximum tuum; et sic de aliis*" (*P* 17:309 var.; Saulnier, 12:97–98). As the New Commandment alone it appears in the episode of the walls of Paris, where the lion of Panurge's obscene fable mentions it to the fox: "Car ainsi nous fault il secourir et ayder l'un l'aultre: Dieu le commande" (*P* 15:298 var.; Saulnier 11:86). And the haughty Parisian lady alludes to it in an attempt to deflect Panurge's pressing suit in chapter 21: "Je ne vous hay poinct, car, comme Dieu le commande, je ayme tout le monde" (*P* 21:330). These are only the most direct allusions and quotations. Many others are implied or latent, and indeed several episodes appear to be predicated entirely on the precept of brotherly love.[25] Never are we allowed to forget that caritas is the central issue of the epic, nor that the hero is a messiah whose mission is to restore brotherly love to the inheritors of fratricide.

But what of the act of redemption promised at the beginning of the *Pantagruel*? Where in the epic does it occur, and what form does it take? The redemptive scheme so clearly set forth in the first chapter, together with the epic teleology of the work as a whole, shows us exactly where to look for this crucial, entelechial moment, and what to look for in it. We know from the beginning that Pantagruel's redemptive act will not consist in a parody of Christ's Crucifixion, for the sin to be redeemed is not a sin against God so great that only the sacrifice of something greater than man can atone for it, but the violent crime of a man against his own brother, a crime that must somehow be undone. Moreover, as the telos of an "*epic* New Testament" his redemptive act must be an act of individual heroism, not an act of divine self-immolation. And finally, we know from chapter 2 that redemption will have come about only when the hero has fulfilled the promise of his messianic name of "dominateur des alterez." According to the overall design of the *Pantagruel*, redemption from Cain's sin must come about at the end, with Pantagruel's final victory in his epic war against the Dipsodes.

Viewed as an integral part of this design, Anarche's invasion of Utopie suddenly appears remarkably relevant to the sin that Pantagruel must redeem. In taking advantage of the Utopians' weakness (Gargantua's "translation" and Pantagruel's absence) to overrun and destroy his just and peaceful neighbors in an unprovoked attack, the usurping king bears a distinct resemblance to Cain, who treacherously rose up against his innocent and unsuspecting brother. As for the Dipsodes, they too appear as worthy inheritors of Cain's sin. As "gens alterez" (*P* 16:348) they are not only thirsty but "deformed" and "angry" as well.[26] In this respect the entire burlesque war of the *Pantagruel* resembles a large-scale, mock-epic reenactment of Cain's archetypal act of invidious aggression against one's own kind. In defeating Anarche and his army of Dipsodes, Pantagruel and the Utopians appear to avenge Abel on an epic scale.

But the specific redemptive act with which Pantagruel fulfills his messianic promise consists in a single, heroic exploit performed at the end of the war in the decisive duel on which the outcome of the entire epic conflict is made to depend. Just as the *Iliad* moves inexorably toward the final showdown between Achilles and Hector that will end the ten-year siege of Troy, and just as the *Aeneid* moves inexorably toward the final duel between Aeneas and Turnus that will end the long war for Lavinia, Latium, and eventual world domination, so the *Pantagruel* moves toward the final single combat between Pantagruel and Anarche's general that will end the hostile occupation of Utopie and determine the future of both Utopie and Dipsodie.

Rabelais does everything possible to point to this fateful encounter as the climax of his epic and the entelechial point at which his hero's redemptive promise will at last be made good. First, Alcofrybas, in mock-heroic imitation of Homer and Vergil, sets the episode apart from the preceding burlesque war by means of an invocation to the Muses of epic poetry and of comedy: "O, qui pourra maintenant racompter comment se porta Pantagruel contre les troys cens geans! O ma muse, ma Calliope, ma Thalie, inspire moy à ceste heure, restaure moy mes esperitz, car voicy le pont aux asnes de logicque, voicy le trebuchet, voicy la difficulté de pouvoir exprimer l'horrible bataille que fut faicte" (*P* 28:358).[27] Then the hero, in the last moments before engaging with Loup Garou, utters a solemn evangelical prayer that contrasts in tone and tenor with everything that precedes and is answered by a highly allusive portent from heaven indicating divine sanction and victory for Pantagruel. Thus the stage is set for the long-awaited showdown between Pantagruel and his ultimate adversary, the villainous Loup Garou.

Everything in Loup Garou identifies him as the hero's predestined antagonist. First, he is a giant. As such he is, like the hero, an inheritor of Cain's original sin. But unlike the messianic hero he remains a typical, unregenerate giant—impious, arrogant, cruel, violent, bloodthirsty, and even cannibalistic. On seeing Pantagruel standing alone he "feut esprins de temerité et oultrecuidance, par espoir qu'il avoit de occire le pauvre bon hommet" (*P* 29:360). He has an overweening confidence in his own unaided strength and even threatens his companions with violent death if they dare to share in the pleasure of massacre and carnage, saying to them: "Par Mahom, si aulcun de vous entreprent combatre contre ceulx cy, je vous feray mourir cruellement. Je veulx que me laissiez combatre seul" (360). He approaches "en grande fierté" (361), "la gueulle ouverte" (362), as if to devour the hero alive and at one point threatens to chop up Pantagruel "comme chair à pastez" (364).[28]

Pantagruel, on the contrary, has become through destiny and education pious, humble, and gentle. He places his hope and trust not in his own considerable strength but in God alone, as he explains to a freed prisoner: "Car de moy, encores que soye puissant, comme tu peuz veoir, . . . toutesfoys je n'espere en ma force ny en mon industrie, mais toute ma fiance est en Dieu, mon protecteur, lequel jamais ne delaisse ceux qui en luy ont mis leur espoir et pensée" (*P* 28:354). Before the fight he humbly "recommends himself to God," reaffirming that "en toy seul est ma totale confiance et espoir" (*P* 29:361). And in a text added in 1533 he states to his prisoner that his purpose in the war against the Dipsodes is not to "piller ny ransonner les humains, mais de les enrichir et reformer en liberté totalle," and sends the prisoner back to Anarche "en la paix du Dieu vivant" (*P* 28:354).

The climactic duel is thus clearly presented as a gigantomachia in which one inheritor of Cain's sin meets another: Pantagruel, the messianic giant born to abolish that sin and redeem his wicked race, and Loup Garou, the "chef" of Anarche's elite corps of three hundred giants, who still represents and embodies the sin in which his race originated.

To emphasize this opposition between the two giants and to clarify its meaning, Rabelais deliberately assimilates their decisive duel to the one between little David of Bethlehem and the giant Goliath of the Philistines. Panurge pointedly recalls that duel in the final moments before the struggle, encouraging Pantagruel to take on Anarche's three hundred giants with only the help of his four companions: "Car quoy? David tua bien Goliath facillement" (*P* 29:359). Loup Garou indeed resembles his and Pantagruel's common ancestor Goliath in that his superior arms give him a distinct advantage over his opponent. Goliath was armed with a bronze coat of mail weighing five thousand shekels, a bronze javelin, and a spear whose shaft "was like a weaver's beam, and his spear's head weighed six hundred shekels of iron" (1 Sam 17.5–7), whereas David was armed only with a sling (1 Sam 17.50). Similarly, Loup Garou is armed with "enclumes Cyclopicques" (*P* 26:347) and an indestructible, all-destroying "masse toute d'acier, pesante neuf mille sept cens quintaulx d'acier de Calibes, au bout de laquelle estoient treze poinctes de dyamans, dont la moindre estoit aussi grosse comme la plus grande cloche de Nostre Dame de Paris" (*P* 29:360–61), whereas Pantagruel is armed only with a ship full of salt and the ship's fragile wooden mast, which the narrator compares to a lady's basket and a pilgrim's staff (*P* 28:356).

More important, Loup Garou resembles Goliath in his arrogance and pride, proposing to make the outcome of the war depend on his valor alone (compare *P* 29:360 and 1 Sam 17.8–10), whereas Pantagruel, though a giant, resembles little David in his humility and faith, trusting in God alone to win the battle for him (compare *P* 29:361 and 1 Sam 17.45–47). Pantagruel's identification with the diminutive David and the promise of God's providential intervention in the battle to come are clear indications that the hero is no longer a true giant, but an agent of God on the point of defeating the arch enemy of his fallen, yet chosen people.

But it is as a "werewolf," or "wolf-man," even more than as a giant, that Loup Garou is most clearly identified as Pantagruel's predestined antagonist. In the animal lore of the Middle Ages the wolf consistently symbolizes rapacity, greed, fraud, and violence. This is evident to us today in the fable tradition that runs continuously from Aesop and Phaedrus through the various Ysopets and Avionnets to La Fontaine, in which the wolf is the cruel enemy of the innocent lamb, the faithful dog, and the good shepherd. The early medieval *Ysengrimus,* which eventually evolved into the vernacular *Roman de Renart,* plays on these characteristics in the sanguinary and brutal character of Ysengrin, the symbol of murder and rapine. Bestiaries elaborate on the same image, characterizing the wolf as rapacious (*rapax*) and bloodthirsty (*cruoris appetens*) and allegorizing him as nothing less than the devil, "who perpetually envies the human race and goes around congregations of the faithful hoping to kill and destroy their souls."[29]

A werewolf, strictly speaking, is nothing more than a man who has the bloodthirsty and rapacious character of a wolf. Both classical medicine and popular legend recognize, each in its own way, the predatory, murderous, and even cannibalistic tendencies of the wolflike man.[30] And a well-known classical proverb identifies man's inveterate cruelty to man as an effect of the wolf in him: *homo homini lupus*.[31] The first man who was a "wolf" to his fellow man was of course Cain, and any wolf-man is merely an imitator of Cain's original wolfishness to his own brother. As a werewolf, then, Loup Garou *is* a kind of Cain.

The identification of Loup Garou with Cain is even more specific than this, however. To see how, we must consider the case of the archetypal wolf-man in literature, Lycaon, whose very name suggests wolfishness (Λυκάων < λύκος = *lupus,* wolf), and whose story is already implicit in the first chapter of the *Pantagruel*. Sandwiched between the two passages of Ovid's *Metamorphoses* that resonate most clearly in that opening chapter—the account of a wicked new race born of the earth "infused with the blood" of the defeated giants (*Met* 1.156–62) and Jupiter's decision to destroy humanity with a universal flood (*Met* 1.240–61; see above)—the story of Lycaon's metamorphosis into a wolf establishes a compelling causal link between those two events: Lycaon is an exemplary member of that blood-born, bloodthirsty race, and his crime is the last straw that provokes Jupiter to destroy his people in the flood. His story is thus implicitly but intimately related to the version of the Fall on which the redemptive scheme of Alcofrybas's epic New Testament is founded.

That story is the following: to verify reports of the atrocities committed by Iron Age men against their own kind, Jupiter takes on a human form and visits the palace of the king of Arcadia. The Arcadians sense the presence of a god and worship him, but the scoffing Lycaon resolves to put the divinity of the stranger to a test by trying to kill him in his sleep. Failing in his attempt, he devises an even more abominable test: he cuts the throat of a hostage and chops him into small pieces that he cooks into a ragout and serves to his guest for dinner. Outraged at the brutality of this crime, Jupiter destroys Lycaon's house with a lightning bolt, while the vicious host himself, fleeing into the countryside, is metamorphosed into a wolf. Ovid carefully points out that Lycaon's character remains unchanged during his metamorphosis and that his physical appearance has simply been modified to correspond more closely to his murderous nature: "He chokes with rage and turns his old lust for carnage against the flocks, and still delights in gore. . . . He becomes a wolf, yet still retains traces of his former shape: he has the same gray hair, the same violence in his face, the same blazing eyes, and remains the very image of savagery."[32] Ovid's fourteenth-century allegorizer Pierre Bersuire makes the same point even more bluntly: "Lycaon was a most wicked tyrant who had the character of a wolf, though he looked like a man. While Jupiter was visiting him in his house, Lycaon killed a man whose flesh he served to the god for dinner, for which Jupiter became enraged and changed him into a wolf. Thus the man who had been a wolf covertly in his inner character became a wolf in appearance as well."[33]

The archetypal man-turned-wolf, then, is a wicked and impious mortal who makes a vicious and unacceptable human sacrifice to the divinity. He is the image of savage brutality (*feritatis imago*), a man whose nature is marked by violence (*violentia*), a lust for carnage (*cupido caedis*), and delight in bloodshed (*sanguine gaudet*) and whose sin is the treacherous and unspeakable murder of an innocent victim entrusted to his safekeeping. The parallels between the murderer Lycaon and the fratricide Cain are evident. Lycaon in fact resembles a classical Cain.

This resemblance did not escape the attention of Rabelais's contemporaries. For proof we need only consult an early sixteenth-century French commentator of the *Metamorphoses,* the Dominican friar Petrus Lavinius.[34] His "tropological enarrations" of Ovid's poem, written during Lent of 1510 (o.s.) in Vienne, were printed along with Raphael Regius's commentaries in the margins of numerous humanist editions of the prestigious Regius text of the *Metamorphoses* published in Lyon between 1510 and 1526. In his commentary on the lines in which Ovid first mentions Lycaon by name (1.163–67) Lavinius identifies the myth as one that "we" Christians, "following Genesis, understand as the story of the fratricide Cain" ("ut Geneseos sequamur historiam, Cayn fratricidam intelligimus" [Ovid, *Libri moralizati,* fol. 14v]). And in his long commentary on the narrative itself he offers three separate allegorical interpretations, the first and most important of which is that "that most wicked man Lycaon . . . is a figure of the unspeakable fratricide Cain" ("sceleratissimus Lycaon . . . nefandissimum illum fratricidam Cayn denotat" [fol. 18v]). Lavinius develops this analogy at considerable length and concludes with the remark: "Ovid therefore wrote under a poetic veil about Cain, very fittingly signified by Lycaon" ("Cayn igitur Lycaone non incongrue significatum scripsit sub velamento Ovidius" [fol. 18v]). For all readers of

Ovid in Rabelais's Lyon and certainly throughout much of the rest of France, the latent suggestive value of wolves and werewolves is made explicit, and the obvious analogies between the first fratricide and the first wolf-man are given the authority and universality of print: as a popular form of Lycaon, Loup Garou is a familiar type of Cain.[35]

If Loup Garou is indeed a type of Cain, and if our sense of the typological design of the epic is right, then Loup Garou must also function as a representative of anticaritas. A well-known passage in the sequel to the *Pantagruel* shows that this is precisely the value given to werewolves in the works of Rabelais. In the world without debts imagined by Panurge at the beginning of the *Tiers Livre,* the theological virtues of Faith, Hope, and Charity will be banished, to be replaced by their opposites Mistrust, Contempt, and Rancor, with the result that "*les hommes seront loups es hommes. Loups guaroux* et lutins comme feurent *Lychaon,* Bellerophon, Nabugotdonosor, briguans, assassineurs, empoisonneurs, malfaisans, malpensans, malveillans, haine portans un chascun contre tous" (*TL* 3:419, emphasis mine). In a world with debts, on the contrary, there will be "entre les humains, *paix, amour, dilection.* . . . Nul procès, nulle guerre, nul debat. . . . Ce sera l'aage d'or, le regne de Saturne, l'idée des regions Olympicques, es quelles toutes autres vertus cessent, *Charité* seule regne, regente, domine, triumphe" (*TL* 4:421, emphasis mine). Here wolves, werewolves, and even Lycaon himself are clearly associated with hatred and violence among men and are explicitly opposed to Christ's New Law of caritas. For Rabelais, Cain was clearly the original "homo homini lupus," and Loup Garou his modern popular hypostasis.

In the climactic, entelechial gigantomachia between Pantagruel and Loup Garou, then, the Christ-like hero born to redeem Cain's original fratricide meets face to face the embodiment of anticaritas and the figure of Cain himself. In this fateful showdown the original encounter between Abel and Cain is reenacted on an epic scale.[36] But this time the outcome is different. By a redemptive reversal it is the unjust aggressor, not the innocent victim, who falls. When the gentle, humble, unarmed hero single-handedly defeats the savage, arrogant, heavily-armed villain, the old score is finally settled. The cry of the brother's blood has been answered (Gen 4.10). Cain and all his giant henchmen lie dead.

In this symbolic reenactment and reversal of Cain's original sin, in this epic "desconfite gigantale" (*P* 30:365), Pantagruel performs his predestined exploit and redemptive act, fulfilling his double role of hero and messiah, completing the salvational scheme set forth in the first chapter, and consummating the overarching redemptive design of Alcofrybas's epic New Testament. Here at last the original fratricide is abolished with the immolation of its type and embodiment. Here the fallen race of giants is redeemed with the annihilation of the Cyclopic, cannibalistic, Goliath-like chief of giants and all his wicked giant henchmen. Here anticaritas—that dark urge that turns brother against brother and lies behind all the violence, depredation, and bloodshed that have plagued humankind ever since the cold-blooded murder of the world's first brother—has been eradicated and the way prepared for a return to a prelapsarian order founded entirely on the New Law of brotherly love, a new Utopian order in which every man is indeed, to answer Cain's self-accusing taunt (Gen 4.9), his brother's keeper.

3

THE EDUCATION OF THE CHRISTIAN PRINCE

In his portrait of the ideal Christian prince, Erasmus borrowed from Plutarch the notion that the good ruler is a living representation of God on earth—a "vivum quoddam Dei simulacrum." As such the ideal prince must be both the best (*optimus*) and the most powerful (*potentissimus*) of men, so that his goodness will make him want to benefit everyone, and his power will enable him to do so.[1] But in adapting this classical idea to the ideal Christian prince Erasmus consistently added to Plutarch's two divine attributes, those of supreme goodness and supreme power, a third, supreme wisdom, in order to forge his God-like prince in the exact image of the triune God of the Christians, whose trinitarian attributes are *potentia, bonitas,* and *sapientia.* Without goodness and wisdom, according to this analysis, power will be pernicious and tyrannical, and the prince who wields it will be a simulacrum of the Devil (*Cacodaemon*), not of God.[2]

The princes of Europe, being hereditary monarchs, are born with supreme power. But being human they are not necessarily born with supreme goodness and are certainly not born with wisdom. Goodness, and especially wisdom, must therefore be acquired—not from experience, for the risks to the political order would be too great in allowing a prince to learn from his youthful mistakes, but rather from study. Hence the crucial importance of education in the formation of the ideal Christian prince.[3]

As a type of Christ predestined to perform a heroic act of moral and political redemption, Pantagruel is presented from the beginning of his epic as a potential "simulacrum Dei" in the most literal sense of the term. But as a giant descended in the flesh from a long line of cruel and fratricidal giants, the hero begins his life with only the first of the three attributes of the God-like prince—a supreme potentia that can lead as easily to the tyranny of his ancestors as to the redemptive pacification for which he is predestined. And indeed the future messianic hero is vividly portrayed in his infancy as a mere brute. The baby Pantagruel "creut en corps et en force" at such a prodigious rate that "estant encores au berseau, feist cas bien espouventables" (*P* 4:235), breaking bindings, snapping thick cables, and finally smashing his cradle in feats of strength greater than those of Hercules, Samson, and Og of Bashan. The impulse behind these feats, moreover, is an appetite that shows a comic propensity toward the savageness of his fallen ancestors. The infant giant devours most of a live cow while his victim "cryoit horriblement comme si les loups la tenoient aux jambes" (236). He even rips to pieces a live bear as easily as if it were a chicken and gulps down its warm flesh as a snack. The baby messiah is truly the inheritor in the flesh of the ancient ancestral sin. Before fulfilling the messianic promise of his genealogy and birth he must therefore be transformed from a mere giant (and potential tyrant) into a perfect simulacrum Dei. To his hereditary power and extraordinary natural force (potentia) must be added a supreme sapientia as well as a supreme bonitas.

This is precisely the role assigned to education in Gargantua's famous letter to his son. Having begotten Pantagruel in the flesh, Gargantua says, he will spare nothing in the education of his son's soul, by which he means specifically the "perfection" of Pantagruel through bonitas and sapientia: "comme si je n'eusse aultre thesor en ce monde que de te veoir une foys en ma vie absolu et parfaict, tant en vertu, honesteté et preudhommie [that is, bonitas], comme en tout sçavoir liberal et honeste [sapientia]. . . . Parquoy, mon filz, je te admoneste que employe ta jeunesse à bien profiter en estudes [sapientia] et en vertus [bonitas]" (*P* 8:258 and 260).

The acquisition and demonstration of these two crucial attributes is the principal subject and unifying theme of a long sequence of chapters leading from the birth of the hero to the accomplishment of his redemptive exploit. These chapters correspond, by their placement and function, to the portion of medieval romance epics traditionally devoted to the hero's early career as a squire and his preparation for an eventual epic role. In keeping with the redemptive design of the *Pantagruel*, the convention of the hero's chivalric apprenticeship is modified to consist entirely in the perfection of a type of Christ through the education of the ideal Christian prince.

In the following pages we shall consider one aspect of this peculiar epic apprenticeship—the process by which Pantagruel's prodigious inherited potentia is supplemented and tempered by a quasi divine sapientia.[4] This process is narrated over the course of eight of the nine chapters that immediately follow the baby Pantagruel's inauspicious beginning. These chapters (5–8 and 10–13) first appear to be so episodic as to be virtually autonomous and even interchangeable—so much so that modern readers have occasionally even ventured hypotheses to explain or "correct" what they perceive to be a faulty sequence of episodes.[5] But as we shall see, each of these eight chapters appears in its proper place within the sequence and contributes in a crucial way to the larger design of the epic. None is superfluous, none is interpolated, none is out of place. Their sequence, moreover, is precisely what will allow us to perceive a perfectly coherent and linear narrative in these chapters, even in the absence of explicit narrational links between them.

For the sake of convenience I shall refer to this entire sequence as the "sapience cycle" of the *Pantagruel*. The eight chapters that compose it are neatly divided into two groups of equal length, corresponding to the hero's acquisition (chapters 5–8) and demonstration (chapters 10–13) of sapientia.[6] In order to perceive the coherence of the entire cycle and its function within the larger design of the *Pantagruel* it will be useful to consider each of these two distinct phases separately and in some detail.

The acquisition phase of the sapience cycle consists of two distinct parts. The first (chapters 5–7) describes a false start in the gothic learning of the Middle Ages that leads only to idleness and ignorance. The second (chapter 8) marks a fresh start in humanistic learning of the Renaissance that leads to both knowledge and wisdom.

Pantagruel's education begins when Gargantua, delighted with Pantagruel's prodigious physical growth and "progress," sends his son to school "pour apprendre et passer son jeune eage." At first the young hero succeeds only in the second of these ends, thanks to the woeful inadequacies of the traditional educational system. Pantagruel's "tour de France universitaire," as it has been called, which begins in Poitiers (*P* 5:239) and ends in Paris (*P* 7:249), is a comic but complete and systematic indictment of the traditional medieval University. Over the course of these three chapters Pantagruel studies briefly at each of the ten great universities of France, only to find that, far from imparting wisdom or even knowledge, they drive bored and abused schoolboys away from serious studies to unproductive idleness and games ("passetemps" and "exercice").

Wherever Pantagruel goes, he finds idle young people wasting the best years of their lives in games and debauchery. Students at Poitiers have so much leisure that they "ne sçav[ent] à quoy passer temps" and are rescued from their boredom only by Pantagruel, who erects the "Pierre levée" so that "quand ilz ne sçauroyent aultre chose faire, passassent le temps à monter sur ladicte pierre" to eat, drink, and write graffiti (*P* 5:239). At Bordeaux there is no other "exercice" than to watch the dockers play cards. At Toulouse students learn to dance and fight with a two-handed sword. At Montpellier they drink (241). At Avignon they spend their time whoring. At Valence they have little "exercice" because the local toughs beat them up at their dances (242). At Orléans, they make a "bel exercice" of the *jeu de paume* and get their *licence en loix* without having acquired any other "science" than that (243). And finally at Paris, queen of all the universities, the arrogant Limousin schoolboy is our witness that students waste their time wandering aimlessly around the capital and cultivating fancy talk, and that they even hock their schoolbooks in order to spend every waking hour in goliardic debauchery in the taverns and whorehouses of Lutèce.[7]

The professors, meanwhile, discourage their students from serious study by their incompetent teaching of futile and outmoded disciplines. Pantagruel wants to study medicine at Montpellier but is repelled by the fact that the profession is "fascheux par trop et melancholicque" and by the stench of old professors who "sentoyent les clisteres comme vieulx diables."[8] He is similarly repelled by law at Montpellier because the entire Faculty of Law there consists of "troys teigneux et un pelé de legistes" (*P* 5:241). He abandons his law studies at Bourges, too, because they consist more in the study of the "tant infame et punaise" Gloss of Accursius than of the "tant beaulx, tant aornés, tant elegans . . . textes des *Pandectes*" (242–43).[9] These remarks on medicine and law clearly identify the University as a place of reactionary, gothic learning. A discrete allusion to the execution of a humanist law professor at Toulouse (241) merely confirms the implications of these remarks on law. The grotesque titles found in the "magnificque" library of Saint Victor have a similar function with respect to theology. Almost all of these titles parody works of scholastic theology and medieval piety. Some of them are attributed to real authors, nearly all of whom are either luminaries of scholastic theology or canon law, or the most notorious opponents of humanism.[10]

What this survey of French universities and their students suggests is that the medieval University is a bastion of gothic incompetence, reaction, futility, and sloth, which educates students only in vices, ranging from the *accidia* of schoolboys "studying" at Poitiers to the gluttony, lust, prodigality, and overweening pride of those "studying" at Paris.[11] The great "profit" Pantagruel is ironically said to derive from this university education is nil. Alcofrybas drives this crucial point home at the end of chapter 5 by stating that at Orléans his hero becomes a "maistre" at the jeu de paume and has fun playing "au jeu du Pouss'avant," but "au regard de se rompre fort la teste à estudier, il ne le faisoit mie, de peur que la veue luy diminuast" (*P* 5:243).

But Gargantua's famous letter to Pantagruel in the last of the four acquisition chapters marks a new beginning in Pantagruel's education. Modern readers rightly sense that the humanist style of the letter, and even its Ciceronian epistolary form, are utterly incongruous in the context of the *Pantagruel*. But this incongruity is not the result of an oversight or an afterthought. It is rather a deliberate narrational device designed to suggest, in an indirect but powerful way, a major turning point in the implicit narrative of the sapience cycle. The style and form of the letter signify humanism, just as unmistakably as the chaotic list of gothic titles cited in chapter 7 signifies barbarism. The shocking contrast between the two chapters thus signals a clean break with the medieval universities and the gothic educational system satirized throughout the three preceding chapters, and a new beginning in the humanistic learning whose center in France had indeed been established at Paris, thanks to the "lecteurs royaux" instituted by François I a mere two years before the publication of the *Pantagruel*.[12]

What Gargantua says in his letter confirms the break implied by its style and form. His thumbnail sketch of the history of learning presents the well-known humanist paradigm of a return to a golden age of *bonae literae* after a millennium of gothic barbarity, a return described in the letter as recent. When Gargantua was a youth "le temps estoit encores tenebreux et sentant l'infelicité et la calamité des Gothz, qui avoient mis à destruction toute bonne literature" (*P* 8:258–59). Only in Gargantua's lifetime ("de mon eage") has "la lumiere et dignité" been "rendue es lettres" and have "toutes disciplines" been "restituées, les langues instaurées, . . . les impressions . . . en usance" (259). That return, moreover, is represented as an effect of divine providence: gothic darkness has now been superseded by the light of humanistic learning thanks to "la bonté divine"; printing has been invented "par inspiration divine" (259); and humanistic learning is a "manne celeste de bonne doctrine" (260). The future restorer of a prelapsarian state of brotherly love is thus to be the first of his long line to reap the God-sent benefits of a providential return to a kind of prelapsarian state of "bonne literature."

The education spelled out at the end of Gargantua's letter confirms in an even more striking way the idea of a radical break with gothic education encountered in the three preceding chapters. The program of studies defined here is actually predicated on a systematic opposition to the antiquated disciplines taught by the medieval University. To perceive this we must recall that throughout the Middle Ages and well beyond the Renaissance, every schoolboy's education began at the Faculty of Arts with a standard course consisting of the seven liberal arts divided into two groups. The trivium, comprising the three verbal arts, consisted of Grammar, which taught the student to read Latin; Rhetoric, which taught him to compose in Latin; and Dialectic, which from the late twelfth century on had taught him to reason and argue in Latin. The quadrivium, comprising the four quantitative arts, consisted of Arithmetic, Music, Geometry, and Astronomy. Having mastered this basic curriculum and graduated from the Faculty of Arts, the Renaissance scholar, like so many generations of medieval scholars since the founding of the first universities in the thirteenth century, could go on to prepare for a career in one of three professions by entering a Faculty of Law, a Faculty of Medicine, or a Faculty of Theology, in order of increasing prestige.[13]

Keeping this curricular structure in mind, we shall discover that in setting forth his program of studies Gargantua follows step by step the canonic sequence of arts and the hierarchy of professions of the medieval university system. But while he respects the traditional order of disciplines scrupulously, Gargantua describes the disciplines themselves in terms that indicate a radical departure from the way they were traditionally constituted and taught by the four Faculties of the medieval University. In doing so he implicitly transforms each of the old gothic disciplines into its antithetical humanistic counterpart.[14]

The letter begins with a systematic humanist revision of the three arts of the trivium: "J'entens et veulx [1] que tu aprenes les *langues* parfaictement: premierement la Grecque, comme le veult Quintilian; secondement, la Latine; et puis l'Hebraïcque pour les sainctes letres, et la Chaldaïcque et Arabicque pareillement; et [2] que tu formes ton *stille,* quant à la Grecque, à l'imitation de Platon; quant à la Latine, à Ciceron. [3] Qu'il n'y ait *hystoire* que tu ne tienne en memoire presente, à quoy te aydera la Cosmographie de ceulx qui en ont escript" (*P* 8:260, emphasis mine). By substituting a perfect knowledge of the famous three languages of Renaissance humanism as they were now beginning to be taught in their pristine purity at the "trilingual" academies of Alcalá, Louvain, and Paris[15]—and two other ancient languages besides[16]—for the barbaric medieval Latin that was taught by the traditional Faculty of Arts, Gargantua in effect replaces gothic Grammar by its humanist counterpart and antidote. By prescribing the direct imitation of classical models of style and eliminating the first two offices of rhetoric, *inventio* and *dispositio,* to make way for the third, *elocutio* ("stille"), he reorients the traditional discipline of Rhetoric away from the *loci communes* and compositional norms, with which the medieval Faculty of Arts continued to pave the way to Dialectic, toward an exclusive preoccupation with the eloquence that had been banished from the scholastic trivium and that was now being practiced and taught, once again, by the Faculty's worst enemies, the humanists.[17]

As for the discipline of Dialectic itself—that quintessentially scholastic art of the syllogism and of the *disputatio pro et contra* on which the entire edifice of gothic learning was built—it is conspicuously absent from Gargantua's program of studies, for reasons not hard to discover. Dialectic is of course the invention, the sign, and the condition sine qua non of scholasticism. Since the assimilation of Dialectic to Aristotelian Logic in the twelfth century, it had become the privileged vehicle for abstract and often metaphysical truth divorced not only from human realities but from linguistic expression, the sole means by which humanists believed that truth could be apprehended and communicated. As such it was considered by humanists to be the most pernicious of all the traditional arts. Nothing of what was taught as Dialectic could be salvaged or put to better use. Gargantua therefore banishes it from the trivium. In its place he substitutes something diametrically opposed to it—that quintessentially humanistic discipline and the centerpiece of the *studia humanitatis,* History. As the invention, the sign, and the condition sine qua non of humanism, History is to humanism precisely what Dialectic is to scholasticism. In this conspicuous substitution of History for Dialectic within the curricular structure of his program, Gargantua is deliberately playing with antitheses in a pointed and polemical way. He is abolishing the scholastics' abstract speculations about the universal, the atemporal, and the transcendent to make room for the humanists' concrete knowledge of the particular, the historical, and the human, and in effect replacing the worst of the old learning with the best of the new.

The four arts of the quadrivium are treated as summarily in Gargantua's letter as they seem to have been in the Faculty of Arts: "Des ars liberaux: [4] *geometrie,* [5] *arismeticque* et [6] *musicque,* je t'en donnay quelque goust quand tu estoys encores petit, en l'eage de cinq à six ans; poursuys la reste, et [7] de *astronomie* saiche en tous les canons; laisse moy l'astrologie divinatrice, et l'art de Lullius, comme abuz et vanitez" (*P* 8:260, emphasis mine). Two points are nevertheless of interest here. One is the condemnation of astrology, as distinct from astronomy, along with other forms of divination and arcane science. This categorical exclusion of the occult provides a negative confirmation of the strictly human orientation that is so evident in the revised trivium. Unlike the scholastics, Gargantua includes all legitimate knowledge of the past and of the natural world. But unlike even some humanists—including Reuchlin, Cornelius Agrippa, Pico della Mirandola, and Lefèvre d'Etaples—he excludes as illegitimate and forbidden all esoteric knowledge of the future and of the supernatural world. The revised program of studies thus conforms exactly to the twin formulae of classical humanism: it embraces everything human ("homo sum: nihil humani alienum a me puto") but explicitly rejects everything that transcends the human or exceeds natural human ken ("quae supra nos nihil ad nos").

The second, less obvious point is the relegation of much of the quadrivium to informal, preschool instruction. Gargantua himself taught Pantagruel most of the rudiments when his son was only a child. Pantagruel's formal education need only supplement this early introduction. The effect of this modification in the canonic sequence of arts is to diminish even further the importance of the quantitative arts and to make them even more subordinate to the trivium than they had been in the medieval curriculum. This shift is entirely consistent with the humanist tendency discernible throughout Gargantua's program to consider human language as the only valid basis for intelligence and the only valid vehicle for knowledge. Numbers express only abstract and general truths and are therefore scarcely more germane than Logic to the disciplines of humanism.

Following this systematic revision of the seven arts taught by the medieval Faculty of Arts, Gargantua proceeds to reform the disciplines taught by the three higher Faculties of the University. First is Law: "Du droit civil, je veulx que tu saiche par cueur les beaulx textes, et me les confere avecques philosophie" (*P* 8:261). Three points are of particular interest in this brief remark. First, the specific mention of "droit civil" clearly implies the elimination of an entire branch of Law as it was taught at the medieval University, and indeed the more prestigious branch—Canon Law. With this simple specification and implied omission Gargantua sweeps away not only one whole Faculty of the medieval University but the Decretals, ecclesiastical authority, and the entire legal basis on which monasticism and all of church hierarchy rest. Second, the explicit mention of the "beaulx textes" of the law implies the elimination of the overwhelming body of Civil Law, too, as it was traditionally taught in the universities of Europe—namely, the myriad glosses of Accursius, Bartolus, Baldus, and others, which, to the humanist way of thinking, had succeeded only in submerging the laws themselves and obscuring and deforming their original meaning. And finally, the exhortation to "conferer" original laws "avecques philosophie" implies the substitution of ancient moral philosophy for the hated glosses of the moderns in interpreting, applying, and reconciling inconsistencies in the laws.

The Law proposed by Gargantua is thus the perfect humanist counterpart and antidote to the gothic Law that had so repelled Pantagruel at Bourges and led him to compare his law books to a resplendent golden robe lined with shit: "Car, disoit-il, au monde n'y a livres tant beaulx, tant aornés, tant elegans, comme sont les textes des *Pandectes* [compare "du droit civil . . . les beaulx textes"], mais la brodure d'iceulx, c'est assavoir la Glose de Accurse, est tant salle, tant infame et punaise, que ce n'est que ordure et villenie" (*P* 5:242–43).

The next recognizably curricular discipline in Gargantua's program is Medicine: "Puis songneusement revisite les livres des medicins Grecs, Arabes, et Latins, sans contemner les Thalmudistes et Cabalistes, et, par frequentes anatomies, acquiers toy parfaicte congnoissance de l'aultre monde, qui est l'homme" (261). It is significant that Gargantua refuses to choose among the various authors—Hippocrates, Galen, and the Arabs—to whom the Faculty of Medicine alternately attributed ultimate authority in medicine, recommending instead the study of all these sources and others besides, which his earlier revision of Grammar will of course allow Pantagruel to study in the original rather than in the unreliable and barbaric Latin translations used by the Faculty. This direct, critical reading of ancient sources accompanied by firsthand observations afforded by frequent dissections implicitly abolishes the entire notion of authority as the University conceived it, and in the process shatters the authority of the Faculty of Medicine itself.[18]

This point is reinforced by the insertion of what first looks like a noncurricular discipline between Gargantua's remarks on Law and Medicine: "Et quand à la congnoissance des faictz de nature, je veulx que tu te y adonne curieusement: qu'il n'y ait mer, riviere, ny fontaine, dont tu ne congnoisse les poissons; tous les oyseaulx de l'air, tous les arbres, arbustes, et fructices des forestz, toutes les herbes de la terre, tous les metaulx cachez au ventre des abysmes, les pierreries de tout Orient et Midy, rien ne te soit incongneu. Puis songneusement revisite les livres des medicins" (261). Natural science as it is presented here does not constitute an independent discipline so much as a kind of propaedeutic necessary to and inseparable from the study of Medicine—the "congnoissance des faictz de nature" that must precede and parallel a "parfaicte congnoissance de l'aultre monde, qui est l'homme" (261).

Two aspects of this association of natural science and medicine are of particular interest. One is the suggestion that the "macrocosm" in which physical man—"l'aultre monde"—must be studied is not the celestial vault that encloses him, represents him, and can influence him from afar through a secret sympathy between homologous parts, but rather the natural, sublunar world in which he actually lives and which provides him with the three classes of "faictz de nature"—animal ("poissons," "oyseaulx"), vegetable ("fructices," "herbes"), and mineral ("metaulx," "pierreries")—that affect him directly in the form of food and remedies.[19] In this way Gargantua implicitly rejects the very basis of astrological medicine, even though he allows the critical examination of Talmudic and Cabalistic sources, thus confirming the naturalistic bias against arcane science expressed in his earlier remarks on Astronomy.

The second important point is that whereas the modern reader may find the link between natural science and medicine so self-evident as to have no particular significance, that link was recognized in Rabelais's day only by medical humanists. The University, for its part, while allowing occasional dissections, forbade as late as 1534 the study of natural science (see Antonioli, *Rabelais,* 50–54). Gargantua's deliberate marriage of natural science and medicine, like his association of ancient medical sources with frequent dissections, thus constitutes a direct humanist challenge to the authority of the traditional Faculty of Medicine and to the kind of medicine it taught.

The third, the highest, and the most gothic of the advanced disciplines represented by the medieval University was Theology—that monstrous creation of dialectical Logic that was taught in Paris by the greatest bastion of scholastic reaction and the most relentless persecutor of humanism in all its forms, the Sorbonne. In place of the abstract and sophistical science to which Dialectic led in the gothic curriculum, Gargantua substitutes a quintessentially humanistic counterpart—direct, personal, daily study of Scripture in the original texts, for which Gargantua's humanist Grammar has been the necessary and sufficient preparation: "Et par lesquelles heures du jour commence à visiter les sainctes lettres, premierement, en Grec, le *Nouveau Testament,* et *Epistres* des apostres, et puis en Hebrieu, le *Vieulx Testament*" (261). With this simple substitution Gargantua in effect abolishes the entire discipline of Theology as the University conceived it—along with the medieval *auctores* on whom it was built, the Faculty of Theology and the hated "sophistes" by whom it was taught,[20] and the human institutions (the Church, the clergy, monasticism, dogma, liturgy) through which it was maintained—to make room for an unmediated, personal, intimate knowledge of Scripture, the only authentic and authoritative source of the Christian faith. Gargantua thus ends his revision of the medieval curriculum with an indirect but powerful expression of Erasmus's familiar claim in the *Paraclesis* that everyone can be a theologian in the true sense of the word, because the Bible is accessible to all and is a far greater authority in matters of faith than all the doctors of the Church put together.[21]

A single principle is at work throughout this portion of Gargantua's letter. In following the canonic order of disciplines and hierarchy of

Faculties of the medieval University, Gargantua systematically replaces each of the gothic disciplines in turn with a direct humanist counterpart to it. The program of studies that results from this systematic transformation is thus not simply a summum of humanistic learning. It is also, and primarily, the *anticurriculum* of an *anti-University* in which "toutes disciplines" (to use the words with which Gargantua himself introduces his program) are indeed deliberately and systematically "restituées" (*P* 8:259).[22] As such it represents the perfect antithesis and antidote to the erratic, slovenly, and aimless education to which Pantagruel had previously been subjected during his tour of the medieval universities of France, and which he had found to be so repugnant and so redolent of the "infelicité et la calamité des Gothz" (*P* 8:258).[23]

Thus Gargantua's Ciceronian letter not only marks a clean break with the old learning of Pantagruel's first education as it has been evoked in the three preceding chapters; it deliberately subverts and rejects that old learning in order to restore it to, or replace it by, its humanistic antithesis—the providential return to a prelapsarian, pregothic "manne celeste de bonne doctrine." In mastering this utopian anticurriculum Pantagruel will be purged of his first education and transformed from the dissolute and ignorant schoolboy of chapters 5 through 7 into something entirely new—not merely a good humanist but humanism incarnate, the physical embodiment of the humanistic, antigothic encyclopedia, a veritable "abysme de science."[24]

The first half of the sapience cycle thus consists of a double education that first introduces Pantagruel to the postlapsarian, gothic learning of his fathers and then purges him of that fallen learning to make him over into the image of the restored learning of humanism.[25] Such is the hero's preparation for the act of redemption that he is destined to perform at the end of the epic. Such is the process that begins to transform him from the mere brute of chapter 4 into the ideal Christian prince he was born to become. Henceforth the messianic hero of the *Pantagruel* will embody not only the supreme potentia he has inherited in the flesh from his fallen ancestors but the divine sapientia of humanist learning as well. Thanks to the providential illumination of gothic darkness he will soon be one step closer to representing the trinitarian God in whose image he must live and rule.

The four chapters devoted to Pantagruel's two contrary educations are balanced and complemented by four chapters that systematically demonstrate the superiority of Pantagruel's new humanistic learning over the gothic knowledge it supersedes. At the conclusion of the acquisition phase Gargantua had enjoined his son to put his new learning to the test by defending theses in all subjects against all comers: "Et veux que, de brief, tu essaye combien tu as proffité, ce que tu ne pourras mieulx faire, que tenent conclusions en tout sçavoir, publiquement, envers tous et contre tous" (*P* 8:261). The demonstration phase begins accordingly, as Pantagruel, having mastered the anticurriculum of the letter, obeys the paternal injunction: "Bien records des lettres et admonitions de son pere," he "voulut un jour essayer son sçavoir" and so "par tous les carrefours de la ville mist conclusions . . . en tout sçavoir, touchant en ycelles les plus fors doubtes qui feussent en toutes sciences" (*P* 10:270–71).[26]

As this last phrase and the well-known precedents of Pico della Mirandola and Martin Luther make plain, this assaying of "sçavoir" constitutes both a test and a challenge. Pantagruel intends not only to prove his own learning but to defy the learning of others by inviting all comers to measure their learning against his. The importance of this challenge in terms of the sapience cycle as a whole is that it presents the demonstration of Pantagruel's learning as a definitive showdown between the gothic curriculum of chapters 5 through 7 and the humanist anticurriculum of chapter 8. Indeed Pantagruel's adversaries are specifically designated as the official representatives and products of each of the four Faculties of the medieval University and of the outmoded gothic disciplines they teach—first the Faculty of *Arts* ("Et premierement, en la rue du Feurre, tint contre tous les regens, artiens, et orateurs"), followed by the three advanced Faculties of the University: the Faculty of Theology ("Puis en Sorbonne tint contre tous les theologiens"), the Faculty of Civil Law ("Et à ce assisterent la plus part des seigneurs de la Court, maistres des requestes, presidens, conseilliers, les gens des comptes, secretaires, advocatz, et aultres"), the Faculty of Medecine ("avecques les medicins") . . . and even the Faculty of Canon Law ("et canonistes") (*P* 10:271).

The result of this showdown is a complete and decisive victory for Pantagruel. In his disputations with the representatives of the Faculty of Arts, Pantagruel "les mist tous de cul." As for the representatives of the higher Faculties, "il les feist tous quinaulx, et leur monstra visiblement qu'ilz n'estoient que veaulx engipponnez," despite their recourse to all the tricks and subtleties of the proscribed scholastic discipline of Dialectic—"nonobstant leurs ergotz et fallaces" (*P* 10:271). What this test is designed to prove is not Pantagruel's mastery of the disciplines represented by his various opponents but the absolute superiority of Gargantua's anticurriculum over the old curriculum it abolishes and supersedes. Pantagruel, we must remember, is not a product of the University but the very embodiment of its antithesis. In overwhelming each of the Faculties and reducing them all to amazed silence he marks the ultimate and definitive victory of the new learning over the old.

This general, symbolic victory of humanism over gothic learning is immediately followed by a more focused and concrete victory in the trial of Baisecul and Humevesne. We are told from the beginning of this episode that the elite of the old-school legal profession—not only the Parliament of Paris but "les plus sçavans et les plus gras de tous les parlemens de France, ensemble le Grand Conseil, et tous les principaulz regens des universitez, non seulement de France, mais aussi d'Angleterre et Italie"—have studied this difficult case for forty-six weeks, without being able to discover even what is at issue, or how they ought to proceed in trying it. They were so humiliated by their failure that they "se conchioyent de honte villainement" (*P* 10:272).

But Pantagruel, now famous for the "sçavoir si merveilleux" he demonstrated during his recent "grandes disputations" (*P* 10:271, 273), succeeds immediately, not only in finding the right way of proceeding in the case but in trying it and sentencing as well. He does so, moreover, by systematically putting into actual practice the restituted learning of his second, humanistic education.

Pantagruel begins by having all the earlier proceedings burned and then proceeds to listen to the litigants themselves, in order to judge their disagreement according to "equité evangelicque et philosophicque" alone (*P* 10:275). The meaning of this gesture is made explicit in a long speech delivered by Pantagruel before accepting the case. The earlier proceedings are invalid, he says, first because they consist entirely of endless dialectical arguments pro and contra, and second because they are based on the obscurantist medieval glosses (the "sottes et desraisonnables raisons et ineptes opinions") of Accursius, Baldus, Bartolus, and others, who "jamais n'entendirent la moindre loy des *Pandectes*" (*P* 10:273–74). Both Dialectic and legal glosses, as we have seen, were banished—implicitly but unmistakably—from Gargantua's humanist anticurriculum.

This crucial point is driven home in Pantagruel's prolonged diatribe against the glossators, which is made up almost entirely of deliberate textual echoes from both his first and second educations. In claiming that laws are "redigées en latin le plus elegant et aorné qui soit en toute la langue Latine" and therefore escape the comprehension of the barbaric glossators (274), he is repeating, almost verbatim, his earlier indictment of the gothic law he studied at Bourges: "Au monde n'y a livres tant beaulx, tant aornés, tant elegans, comme sont les textes des *Pandectes,* mais . . . la Glose de Accurse, est tant salle, tant infame et punaise, que ce

n'est que ordure et villenie" (*P* 5:242–43). As for his long enumeration of the various disciplines that are "nécessaire[s] à l'intelligence des loix" but of which the glossators are totally ignorant (274), it is nothing more than a recapitulation of all the relevant disciplines of Gargantua's humanistic anticurriculum—Grammar, Rhetoric, History, and Law—described, moreover, in exactly the same terms, as a simple juxtaposition of the two passages will clearly show. The glossators, says Pantagruel,

> n'avoyent congnoissance de *langue ny Grecque, ny Latine,* mais seullement de Gothique et Barbare; et toutesfoys les loix sont *premierement* prinses des *Grecz;* . . . et *secondement* sont redigées en *latin* le plus *elegant et aorné* qui soit en toute la langue Latine, et n'en excepteroys voluntiers ny Saluste, ny Varron, ny *Ciceron,* ny Senecque, ny T. Live, ny Quintilian. Comment doncques eussent peu entendre ces vieulx resveurs le *texte des loix,* qui jamais ne virent bon livre de langue Latine, comme manifestement appert à leur *stille,* qui est stille de ramonneur de cheminée ou de cuysinier et marmiteux, non de jurisconsulte?
>
> Davantaige, veu que les loix sont extirpées du mylieu de *philosophie moralle* et naturelle, comment l'entendront ces folz qui ont, par Dieu, moins estudié en philosophie que ma mulle? Au regard des *lettres de humanité* et congnoissance des *antiquitez et histoire,* ilz en estoyent chargez comme un crapault de plumes, dont toutesfoys les droictz sont tous pleins et sans ce ne pevent estre entenduz, comme quelque jour je monstreray plus apertement par escript. [*P* 10:274, emphasis mine throughout]

> GRAMMAR: "que tu aprenes les *langues* parfaictement: *premierement* la *Grecque* . . . *secondement,* la *Latine.*"
> RHETORIC: "que tu formes ton *stille,* quant à la Grecque, à l'imitation de Platon; quant à la Latine, à *Ciceron.*"
>
> LAW: "que tu saiche par cueur les beaulx *textes* [du] droit civil."
> RHETORIC: "que tu formes ton *stille.*"
>
> LAW: "et me les confere avecques *philosophie.*"
>
> INTRODUCTION: "la lumiere et dignité a esté de mon eage rendue es *lettres.*"
> HISTORY: "qu'il n'y ait *hystoire* que tu ne tienne en memoire presente." [*P* 8:259–61, emphasis mine throughout]

The purpose of these precise textual echoes is to establish as clearly as possible the fact that the Parliament, the Grand Conseil, and the "principaulx regens des universitez" of Europe have approached the case of Baisecul vs. Humevesne as practitioners of the old gothic Law of the University, and that Pantagruel proposes to proceed, on the contrary, as a practitioner of the newly restored Law of Gargantua's humanistic anticurriculum.

Thus, from the beginning of the episode, Baisecul vs. Humevesne is presented as a case so complex and difficult—a "controverse . . . si haulte et difficile en droict" (*P* 10:272), a "jugement tant difficile et espineux" (*P* 13:287)—that even the most illustrious representatives of traditional medieval jurisprudence have failed utterly in their long attempts to resolve it. As the great stumbling block of old gothic Law it functions within the larger design of the *Pantagruel* as a particularly revealing test both of Pantagruel's new Law and of the humanistic sapientia he has come to represent.

The case is indeed obscure. Rabelais convinces us of its difficulty by allowing us to hear viva voce the full statements of both the plaintiff and the defendant and by guaranteeing, through the use of deliberately incomprehensible language, that we will understand no more what is at issue or how to proceed than had the Parlement de Paris, who "n'y entendoi[en]t que le hault alemant" (*P* 10:272), or than do the assembled "presidens, conseilliers et docteurs," who exclaim, as indeed we must: "Nous l'avons veritablement ouy, mais nous n'y avons entendu, au diable, la cause" (*P* 13:285).[27] Even Pantagruel must strain to see clearly to the bottom of the case: "Je sue icy de haan pour entendre la procedure de vostre different," he says at one point of the testimony (*P* 11:278), and at the end "il se pourmena un tour ou deux par la sale, pensant bien profundement, comme l'on povoit estimer, car il gehaignoyt comme un asne qu'on sangle trop fort" (*P* 13:285).

But in the end Pantagruel's miraculous humanistic sapientia triumphs. His judgment, which exceeds our comprehension as much as the statements of the two litigants have done, is so brilliant and so equitable that both litigants—mirabile dictu—are equally satisfied with it, and the old-school "conseilliers et aultres docteurs . . . demeurerent en ecstase esvanoys bien troys heures, et tous ravys en admiration de la prudence de Pantagruel plus que humaine" (*P* 13:287). The burlesque humor of the trial is an impressive tour de force on Rabelais's part, but we must not allow it to distract us from the crucial point of the episode, which is that Pantagruel's approach to the case reflects exactly the content, the orientation, and even the diction of Gargantua's humanistic program of studies, and that it is the new anticurriculum in action that confounds once again the gothic curriculum, this time in the persons of the most distinguished products of the traditional Faculty of Law.

The episode of Baisecul and Humevesne thus works in tandem with that of Pantagruel's Mirandolesque defense of theses to establish once and for all the superiority of the hero's humanistic sapientia over the gothic learning of the University. In spite of what modern readers have tended to assume, the sapience cycle is complete, coherent, and meticulously, even symmetrically, composed. The two-part demonstration of Pantagruel's learning balances and complements the two-part section devoted to its acquisition, and the four demonstration chapters are linked to the four acquisition chapters by consistent textual and thematic echoes that constitute them as equal, corresponding panels in a perfectly rational diptych. By the end of this remarkably ordered sequence of chapters in which nothing is missing, nothing is superfluous, nothing is out of place, the messianic hero of the *Pantagruel* has become the incarnation of the new humanistic learning that triumphs over medieval darkness and the "calamité des Gothz."

But what, precisely, is the relevance of this sapience cycle to the larger design of the *Pantagruel*? Given the heroic exploit that Pantagruel is destined to perform at the end, humanistic learning and its triumph might first seem a rather peculiar form for his requisite apprenticeship to take. In fact, that apprenticeship is a most appropriate one for a number of reasons. First, as we have seen, it transforms the future hero from a fallen cannibalistic brute into an "image of God" by tempering his native potentia with the requisite sapientia and bonitas (see note 4 above). This transformation is precisely what was required to complete his identity as a type of Christ and to prepare him for the messianic act of redemption he was born to perform. At the same time, the topical realism of this apprenticeship adds an entirely new dimension to Pantagruel's character. Henceforth the hero will function not only typologically but in a more broadly allegorical way as well, as an exemplar of the Erasmian Christian prince whose divine attributes of sapientia and bonitas are the necessary qualities that will allow him to establish a new order at the end of the epic. As we shall see in chapter 5, this added dimension will have important consequences for the meaning of the overall design.

The most compelling relation, however, is revealed through a biblical analogy drawn at the end of the sapience cycle. Chapter 14 begins by retrospectively assimilating the difficult case of Baisecul vs. Humevesne to the juridical dilemma presented to Solomon in 1 Kings 3.16–28: "Salomon, qui rendit par soubson l'enfant à sa mère, jamais ne montra tel chief d'oeuvre de prudence comme a faict le bon Pantagruel" (*P* 14:288). Solomon's miraculous judgment in the irresolvable case of the two harlots appears in its original context as proof that God has answered Solomon's modest wish for nothing more than the practical political wisdom (that is, the sapientia) necessary to become a fitting ruler of God's chosen people (a "Judge" of Israel): "an understanding mind to govern [*iudicare*] thy people, that I may discern between good and evil," "understanding [*sapientiam*] to discern what is right [ad discernendum *iudicium*]," a "wise and discerning mind [cor *sapiens* et intelligens]" (1 Kgs 3.9, 11, 12).[28] And indeed, "when all Israel heard of the judgment which the king had rendered . . . they stood in awe of the king, because they perceived that the wisdom of God [*sapientiam Dei*] was in him, to render justice [ad faciendum *iudicium*]" (1 Kgs 3.28).

The parallels between the episode of Baisecul and Humevesne and its biblical analogue are many and obvious. Pantagruel, like Solomon, has been divinely ordained as the ruler of a chosen people. To fulfill his role he, like Solomon, acquires a sapientia Dei through the intervention of God—in Pantagruel's case indirectly through the "manne celeste de bonne doctrine" of humanism which, "par la bonté divine," has restored light and dignity to letters (*P* 8:260 and 259). Once acquired, his sapientia, like Solomon's, is revealed to his people through a miraculous judgment in a "controverse merveilleusement obscure et difficile" (*P* 10 title:270), with identical results: like "all Israel," the "conseilliers et aultres docteurs" perceive the "wisdom of God" in his judgment: they swoon and faint dead away for three hours, "tous ravys en admiration de la prudence de Pantagruel plus que humaine, laquelle avoyent congneu clerement en la decision de ce jugement tant difficile et espineux" (*P* 13:287). Clearly, an important function of the episode, and indeed of the entire sapience cycle, is to identify the hero of the *Pantagruel* as a kind of latter-day Solomon.[29]

This deliberate identification, which was already suggested at the end of Gargantua's letter ("Mais, parce que selon le saige Salomon, Sapience n'entre poinct en ame malivole et science sans conscience n'est que ruine de l'ame" [*P* 8:261–62]) and will come into play again before Pantagruel embarks on his epic exploit, is a crucial one for understanding the relevance of Pantagruel's unorthodox epic apprenticeship to the heroic exploit he will ultimately perform. First and most obviously, it recalls a model for the proper and necessary relationship between sapience and enlightened rule. Solomon is not only the best-known biblical exemplar of wisdom—"le saige Salomon" referred to in *P* 8:261 and again in *P* 18:313—but, as the explicit biblical analogue of the episode of Baisecul and Humevesne reminds us, he is a *king* designated by God to rule over his chosen people. He seeks sapientia from God not as an end in itself, but as the understanding necessary to fulfill his divinely appointed role in a way befitting its dignity: "to govern thy people, that I may discern between good and evil; for who is able to govern this thy great people?" (1 Kgs 3.9). Pantagruel, too, is a prince designated by God to rule a chosen people. His sapientia, too, is presented as the divine understanding—the "prudence plus que humaine"—necessary to fulfill his appointed role. Far from being either an end in itself or the occasion for an extraneous piece of antischolastic propaganda inserted willy-nilly into a formless Menippean satire, Pantagruel's encyclopedic learning is strictly a means to a political end, and as such forms an integral part of the larger design of the epic. The humane learning of the *studia humanitatis,* as opposed to the abstract, contentious, and suprahuman learning of the gothic University, is the kind of sapientia that will allow the hero to rule the chosen people of the *Pantagruel* in the image not only of the trinitarian God of the Christians but of the most wise and just king of the Old Testament.

Second and less obvious to the modern reader, perhaps, is that Solomon represented for Christian humanists the most important Old Testament type of Christ. As such, he was also the most suitable Old Testament exemplar for ideal Christian prince. "If only," writes Erasmus, alluding to the same biblical episode that Alcofrybas does, "all Christian princes would imitate that wisest of Kings who, given the opportunity to ask for anything he wanted from Him who could give everything, asked for nothing other than wisdom [sapientia], the wisdom by which he might justly govern the people who had been entrusted to him."[30] By associating Pantagruel with Solomon, the sapience cycle thus confirms his typological identity as a type of Christ while at the same time conferring upon him an exemplary identity as an Erasmian Christian prince.

Third and most important is the quality that made Solomon such a satisfactory type and exemplar to the Erasmian, evangelical way of thinking. "Solomon," as Erasmus never tired of repeating, means "peacemaker" in Hebrew (1 Chr 22.9), and it is precisely because Solomon was a peacemaker and ruled the chosen people in perfect peace that God chose him, and not his father, the blood-stained warrior David, to build his Temple (1 Chr 22.6–10 and 28.2–6) and most perfectly to foreshadow Christ, the messianic "Prince of Peace" prophesied by Isaiah (Is 9.6). The following passages are typical:

> Christ called only one precept his own, the precept of *caritas.* What is more contrary to *caritas* than war? . . . The type of Christ was Solomon, whose name means "peacemaker" in Hebrew. God chose

> him to build his Temple. He prevented David, who was in other respects incomparably glorious for his various virtues, from building his Temple for the sole reason that he was bloody. . . . When Christ was born the angels sang not of war or triumphs, but of peace [Lk 2.14: "and on earth peace among men of goodwill"]. Even before he was born that mystical prophet sang of him: "His abode has been established in Salem ['peace,' Ps 76.2]." [*Adagia* 4.1.1 ("Dulce bellum inexpertis")][31]

> David was most pleasing to God for his other virtues, and yet God forbade him to build his Temple, for no other reason than that he was bloody—that is, a warrior. He chose for this purpose the peacemaker, "Solomon." If it was thus among the Jews, how shall it be with us Christians? They had a shadow of "Solomon," we have the true "Solomon," the peacemaker Christ, conciliator of all things celestial and terrestrial. [*Institutio principis christiani* 11][32]

> Whoever proclaims Christ proclaims peace. Whoever preaches war preaches the opposite of Christ. Come now, for what purpose was the Son of God enticed down to earth if not to reconcile the world to the Father, to bind men together with a mutual and indissoluble *caritas,* and to make man a friend to himself? He was sent for *my* [Peace's] sake, to do *my* business. And for that reason he wanted his type to be Solomon, which in our language means εἰρηνοποιός, that is "peacemaker." As great as David was, nevertheless because he was a warrior, because he was defiled with blood, he was not permitted to build the house of the Lord; he did not deserve in this respect to be the type of Christ the peacemaker. [*Querela Pacis*][33]

Such passages help to reveal the most profound relation between Pantagruel's humanist education and the larger design of the epic. It is specifically as a *pacificus* that the hero of the *Pantagruel* has been cast in the role of Christ. Destined to redeem the original sin of fratricide, to reconcile brother to brother, and to reestablish a prelapsarian reign of caritas, Pantagruel's function is that of the messianic Prince of Peace whose archetype is Christ and whose prototype is the Old Testament king named "Peacemaker." Only by becoming as wise as Solomon will he be able to fulfill that role, not only to redeem, like Christ, a fallen race but also to govern in peace, like Solomon, the people entrusted to him. Behind the rather schematic typology of a redemptive design that culminates in the duel with Loup Garou and the pacification of Dipsodie lies a clear suggestion that in the real world of men such a redemption and such a reign of brotherly love can be brought about only by the kind of Erasmian prince whom humanistic, humane learning has made wise enough to govern God's people in peace, as a Solomon.

Pantagruel's judgment in the case of Baisecul and Humevesne confirms this crucial point. What is said to be truly miraculous in his judgment is not simply that it shows the hero to be wiser than the professional judges of the old school, or even that the judgment is more just and "prudent" than Solomon's, but specifically that it *reconciles two feuding neighbors* and reestablishes caritas between them, sending them away "amis comme devant, sans depens, et pour cause" (*P* 13:287). In sentencing, moreover, Pantagruel begins by declaring both parties innocent of the charges they have made against each other. The plaintiff is found to have had "juste cause" in doing whatever it is he did and is likewise "déclairé innocent" of some other "cas . . . qu'on pensoit qu'il eust encouru." Similarly, the charge made against the defendant "n'a esté en brimbalant trouvé vray" (*P* 13:286). Having declared both parties innocent, Pantagruel then sentences each to make amends for his unfounded charges against the other by an exchange of highly significant gifts. The plaintiff must provide the defendant with drink, the defendant must provide the plaintiff with food: "La court condemne [le demandeur] en troys verrassées de caillebottes . . . envers ledict defendeur. . . . Mais ledict defendeur sera tenu de fournir de foin et d'estoupes à l'embouchement des chassetrapes gutturales" (*P* 13:286–87). In other words, Pantagruel's sentence "condemns" the two burlesque antagonists to nothing more than a fittingly burlesque *convivium,* or agape, in which the reconciled feuders will eat and drink together in friendship and fraternal communion.[34]

The litigants' reaction to this sentence is indeed unprecedented: "Les deux parties departirent toutes deux contentes de l'arrest." This is an almost unbelievable thing, states the narrator—"quasi chose increable"—for, as he observes in a 1542 addition, never had it happened before and never would it happen again: "venu n'estoyt despuys les grandes pluyes et n'adviendra de treze jubilez que deux parties, contendentes en jugement contradictoires, soient egualement contentez d'un arrest diffinitif" (*P* 13:287). Strictly speaking, Pantagruel does not *judge* the great controversy between Baisecul and Humevesne at all. He literally *resolves* it by absolving and reconciling the opposing antagonists.

Thus, in the fullest sense of the word, Pantagruel may be said to make his Solomonic judgment according to "equité evangelicque et philosophicque" (*P* 10:275). The equity of his judgment is truly evangelical in that it reestablishes between two feuding neighbors the one evangelical precept that Christ called his own and the one principle that Pantagruel, the messianic Prince of Peace, is destined to restore to the fallen world—namely, the caritas that is peace among men.

With this in mind we may begin to discern remarkable resonances in the episode that concludes the sapience cycle of the *Pantagruel*. Lawsuits, as every Christian humanist knew, are the effect of enmity between brothers in a world tainted by Cain's sin. As such they are diametrically opposed to caritas, which is the love between brothers. Paul suggests as much in his first Epistle to the Corinthians (6.1–8), and Marot states it clearly in his *Enfer*, where lawsuits are represented as serpents descended from the Hydra who

> Les engendra dès l'aage et dès le temps
> Du *faux Cayn*. Et si tu quiers raison
> Pourquoy Procès sont si fort en saison,
> Sçaiche que c'est *faulte de charité*
> Entre Chrestiens.
> [lines 186–90, emphasis mine]

Lawsuits are in fact so incompatible with the nature of a "vray Chrestien, qui de touts se dict *frere*" that it is strictly impossible "D'estre Chrestien et playdeur tout ensemble" (lines 195–98, emphasis mine). As litigants locked in an interminable legal battle, Baisecul and Humevesne behave as exemplary heirs of Cain and inheritors of the original sin of fratricide.

But if this is the case, the old, gothic "Law" of the University, which proved to be incapable of adjudicating the dispute between Baisecul and Humevesne, begins to look very much like the *Old Law* of interdiction and of judgment. In attempting to *judge* according to overglossed laws, the old-school doctors of Law actually proceeded according to the veiled Law of Moses and thereby succeeded only in aggravating and perpetuating the great "controverse" between antagonistic neighbors. The new, restored "Law" of humanism, on the other hand, begins to look very much like the *New Law* of love and of pardon. By putting into practice the God-given sapience and jurisprudence of humanism, Pantagruel succeeds immediately in resolving the great controversy because in fact he does not "judge" at all but does justice to each party "sans varier ny accepter personne" (*P* 13:285) and absolves and reconciles them through caritas, "selon equité evangelicque" (*P* 10:275).[35] It is nothing less than Christ's New Law working through the new "Law" of the humanists that puts an end to the feud between neighbors by miraculously dissolving the fratricidal enmity that motivated it and by returning the antagonists to communion and a prelapsarian brotherly love, "amys comme devant." Seen in this light, the episode of Baisecul and Humevesne could hardly be more germane to the redemptive design of Alcofrybas's epic New Testament.

We may now see how completely the education chapters are integrated into the larger epic design of the *Pantagruel*. By the end of the sapience cycle Pantagruel is fully prepared for his predestined role and for the act of redemption that is the telos of the epic. Having acquired and literally incorporated the complete encyclopedia of restituted humanistic learning, the hero has become a complete image of God on earth and an ideal Christian prince. And in demonstrating the effects of that learning he has shown himself to be a new Solomon—both a wise ruler, or judge, and a Peacemaker—who, in "judging" the irresolvable legal conflict between feuding brothers, simultaneously puts into practice his new learning, new Law, and the New Law. The hero is now a full-fledged Prince of Peace ready to redeem Cain's sin on an epic scale and, in accordance with Isaiah's messianic prophecy (Is 9.6–7), to take upon his shoulder the government in an everlasting reign of brotherly love.

4

PANURGE

One of the greatest obstacles to a coherent interpretation of the *Pantagruel* has always lain in its richest and most conspicuous character. The mercurial and elusive Panurge seems to wreak havoc not only in the fictional world he inhabits but in the narrative logic and overall economy of the book as well. His character, his name, even the timing of his first appearance in the book are so many puzzles and so many apparent anomalies in the otherwise comprehensible design of Rabelais's first epic.

Variously associated with Hermes, the god of magic, arcane knowledge, rhetoric, subterfuge, and theft; with Tyl Ulenspiegel and Maistre Pierre Faifeu, the merry pranksters of folk legend; with the Devil, that malevolent worker of mischief in the world who leaves behind him fire and the smell of sulfur; and with Ulysses, the classical exemplar of worldly curiosity, Panurge has been identified as an essentially negative—but at the same time a curiously attractive—character, and perhaps even the antihero of the *Pantagruel*.[1] His pranks, though frequently malicious and sometimes even vicious, are tolerated and even overtly approved by both Pantagruel and the narrator. Is Panurge a good character or bad, the enemy or the hero of the *Pantagruel*?

This fundamental ambivalence in Panurge's character is reflected even in his name, since the word πανοῦργος allows moral connotations that are almost diametrically opposed. In classical usage the negative meanings ("cunning," "malicious," "fraudulent") seem to take precedence over the positive ("clever," "skilled," "experienced").[2] More germane to the problem of Panurge, perhaps, is the biblical use of πανοῦργος and its cognates. In the sapiential books of the Septuagint πανοῦργος is used in a predominantly positive sense to denote the prudent boy or man (*astutus, callidus, sapiens*) who will learn, or has learned, the wisdom of his father, as opposed to the foolish boy or man (*fatuus, stultus,* or *innocens* in a negative sense) who refuses to heed paternal counsel.[3] But in the Epistles of Paul the abstract noun πανουργία is used in an exclusively negative way, to refer to the foolish wisdom of the world that is confounded by the wisdom of God (1 Cor 3.19), the deceitfulness and prevarication of disseminators of false doctrines (2 Cor 4.2 and Eph 4.14), and even the craftiness by which the serpent deceived Eve and the scribes attempted to deceive Christ (2 Cor 11.3 and Lk 20.23).[4] Is Panurge then a clever man or a fraudulent one, the prudent lad of the Old Testament or the fool, the deceiver, and the enemy of truth of the New?

The moment of Panurge's first entrance into Pantagruel's gesta, too, appears to be so incongruous that many have claimed that chapter 9 of the *Pantagruel* is misplaced and have advanced ingenious hypotheses to explain why it does not appear where it should (see chapter 3, note 5). As we have seen, the chapter in which Panurge is introduced interrupts a natural sequence of episodes in what I have called the sapience cycle of the *Pantagruel*, separating Gargantua's exhortation to defend theses publicly from Pantagruel's execution of his father's wishes.[5] To make matters worse, the intervening chapter 9 ends with Panurge's promise of a full narration of his past misfortunes, which is similarly forgotten during the second half of the sapience cycle, only to be fulfilled five chapters later.[6] Worse still, once Panurge's autobiographical narration is finished at the end of chapter 14 the narrator, rather than returning to the gesta of his hero, goes on to relate the witticisms, "meurs et condictions de Panurge" (*P* 16 title:300) at such length that Panurge seems to replace the messianic hero as the focal character. The presentation of Panurge thus not only interrupts the natural sequence of two logically consecutive chapters but introduces another sequence that will in turn be interrupted by the return to the first sequence, in the following way:

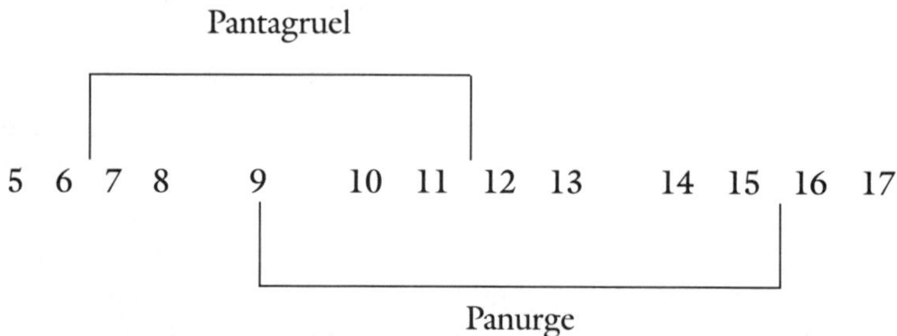

Why does Panurge not simply appear for the first time after chapter 13? Is his untimely appearance a printer's error? or an effect of Rabelais's perverseness?[7]

These difficulties have given rise to much confusion. The negative aspects of Panurge's character have led some readers to make him the villain of the book, while his inexplicable appeal has led others to make him the hero. Yet others have found him to be so ambivalent and anomalous as to have no other function than to defy stable interpretation and to throw into radical question any serious reading one might wish to make of the rest of the "horribles et espoventables faictz et prouesses du tres-renommé Pantagruel." Whichever of these interpretations we might prefer, Panurge would seem to weaken and perhaps even sabotage from within the redemptive design we have discerned in the broad lines of the rest of Pantagruel's gesta.

But the notorious difficulty of interpreting Panurge is in large part merely an effect of the anachronistic way the problem has traditionally been posed, and of mistaken assumptions about the nature of the book as a whole. If the *Pantagruel* were a free-form Menippean satire, as it has so often been taken to be, then it would be entirely legitimate to consider Panurge as a character in the classical sense of the word—that is, as a moral type (χαρακτήρ). If it were a novel, as many prefer to call it, then it would perhaps be legitimate to consider Panurge as a character in the nineteenth-century sense of the word—that is, as a coherent psychological persona. But the *Pantagruel* is neither a Menippean satire nor a novel. It is, as we have seen, a heroic work of unmistakable and insistent epic pretensions, and as such demands to be understood in the light of the conventions of epic. If we approach Panurge not as a problematic character but simply as an *epic function,* his role and even the timing of his appearance appear far less anomalous than a naïve reading might lead one to think.

In classical epic, and in ancient legend in general, the hero is typically accompanied by a true and faithful friend called an ἑταῖρος, or *comes.* Theseus is accompanied and aided by Pirithoos, Heracles by Theseus, Orestes by Pylades, Achilles by Patroclus, Odysseus by Diomede, and of course *pius Aeneas* by *fidus Achates.* In medieval epic the function of the classical *comes* evolved from the rather minor role of friend and silent partner into a crucial foil character that serves to reveal through complementarity, contrast, and opposition the heroic character or even the tragic flaw of the hero. Roland and Olivier, Yvain and Gauvain, Perceval and Gauvain are typical pairs of this kind. Because the *Pantagruel* is presented as an epic conspicuously inscribed in the classical-medieval tradition, Rabelais was virtually required by the conventions of that tradition to provide his epic hero with a *comes.*

Panurge is of course that *comes.* He is deliberately presented as such during his first appearance, when the hero designates him as his companion by casting him in the role of Achates, the *comes* of the epic on which the *Pantagruel* is most closely modeled (*P* 9:269). The only novelty in this epic companionship, as we have seen, is that because the *Pantagruel* is also a kind of New Testament and its hero a messianic type of Christ, Pantagruel's epic companion is presented in the rather curious role of disciple as well (*P* 9:270). From the beginning Panurge is thus presented as an ally in a common epic-messianic cause—as an Achates-disciple to Pantagruel's Aeneas-Christ. In the tradition of his more immediate forebears, however, Pantagruel's companion-disciple plays a much more important role than that of a pale subordinate like Achates, Patroclus, or a disciple. Like most medieval epic companions he acts as foil as well as counterpart, functioning dialectically both to define the hero's character and to bring a particular issue into clear focus. Just as the dispute that opposes Roland and Olivier ("Rollant est proz e Olivier est sage") is designed to reveal the nature of Roland's heroism and to probe the ideal of feudal valor, for example, so the curious friendship between Pantagruel and Panurge is designed to reveal something important about the hero and the nature of his epic exploit.[8]

Before even considering Panurge's character, we know from purely generic considerations that he cannot possibly be an evil or entirely negative character, or an antihero in any modern sense of the word. As an epic *comes* and disciple he is, on the contrary, a companion, an ally against a common adversary, and a crucial foil and counterpart whose character and role must be considered in close relation to those of the hero and to the predestined establishment of a new order. With this in mind we must look more closely at the moment and the manner of Pantagruel's first encounter with his *comes,* in order to discover what role this paradoxical foil and ally will play within the larger epic design of the *Pantagruel.*

The diverse tongues spoken by Panurge in response to Pantagruel's straightforward questions—"Qui estes vous? Dont venez vous? Où allez vous? Que querez vous? Et quel est vostre nom?" (*P* 9:264)—first appear to contribute to Panurge's general ambivalence. They recall the confusion of tongues by which God punished the presumption of Pantagruel's own ancestor Nimrod (*P* 1:224) and scattered his people over the face of the earth (Gen 10.8–12 and 11.1–9). But they also recall the converse, compensatory gift of tongues by which the Holy Spirit of Pentecost allowed the Apostles to bring the Word to the diverse and scattered peoples of the world (Acts 2.1–11). And at the same time they recall the languages by which the trickster Pathelin contrived to block communication and cheat the merchant Guillaume Joceaulme out of his due.[9]

To understand the implications of this curious first meeting we must begin by considering not the superficial fact that Panurge speaks many foreign languages before answering in his native French, but what Panurge actually *says* in those various languages. For although Pantagruel and his companions do not seem to understand Panurge's meaning, the reader is able to understand a great deal of what he says with no difficulty. Any reader of the original 1532 edition, especially, could easily have understood at least three of the original nine languages (which were German, "langaige des Antipodes," Italian, Dutch, Spanish, Hebrew, Greek, Utopian, Latin), because Latin was the native written language of all literate people, and because anyone who knows both Latin and French can make perfect sense of Panurge's very Latinate Italian and Spanish, even if he has no knowledge of either language. In addition, Rabelais could have expected many of his readers to know enough Greek, and some to know enough Hebrew, to understand yet a fourth and possibly a fifth language. And if a reader happened to know the language of the Holy Roman Empire he could not only have understood the German but also have deciphered the Dutch. Of all of Panurge's original nine languages, then, only two—the fictional "Antipodian" and "Utopian" languages—were certain to defy comprehension. Readers could be expected to understand anywhere from three to all of the remaining seven.[10] Even one or two would be sufficient, however, because Panurge says essentially the same thing in each of them. Moreover, he gives fullest expression to his crucial, highly charged message in precisely those languages that were most accessible to Rabelais's original readers—Latin, Spanish, Italian, and Greek.

His message may be divided into two separate but mutually reinforcing propositions. The first is simply that Panurge is hungry and that Pantagruel should therefore have *pity* on him by giving him something to eat: "Das . . . ist ein arm unnd *erbarmglich* ding. . . . [Tholb suld of me *pety* have]. . . . Ggheest my unyt *bermherticheyt* yet waer un ie ghevoet mach zunch. . . . Sy ellos non bastarent para mover Vostra Reverentia a *piedad,* supplico que mire a la *piedad* natural, la qual yo creo que le movra como es de razon. . . . [Hwarfor *forbarme* teg omsyder offvermeg]. . . . Laah [sic] al Adonai *chonen* ral [sic for 'dal'] (לָוָה [!] עַל־אֲדֹנָי חוֹנֵן דָּל). . . . Ce en to metaxy eme uc *eleis* udamos (*καὶ ἐν τῷ μεταξὺ ἐμὲ οὐκ ἐλεεῖς οὐδαμῶς*). . . . Obtestatus sum, ut, si qua vos *pietas* permovet, egestatem meam solaremini" (*P* 9:264–69, emphasis mine).[11] The relevance of this simple message to the larger redemptive design of the *Pantagruel* is obvious. While even pagan cultures place a high value on charity to the unfortunate ("piedad natural," "pietas"), such charity as an effect of evangelical caritas forms the very basis of all Christian ethics. The "preceptos evangeliquos" (*P* 9:267) to which Panurge so pointedly refers in one of his most immediately comprehensible tongues are none other than those of the single Great Commandment of the New Testament: "Dilige proximum tuum sicut teipsum." In his first, unexpected appearance in the epic, then, Panurge is presented, and explicitly presents himself, as an *object of Pantagruel's caritas*—that is, as an object of the brotherly love that the messianic hero is destined eventually to restore to a fallen world of brotherly hatred and fratricide.

Pantagruel immediately recognizes this and states that he has already taken pity on this unfortunate man and is naturally disposed to do everything in his power to help him. His first words to the bedraggled stranger are: "Mon amy, je vous prie que un peu veuillez icy arrester et me respondre à ce que vous demanderay, et vous ne vous en repentirez point, car j'ay affection très grande de vous donner ayde à mon povoir en la calamité où je vous voy: car vous me faites grand *pitié*" (*P* 9:263–64, emphasis mine). His last words of the episode show that his pity is indeed an effect of caritas: "Par ma foy, je vous ay ja prins en *amour* si grand que, si vous condescendez à mon vouloir, vous ne bougerez jamais de ma compaignie, et vous et moy ferons un nouveau pair d'amitié telle que feut entre Enée et Achates" (*P* 9:269, emphasis mine).

But by inquiring into the particulars of the stranger's identity and circumstances, and by linking charity to simple information—"Vous me faites grand pitié. Pour tant, mon amy, dictes moy: Qui estes vous? Dont venez vous, etc. [264]. . . . Racomptez nous quel est vostre nom, et dont vous venez: car, par ma foy, je vous ay ja prins en amour si grand, etc." (269)—Pantagruel puts knowledge before caritas, thereby delaying an act of charity he knows is urgently needed and that he is already prepared to perform regardless of the answers to his questions.

The second proposition contained in Panurge's various speeches points out this initial imperfection in Pantagruel's caritas. It is simply that language is superfluous in the present circumstances because Panurge is too hungry to talk ("non vi saprei contare le mie fortune, se prima il tribulato ventre non a la solita refectione"), because he is too hungry to listen ("venter famelicus auriculis carere dicitur"), and most important, because his need speaks for itself, and indeed speaks far more eloquently than any words could possibly do: "My dunct nochtans, al en seg ie u *niet een wordt*, mynen noot verklaart ghenonch wat ie beglere. . . . [Endog ieg med *inghen tunge* talede . . . myne Kleebon och myne legoms magerhed uudviser allygue klalig huvad tyng meg meest behoff girereb]" (265–69, emphasis mine). This last point is made most explicitly in Greek, which contains a miniature treatise on the uses and abuses of language. "All men of letters agree that speech and language are altogether superfluous when the thing itself is obvious to everyone. Speech is necessary only in situations in which the things we are discussing are not clearly apparent": "φιλόλογοι πάντες ὁμολογοῦσι τότε λόγους τε καὶ ῥήματα περιττὰ ὑπάρχειν, ὁπότε πρᾶγμα αὐτὸ πᾶσι δῆλόν ἐστι. Ἔνθα γὰρ ἀναγκαῖοι μόνον λόγοι εἰσὶν, ἵνα πράγματα, ὧν πέρι ἀμφισβητοῦμεν, μὴ φωσφόρως ἐπιφαίνηται." Because Panurge's hunger is obvious, there should be no need for him to say that he is hungry. Pantagruel's question "Que querez vous?" is answered by observable reality before he even asks it.

The interest of these two simple propositions is that they work together in their immediate context and against several well-known biblical contexts to constitute a subtle, ironic lesson in practical caritas. Panurge's profusion of languages is not primarily Babelic or even Pentecostal. Nor is it Pathelinesque or an effect of idle virtuosity or perverseness. Rather it is a deliberate stratagem designed to show his rich and well-meaning interlocutor that when the time comes to love one's brother and help him in his need, information about particulars like name, birth, profession, and circumstances ("Qui estes vous? Dont venez vous? Où allez vous? Que querez vous? Et quel est vostre nom?") are of no consequence, for caritas must act first and ask questions later, and in any case must act without partiality or distinction according to person (Jas 2.1 and 9)—"sans accepter personne," as a wiser Pantagruel will himself state at the end of the following episode (*P* 13:285; see above, chapter 3, note 35). The point of Panurge's glossolalia is simply that one need not understand his *words* to understand his *meaning* perfectly. Panurge speaks incomprehensible tongues precisely in order to force Pantagruel to the realization that he has already understood what is to be done even before resorting to language. The very incomprehensibility of his words conveys his most important meaning.

By allowing his readers to understand so many of Panurge's various tongues, Rabelais makes sure that we see this crucial, ironic point of Panurge's glossolalia. In languages that we can understand but that the Pantagruelians apparently cannot, Panurge tells us explicitly that his own words are indeed superfluous to the higher meaning toward which they are intended to point. Given the privileged position in which this autocommentary puts the reader, it seems likely that Rabelais's reason for including invented languages, which are by definition and by design indecipherable to everyone, is to put the more comprehending reader, at least momentarily, in the awkward position of the Pantagruelians.[12] By guaranteeing in this way that we understand virtually nothing of at least these three languages (Antipodian, Utopian, and later Lanternois) Rabelais forces even the best linguists among us to reveal whether or not we have understood not only Panurge's words but the intention behind those words. Will we be wise enough to understand that the precise meaning of these words is irrelevant to Panurge's higher, moral meaning? Or will we be so foolish as to stick at the opacity of these languages *as languages* and seek to understand the literal meaning of the words themselves, as the Pantagruelians persist in doing? Modern commentaries on the episode and various misguided attempts to decipher its deliberately indecipherable languages are ample proof that the lesson is by no means an easy one to learn.

The crucial point of Panurge's polyglot answers is driven home toward the end of the episode, when Panurge at last speaks languages that even Pantagruel and his companions can understand—Hebrew ("A ceste heure ay je bien *entendu,*" says Epistemon, "car c'est langue Hebraïcque bien rhetoricquement prononcée"), Greek, ("Quoy? dist Carpalim, . . . c'est Grec, je l'ay *entendu*"), Utopian ("J'*entends,* se me semble, dist Pantagruel: car ou c'est langaige de mon pays de Utopie, ou bien luy ressemble quant au son"), and the universally understood Latin (268–69, emphasis mine). Yet even when they understand the literal, self-glossing meaning of Panurge's words the Pantagruelians fail to understand the moral meaning that his recourse to tongues is designed to convey—that literal comprehension is neither necessary nor sufficient in matters of caritas.

Thus Panurge enters the epic as a crafty teacher and an object lesson in practical caritas. This initial role is not without precedent. It corresponds exactly to the role attributed to the apostle Paul in the single passage of the entire New Testament in which the adjective "πανοῦργος" appears. Writing to the Corinthians Paul recalls how he managed to convert them to Christianity: "I was crafty [πανοῦργος], you say, and got the better of you by guile" (2 Cor 12.16). This is precisely the sense in which "Panurge" is "πανοῦργος." When Pantagruel's teacher of caritas and future disciple first comes to Paris he is πανοῦργος in the same way, and to the same end, that the evangelizer of the Gentiles was in Corinth.

Panurge's Pauline craftiness consists, moreover, in an ironic playing out of the fullest and best-known definition of caritas offered by the same Paul to the same Corinthian converts:

> If I *speak in the tongues* of men and of angels, but have not love [caritas], I am a noisy gong or a clanging cymbal. . . . Now [brothers], if I come to you *speaking in tongues,* how shall I benefit you unless I bring you some revelation of knowledge or prophecy or teaching? . . . If you *in a tongue* utter speech that is not intelligible,

> how will any one know what is said? For you will be speaking into the air. There are doubtless *many different languages* in the world, and none is without meaning; but if I do not know the meaning of the language, I shall be a foreigner to the speaker and the speaker a foreigner to me. [1 Cor 13.1, 14.6 and 9–11, emphasis mine]

In subsequent chapters Panurge may prove to be a man without love, a noisy gong and a clanging cymbal. He may even "[wander in] cunning" ("*μὴ περιπατοῦντες ἐν πανουργίᾳ*," "non *ambulantes in astutia*") and "tamper with God's word" instead of stating the truth openly (2 Cor 4.2). But at the moment of his first appearance he does so, speaking the unintelligible tongues of men and angels, not to prevent understanding but to create it, not to hide his own lack of love but to teach love to others. And even in this Panurge conforms to a model set forth by Paul. At the conclusion of the same passage to the Corinthians Paul quotes Isaiah to say that "in the law it is written, 'By men of strange tongues and by the lips of foreigners will I speak to this people, and even then they will not listen to me, says the Lord'" (1 Cor 14.21 [Is 28.11–12]). Panurge is clearly such a man of strange tongues. The paradox of Panurge is thus a perfectly evangelical one. The apparently godless stranger encountered so unexpectedly by Pantagruel in the midst of the sapience cycle is actually a crafty, ironic, Pauline agent of God, speaking in strange tongues to teach the New Law of caritas without partiality to a people who hear but do not listen.

We are now in a position to resolve all the difficulties arising from Panurge's character and initial appearance in the epic. First, Panurge's crafty, Pauline lesson is none other than the one stated by John in the crucial passage of his first Epistle on the opposition between Cain's fratricide and the New Commandment of brotherly love, on which we have found the entire redemptive design of the *Pantagruel* to be predicated: "For this is the message which you have heard from the beginning, that we should love one another, and not be like Cain who was of the evil one and murdered his brother. . . . But if any one has the world's goods and *sees his brother in need,* yet closes his heart against him, how does God's love abide in him? Little children, let us not love *in word or speech* but *in deed and in truth*" (1 Jn 3.11 and 17–18, emphasis mine). By the end of the episode Pantagruel has learned that lesson, having not only declared his undying love for Panurge in speech, but translated that love into action by feeding him, clothing him, and taking him on as his constant companion in a "nouveau pair d'amitié" (*P* 9:269–70).

Second, the fact that the encounter with Panurge constitutes a lesson in practical caritas makes its placement in the epic perfectly comprehensible. Chapter 9 appears where it does because it marks the completion of Pantagruel's education. In chapter 8, as we have seen, the young giant's extraordinary potentia was tempered and supplemented with an equally extraordinary sapientia, thanks to the antischolastic, humanistic education that made of him a veritable "abysme de science." But as Gargantua had warned, "Science sans conscience n'est que ruine de l'ame." Knowledge must be accompanied by the caritas of the Great Commandment: "Il te convient servir, aymer et craindre Dieu, et en luy mettre toutes tes pensées et tout ton espoir. . . . Soys serviable à tous tes prochains, et les ayme comme toymesmes" (*P* 8:262; compare Mt 22.37–39). In chapter 9, Pantagruel's newly acquired sapientia is accordingly tempered and supplemented in turn by bonitas, thanks to an object lesson in practical caritas in the person of the wandering Panurge. By the end of chapter 9, the formation of the messianic hero of the *Pantagruel* is at last complete. Pantagruel is now the perfect Christian prince whose attributes—potentia, sapientia, bonitas—are those of the trinitarian God in whose image he is to reign on earth. Only now may he put his education into practice by defending theses and intervening actively to restore brotherly love to the feuding Baisecul and Humevesne.

The unsettling encounter with Panurge is thus not at all misplaced or digressive. It appears precisely where it should, forming not only an integral and crucial part of the prince's education but the keystone of the entire symmetrically composed sapience cycle. In addition to separating the four chapters devoted to the hero's acquisition of sapientia from the four chapters devoted to the demonstration of his now-perfect sapientia and bonitas, chapter 9 also narrates the acquisition *and* preliminary demonstration of the hero's evangelical bonitas.

Finally, to return to the question of Panurge's character, it has become even more obvious that Pantagruel's epic *comes* and disciple is not principally a demonic or diabolical character, or even a simple negative counterpart to Pantagruel. He is the first object, and even the teacher, of the hero's brotherly love. Even the title of the chapter points to this crucial fact: "Comment Pantagruel trouva Panurge, lequel il *ayma* toute sa vie" (*P* 9 title:263, emphasis mine).

And yet Panurge himself is far from being a perfect practitioner of caritas, as we learn when the narration eventually returns to him five chapters later (*P* 14–17). He ignores the Parisian lady's grudging attempt at caritas—"Quant est de moy," she says in repelling his advances, "je ne vous hays poinct, car, comme Dieu le commande, je ayme tout le monde" (*P* 21:330)—and takes revenge on her for her refusal. He abuses the nominal "pardons" offered by sellers of indulgences and "tampers with God's word" (2 Cor 4.2) by invoking the New Law of brotherly love, which he represents moreover as a strictly Judaic law: "car *accipies* est dit selon la maniere des Hebrieux, qui usent du futur en lieu de l'imperatif, comme vous avez en la Loy: *Dominum deum tuum adorabis, et illi soli servies; diliges proximum tuum; et sic de aliis*" (*P* 17:309 var.; Saulnier *P* 12:97–98)—only to justify his theft of twelve pocketfuls of silver coins from the Church. And he exploits the natural caritas—what he himself had called "pietas" and "piedad natural" (*P* 9:269 and 267)—of the Turks in order to bring them to utter ruin: "me voyans ainsi à demy rousty, eurent *pitié* de moy *naturellement* et me getterent toute leur eau sur moy et me refraicherent joyeusement. . . . Ce pendent qu'ilz se amusoyent à moy, le feu triumphoit . . . à prendre en plus de deux mille maisons" (*P* 14:292–93, emphasis mine). What is worse, he exults uncharitably in the Turks' calamity which their own natural caritas and his conspicuous lack thereof have brought about: "[Je] vys toute la ville bruslant, dont je fuz tant aise que je me cuydé conchier de joye. . . . Je regardoys en grand liesse ce beau feu, me gabelant et disant: 'Ha, pauvres pulses, ha, pauvres souris, vous aurez maulvais hyver, le feu est en vostre paillier'" (*P* 14:293). Panurge is thus explicitly and consistently portrayed in terms of the New Commandment and shown to be as deficient in brotherly love as anyone can possibly be without joining the hostile ranks of Anarche and Loup Garou.

But this is precisely the point that makes Panurge's relation to the hero of the *Pantagruel* most significant. As the most flawed and imperfect of mortals who falls so woefully short of the ideal represented by Pantagruel, Panurge functions not only as the teacher and first object of Pantagruel's own caritas but as proof of the absolute perfection of that caritas in the Christ-like hero of Alcofrybas's epic New Testament. He is the limiting case of the kind of imperfect brother that Pantagruel's caritas must stretch to embrace.

And indeed the messianic redeemer of Cain's fratricide will go out of his way throughout the epic to tolerate, to include, and to *love* his wayward and often not very lovable companion, laughing heartily at all Panurge's untimely obscenities ("Ho, ho, ha, ha, ha! . . . Vrayement, dist Pantagruel, tu es gentil compaignon" [*P* 15:296 and 299]; "Ha, ha, ha, dist Pantagruel. . . . Et le bon Pantagruel ryoit à tout" [*P* 26:348–49]) and taking in good part his pranks ("A quoy voluntiers consentit Pantagruel, et veit le mystere, qu'il trouva fort beau et nouveau" [*P* 22:334]; "Et Pantagruel prenoit à tout plaisir" [*P* 31:376]). For Panurge is not an agent of anticaritas to be neutralized before the new order of brotherly love can be restored but an extreme case of the kind of flawed Everyman who must somehow be redeemed and incorporated into that Utopian order.[13] What makes the postlapsarian world of the *Pantagruel* the Caïna it is, is precisely that it is inhabited not by ideal types like Pantagruel but by flawed and imperfect mortals like Panurge, and that such "brothers" are so damnably hard to love. Without the Panurges there would be no need for a messianic hero like Pantagruel, and caritas would not be a heroic virtue. Loving a man like Panurge is the greatest proof of that virtue in the Christ-like hero Pantagruel.

But there is even more to Panurge than a teacher, an object, and a limiting test case of all-embracing caritas in Pantagruel. As a *comes* to the messianic hero, even this most imperfect practitioner of brotherly love will play a positive role in the epic struggle to come. In spite of first appearances, Panurge is perfectly integrated into the larger redemptive design of the epic and contributes something crucial and even indispensable to it. By loving this loveless and unlovable companion and counterpart, Pantagruel discovers in him an indispensable ally whose very faults can be put to good use in his heroic battle against anticaritas.

When the narration returns to Panurge at the end of the sapience cycle, we are shown a thief and a prankster whose victims are almost without exception the rich, the proud, and the powerful, and the guardians of the old order. He persecutes without remorse the "sergeans" and the "guet" who patrol the section of the Latin Quarter where students at the Faculty of Arts are lodged; the old-school "maistres es arts et theologiens";[14] monks who say Mass for the bigwigs at the courts of law; moneychangers; and noble ladies and gentlemen (*P* 16).

All of Panurge's pranks involve the debasement of assumed grandeur. This is most obvious in his treatment of rich nobility. Panurge's favorite targets are ladies whose fine clothing sets them apart as socially superior—"les plus sucrées damoiselles qu'il trouvoit," "mesmement celles qui portoyent robbes de tafetas armoisy," "les femmes qu'il voyoit les plus acrestées," "femme ou homme qui eust quelque belle robbe," etc.—especially when they are showing off in church (*P* 16:303, 305). He never harms these victims physically but contrives to expose their baser humanity by making them sneeze, disrobe, or lose countenance in church or, more frequently, by staining, tearing, or befowling the fine clothing that is the sign of their presumed distinction from hoi polloi. When Panurge takes his revenge on the haughty Parisian lady, he debases her in exactly this way, choosing the feast of Corpus Christi, "à laquelle toutes les femmes se mettent en leur triumphe de habillemens"; when his lady "s'estoit vestue d'une très belle robbe de satin cramoysi et d'une cotte de veloux blanc bien precieux," to contrive to have all the dogs of Paris "compiss[er] tous ses habillemens" and "gast[er] tous ces beaulx acoustremens" (*P* 22:332, 333, and 334).

The purpose behind all Panurge's pranks is to turn the social order upside down by elevating the poor and wretched and by humbling the rich and powerful. Thus, through a kind of misdirected caritas he dissipates ill-acquired fortunes in marrying off unmarriageable old hags and in offering banquets to poor pageboys. Conversely, through a complementary vindictiveness, he devises lawsuits against the rich "damoyselles" of Paris in favor of their poor suitors, against the theologians "es escholes de Sorbone" in favor of the cesspool cleaners, and against the "Presidens et Conseillers" in favor of their pages (*P* 17).

This systematic inversion of high and low stations—and particularly the debasement of the exalted—is fundamental to Panurge's role. It comes into play in most of Panurge's parodic imitations of Pantagruel, as for example in his obscene reply to the prince's suggestion that the best walls for a city are the "bones" of its male citizens (*P* 15:295); in his treatment of the haughty Parisian lady and of the conventional language of love (*P* 21:327); and in his culinary parody of Pantagruel's trophy and "dicton victorial" (*P* 27:350–51). As we shall see in chapter 6, this essential aspect of Panurge's character will play a crucial role at the epic conclusion of the *Pantagruel* and will serve to integrate Panurge even further into the larger redemptive design of the epic.

Before aiding Pantagruel in his predestined exploit, however, this paradoxical epic *comes* and counterpart proves to be an indispensable complement and ally in other ways. The episode that establishes most clearly Panurge's usefulness to Pantagruel is the famous debate by signs with the Englishman Thaumaste. Here the trickster Panurge intervenes at a critical moment to defend his lord against a serious challenge to his divine sapience and in the process proves even to doubters that Pantagruel is a type of Christ.

It will be recalled that in the second half of the sapience cycle Pantagruel demonstrated his extraordinary sapientia by putting it to the test—"essayer son sçavoir" (*P* 8:261 and *P* 10:270)—first in defending theses against all comers, and second in the admirable judgment by which he reestablished brotherly love between two litigants in an impossibly complex lawsuit. Those tests won him a universal reputation for his "sçavoir merveilleux" (*P* 10:271) and "prudence plus que humaine"

(*P* 13:287)—greater even than Solomon's (*P* 10 title:270 var.; Saulnier *P* 9 bis:55 and *P* 14:288). After four chapters devoted to Panurge's tricks (*P* 14–17) a new challenge arises to that reputation. Having heard the "bruict et renommée" of Pantagruel's "sçavoir incomparable" and "tant inestimable" (*P* 18:312 and 314), the Englishman Thaumaste has made the long voyage to Paris to test that Solomonic wisdom with certain "problemes insolubles" (*P* 20:324)—"en ceste seule intention de veoir Pantagruel et le congnoistre et esprouver si tel estoit son sçavoir comme en estoit la renommée" (*P* 18:312)—exactly as the Queen of Sheba had once made the long voyage to Jerusalem to "test" the wisdom of Solomon "with hard questions": "Sed et regina Saba, audita fama Salomonis in nomine Domini, venit tentare eum in aenigmatibus" (1 Kgs 10.1 and 2 Chr 9.1; compare *P* 18:313). The episode of Thaumaste thus parallels that of Baisecul and Humevesne[15] and constitutes a virtual reprise of the second half of the sapience cycle in which Panurge, the epic companion and disciple, acts as the indispensable stand-in for his lord to demonstrate once again not only the Christological nature of Pantagruel but his own usefulness to him.

Two aspects of this new challenge to Pantagruel's prudence are significant. First, Thaumaste's challenge is an act of pride. In spite of Pantagruel's invocation of the humanistic ideal of "celeste manne de honeste sçavoir" (*P* 18:315; compare *P* 8:260: "manne celeste de bonne doctrine"), in spite of the prince's explicit admonition to seek not "honeur ny applausement des hommes, mais la verité seule" (*P* 28:315), the Englishman, for his part, is clearly motivated by pride alone. His purpose is to dethrone the embodiment of wisdom, the "imaige de science et de sapience" (*P* 18:313), by tripping him up with his *aenigmata* and conundra. The explicit analogy with the Queen of Sheba who "tempts" wise Solomon at the beginning of the episode, and the implicit extension of this analogy at the end of the episode to include the scribes and Pharisees of an "evil and adulterous generation" who "tempt" Christ (*P* 20:324; see below), are already clear indications of Thaumaste's invidious pride.

These indications are confirmed by Thaumaste's speech. In striking contrast to the generous and honorable modesty of Pantagruel's reply—"Seigneur, des graces que Dieu m'a donné je ne vouldroyes denier à personne en despartir à mon pouvoir; car tout bien vient de luy" (*P* 18:315)—the words with which Thaumaste first lays down his challenge betray the conceit of a man who is certain that no one can solve the problems he has been unable to solve, and for whom, moreover, there is nothing of greater worth than himself: "si tu me peulx souldre [aulcuns passages de philosophie], je me rens dès à present ton esclave, moy et toute ma posterité, car aultre don ne ay que assez je estimasse pour la recompense" (*P* 18:314). These words, presumptuous and vain enough in themselves, are doubly significant in that they echo the boastful challenge by which the Philistine Goliath offered to fight any Israelite in single combat: "Am I not a Philistine, and are you not servants of Saul? Choose a man for yourselves, and let him come down to me. If he is able to fight with me and kill me, then we will be your [slaves] [*erimus vobis servi*]; but if I prevail against him and kill him, then you shall be our [slaves] and serve us. . . . I defy the ranks of Israel this day; give me a man, that we may fight together" (1 Sam 17:8–10). In defying the giant Pantagruel, the "grandissime clerc" (*P* 18:312 var.; Saulnier *P* 13:102) paradoxically casts himself in the role of the hubristic Philistine giant, and Pantagruel in the role of the diminutive David who was destined to slay him.

Lest we mistake the implications of these echoes and analogies, Panurge neatly sums them up by referring to Thaumaste at a critical moment midway through the episode as "ce *glorieux* Angloys" (*P* 18:317, emphasis mine).

A second and even more important aspect of Thaumaste's challenge is that the challenger is a sophistical dialectician whose real purpose is to confound the humanistic prince with his subtle problems and farfetched dialectical disputations and thereby to avenge the old scholastic disciplines that Pantagruel had so soundly defeated in defending his theses against them. The people of Paris expect to witness the revenge of scholasticism when they think to themselves: "Ce diable de Pantagruel, qui a convaincu tous les ruseurs et bejaunes sophistes [1532: tous les Sorbonicoles], à ceste heure aura son vin, car cest Angloys est un aultre diable de Vauvert. Nous verrons qui en gaignera" (317). So too do the "grimaulx, artiens et intrans," who raise a clamor as Pantagruel and Panurge enter the great hall of the notorious Collège de Navarre for the momentous showdown between a "grand clerc" (*P* 18 title:312) and the Solomonic sage (317–18). This aspect of the challenge is confirmed by the challenger's nationality. Thaumaste is English not because Thomas More is English—for as we shall see "Thaumaste" has nothing whatever to do with this "Thomas" (see below, note 23)—but because England enjoyed an unfortunate reputation in the Renaissance as the home of the two most notorious dialectician-philosophers of the gothic age, the two sophists whom Rabelais, like all humanists, hated with a particular loathing, Duns Scotus and William of Ockham.[16]

Thaumaste's sophistical test is a serious one indeed, for it challenges Pantagruel on specific subjects and through a specific medium of communication for which the humanistic prince is not at all prepared. The subject of the debate is explicitly identified both at the beginning and the end of the episode as "aulcuns passaiges de philosophie, [de *magie*, de *alkymie*][17] de *geomantie* et de *caballe,* desquelz je doubte et ne puis contenter mon esprit" (*P* 18:314 var.; Saulnier *P* 13:104), "des problemes insolubles, tant de *magie, alchymie,* de *caballe,* de *geomantie,* de *astrologie,* que de philosophie, lesquelz je avoys en mon esprit" (*P* 20:324, emphasis mine). We know that these are indeed the subjects that Thaumaste raises in his debate, for when in the heat of the discussion the cleric forgets himself and inadvertently begins to speak, his words show that he is debating a point of astrology: "Et si Mercure . . ." (*P* 19:320). Later in the debate Thaumaste seems to be "ravy en haulte contemplation" (*P* 19:322) and near the end cries out, in response to one of Panurge's signs: "Ha, Messieurs, le grand secret!" (*P* 19:323). Here the debate has moved on to the Cabala and alchemy.

The importance of these disciplines is that they are the only ones explicitly and vigorously excluded from the humanistic program of studies set forth in Gargantua's letter: "Laisse moy *l'astrologie* divinatrice, et *l'art de Lullius* [that is, alchemy], comme abuz et vanitez" (*P* 8:260, emphasis mine). The dialectician Thaumaste has thus come to test Pantagruel not only about "insoluble problems" but about those illegitimate, arcane sciences that transcend the human realm and are therefore most alien to humanistic learning. These are the very disciplines about which Pantagruel, who embodies the totality of humanistic learning, can—and indeed should—know absolutely nothing.[18]

As for the mode of the proposed debate, it is determined by the subject and is entirely consistent with it. The arcane sciences that transcend human ken must necessarily transcend human language as well. They are "tant ardues que les parolles humaines ne seroyent suffisantes à les expliquer à mon plaisir" (*P* 18:314). Thaumaste therefore proposes to dispense with words altogether and to debate "sans parler," by mute signs alone. This new form of disputation is as alien to Pantagruel's humanistic learning as are the particular subjects proposed by Thaumaste. Pantagruel's formation is, as we have seen, entirely logocentric, being firmly grounded in Grammar and Rhetoric—the sole arts through which good humanists believed that legitimate human knowledge may be acquired and communicated. As a humanist sage Pantagruel is by definition prepared to dispute only through the medium of "parolles humaines," and "en la maniere des academicques par declamation" (*P* 18:314). By precluding recourse not only to humanistic declamation but to words of any kind, even to the less perfect human languages of Dialectic or the quadrivium—"je ne veulx disputer *pro* et *contra,* comme font ces sotz sophistes de ceste ville et de ailleurs . . . ny aussi par nombres, comme faisoit Pythagoras et comme voulut faire Picus Mirandula à Romme" (*P* 18:314)—he leaves Pantagruel utterly defenseless, stripping him in advance of the arms by which he had earlier defeated the representatives of the outmoded scholastic disciplines.[19]

Thus the "glorieux" English dialectician has laid a perfect trap for the humanist hero. He has in effect contrived to challenge humanism with insoluble enigmas that lie beyond the scope of humanism, and with weapons that humanism is by definition forbidden to wield, defining both the subject and the manner of the debate in such a way that Pantagruel cannot possibly win. Pantagruel himself is acutely aware of this double trap. "Abysme de science" though he is, he "entr[e] en la haulte game" and, "esmeu en [son] esprit," prepares to master in one night the antihumanistic disciplines necessary to meet this insidious challenge of Dialectic and arcane sciences to humanism by poring over forbidden books on magic, signs, and ineffable things (*P* 18:316).

He is spared these efforts, however, and saved from certain defeat by the intervention of that most imperfect object of his brotherly love, his companion and counterpart—his "other" as some moderns would call him, his epic ἑταῖρος as he should more appropriately be called—Panurge. Instead of dealing with Thaumaste on his own terms, as Pantagruel would have done to his own peril, the trickster Panurge uses his now-famous wiles (*πανουργία*) to turn the tables on him and catch him in his own trap. First, he tricks the sophist into accepting the substitution of disciple for master by playing on the presumptuous cleric's false pretense to a genuine desire for knowledge: "Seigneur," he asks, echoing Pantagruel's words of the day before, "es tu icy venu pour disputer contentieusement de ces propositions que tu as mis, ou bien pour aprendre et en sçavoir la verité?" (*P* 18:318; compare 315). Thaumaste answers, as he must in the circumstances, by claiming to be motivated only by a "desir de apprendre et sçavoir" and pretending to dissociate himself completely from the "maraulx sophistes" whose cause he is championing (318). Having forced Thaumaste to this statement, Panurge uses it to cut him off from a direct showdown with Pantagruel: "Doncques," he concludes dialectically, "si je, qui suis petit disciple de mon maistre Monsieur Pantagruel, te contente et satisfays en tout et par tout, ce seroit chose indigne d'en empescher mon dict maistre" (318). Thaumaste cannot deny the logic of this conclusion. Nor can he insist on the desired showdown with Panurge's master without belying his pretensions to a purely "studieux desir." He has been outmaneuvered by a wilier dialectician than himself and prevented from confounding Pantagruel with his extrahumanistic traps. He is now at the mercy of Panurge alone.

The means by which Panurge proceeds to defeat Thaumaste in his own debate by signs are more obvious. Using unequivocally obscene gestures that anyone can easily understand, he tells his too-clever and self-satisfied opponent, quite literally, to go fuck himself.[20] But the Englishman is so caught up in the dialectical subtleties and extraterrestrial enigmas with which he thought to trap Pantagruel that he understands these gestures as the revelation of high mysteries and great secrets. This blatant misreading of Panurge's intention, and the cleric's obvious expressions of "angustie" (*P* 19:322) as he begins to realize Panurge's mastery toward the end of the debate, contribute to one of the most successful moments of high comedy in all of Rabelais.[21]

While the humor of the episode requires no explanation, the fundamental comic mechanism at work here does. It is essential to realize that what is involved in the debate is not simply a satire of disputation but the old theme of the *trompeur trompé*. By playing to perfection his now-familiar double role of uncharitable trickster and debaser of the proud, Panurge simultaneously catches an enemy trickster in his own trap and brings down a "grandissime" and "glorieux" cleric. With obscene gestures, which Thaumaste in his esoteric cleverness does not even understand, he not only forces the presumptuous challenger humbly to recognize the supreme authority of the sage he had come to dethrone but reduces him to the lowest level of his humanity by making him "se conchi[er] de angustie" (*P* 19:322).

In so doing Panurge reveals both the full significance of his ambiguous name and the true nature of his ambiguous role in the *Pantagruel*. Both find their explanation in one of the best-known passages of Paul's first Epistle to the Corinthians. "Let no one deceive himself," says Paul. "If any one among you thinks that he is wise in this age, let him become a fool that he may become wise. For the wisdom of this world is folly with God. For it is written, 'He catches the wise in their craftiness [*astutia, πανουργίᾳ*]'" (1 Cor 3.18–19; compare Job 5.13). The sophistical dialectician and arcane scientist Thaumaste is one of those arrogant self-deceivers who, thinking he is wise in this age, has traveled great distances to entrap the Christ-like Pantagruel who now embodies not only potentia and bonitas but the sapientia that consists of "la manne celeste de bonne doctrine." But thanks to Panurge, Thaumaste is caught in his own trap. The "craftiness" in which he is caught is none other than Panurge's astutia, the very "πανουργία" from which Panurge derives his name. In humiliating Thaumaste and turning his own *πανουργία* against him, the wily trickster Πανοῦργος, whatever his faults and defects, proves an active agent of divine sapientia and an indispensable defender of the Christ-like Pantagruel.

Panurge's victory over Thaumaste not only foils an insidious challenge to the messianic hero of the *Pantagruel* but actually augments the reputation of his master and confirms yet again his identity as a figure of Christ. In an act of homage at the conclusion of the debate, the outwitted and humbled (though still deluded) Thaumaste makes Panurge's victory (whose nature he still does not understand) redound not to the glory of Panurge himself but to the even greater glory of Pantagruel, by recalling Panurge's earlier claim to be only the "petit disciple de [son] maistre Monsieur Pantagruel" (*P* 18:318): "Seigneurs, . . . vous avez icy un thesor incomparable en vostre presence; c'est Monsieur Pantagruel. . . . Vous avez veu comment son seul disciple me a contenté . . . d'ont povez juger ce que eust peu dire le maistre, veu que le disciple a faict telle prouesse" (*P* 20:324–25). In so doing he quotes the precise words by which Christ referred to his own supremacy over his disciples: "*Non est discipulus super magistrum*" (*P* 20:325; Mt 10.24 and Lk 6.40). "Mon maistre" Pantagruel is none other than the *magister* that is Christ.

The implications of this biblical echo are confirmed by those of another: "*Et ecce plus quam Salomon hic*" (*P* 20:324; Mt 12.42 and Lk 11.31). As has long been recognized, this "mot evangelicque" is the one pronounced by Christ to the hypocritical scribes and Pharisees who had come to test him with their insidious request for a miracle (Mt 12.38 and Lk 11.16; compare Mk 8.11, Mt 16.1). Thus the divine sapience of Pantagruel, which has consistently and deliberately been associated with that of "le saige Salomon" from the beginning of his humanistic formation (compare *P* 8:261, *P* 10 title:270 var.; *P* 14:288, *P* 18:313), is shown through Thaumaste's Sabaean challenge to be even greater than Solomon's, and Pantagruel himself to be a "more-than-Solomon"—that is, a Christ.

But as the context of Thaumaste's final biblical allusion makes clear, much more is involved than a simple reaffirmation of Pantagruel's well-established identity as messianic hero. Thaumaste, having earlier cast himself in the Old Testament roles of Goliath relative to David, and of Queen of Sheba relative to Solomon, concludes by casting himself in the role of Goliath's and the queen's New Testament counterparts, the scribes and Pharisees, relative to a "plus quam Salomon." Typologically speaking the English cleric and sophist is a scribe and a Pharisee—a hypocritical representative and defender not only of the old guard but of the Old Law as well. Exactly like them Thaumaste lays a trap for the Christ-like Pantagruel in a malicious attempt to bring him down. Exactly like them, he treacherously seeks a "sign"—"Magister, volumus a te *signum* videre" (Mt 12.38, emphasis mine; compare Lk 11.16)—that is, nothing short of a miracle.

This crucial aspect of Thaumaste's role is summed up in the very name he bears. Θαυμαστός means "marvelous," and ϑαυμαστά are "marvelous things." Such indeed are the transcendent, arcane problems that Thaumaste proposes to Pantagruel. But as any sixteenth-century biblical humanist would have known, the verb ϑαυμάζω (to marvel) is used throughout the New Testament to denote the reaction of witnesses to the *words and deeds of Christ*—sometimes to his marvelous teaching (Lk 4.22, Jn 7.15 and 21), but most often to the various miracles (*signa*) he performs: the calming of the great storm on the sea (Mt 8.27 and Lk 8.25), the casting out of demons (Mt 9.33 and Lk 11.14), the curing of the lame, the maimed, the blind, and the dumb (Mt 15.31), the healing of an epileptic child (Lk 9.43), the withering of the fig tree (Mt 21.20), the healing of a paralytic on the Sabbath (Jn 5.20), and so forth.[22] The adjective ϑαυμαστός is similarly used to evoke the miracle that is Christ himself: "The very stone which the builders rejected has become the head of the corner; this was the Lord's doing, and it is marvelous [ϑαυμαστή] in your eyes" (Mt 21.42 and Mk 12.11); "Why, this is a marvel [ϑαυμαστόν]! You do not know where he comes from, and yet he opened my eyes" (Jn 9.30); "But you are a chosen race, a royal priesthood . . . that you may declare the wonderful deeds of him who called you out of darkness into his marvelous [ϑαυμαστόν] light" (1 Pet 2.9).

The essence of Thaumaste's role is to be found at the intersection of these two meanings of his name, the general and the specifically biblical. In testing Pantagruel with insoluble problems about arcane sciences (ϑαυμαστά), Thaumaste is like a Pharisee testing Christ with the hypocritical request for a signum, or miracle, at which to marvel (ϑαυμάζειν). But Thaumaste's trap, like those of all the scribes and Pharisees of the New Testament, is foiled and serves only to reveal the truly divine wisdom of Pantagruel. For the only "signum" Thaumaste will receive is of course Panurge's obscene gesticulations in the course of his debate "par signes." And the only "miracle" he will witness is the "thesor incomparable" of the more-than-Solomonic, Christ-like Pantagruel, at whom he must marvel just as the plotting scribes and Pharisees had to marvel at Jesus.

Keeping all these things in mind we shall discover that, together, Panurge and Thaumaste play out the roles suggested by their names in the single most famous trap laid for Jesus in the New Testament—the loaded question about paying taxes to Caesar as it is related in the Gospel of Luke. "Pretending to be sincere," certain Pharisees, scribes, and chief priests attempted to "catch him by what he said" by asking, with hypocritical deference: "Teacher, we know that you speak and teach rightly, and show no partiality, but truly teach the way of God. Is it lawful for us to give tribute to Caesar, or not?" But Jesus "perceived their *craftiness*"—their πανουργία—and evaded their trap with the famous trick of his own. And when they heard his answer that was both clever and wise, "*marveling* at his answer [θαυμάσαντες] they were silent" (Lk 20.19–26, emphasis mine; compare Mt 22.15–22).

The episode of Thaumaste is undoubtedly designed to recall and derive its meaning from this well-known episode in the life of Christ. Once we have realized this we may readily see that Panurge is not only the craftiness (πανουργία) in whom the wise of the world—in this case the "sçavant" Thaumaste—are caught (1 Cor 3.19). He plays an even more specific and germane role as the particular πανουργία consisting of marvels, miracles, and signs (θαυμαστά) by which Christ—or in this case the Christ-like hero of this epic New Testament—reduces to amazed silence the crafty scribes and chief priests of the Old Law, here played by the hypocritical English dialectician come to avenge his fellow sophists of the old school (Lk 20.19–26). Put more simply, Panurge is the "craft" by which Christ-Pantagruel confounds a crafty scribe-cleric; his signs are the trick by which an insidious request for a "sign" is answered and the Pharisee-sophist Thaumaste is "amazed."[23]

This crucial, unnoticed subtext confirms in a striking way what the other biblical allusions of the episode and the overall design of the epic have already suggested. For all his unsettling ambiguity and even his unambiguously negative aspects, Panurge has a decidedly positive role to play in the *Pantagruel*. His tricks are not gratuitous and undirected, as they tended to be before his meeting with Pantagruel. Having become Pantagruel's epic companion and disciple he puts his once-dubious wiles at the service of his master, using them, as a necessary counterpart and an indispensable ally, to defend and further the cause of the messianic hero.

The Thaumaste episode thus marks a crucial moment. As a reprise of the earlier episode of Baisecul and Humevesne in which the trickster Panurge now craftily defends a helpless Pantagruel against an insidious counterattack from the old school and the Old Law, it signals the point at which the heretofore distinct stories of the perfect prince and his imperfect ally combine to form a single story. In this reprise, and in this joining of two separate, interwoven narrative strands, we may discover the logic of a narrative sequence that has troubled so many of Rabelais's readers.

The order in which Rabelais has arranged the various episodes of these first twenty chapters is neither random nor corrupt but the perfect expression of an intertwining of parallel destinies in which the meticulously wrought design of the *Pantagruel* may once again be discerned:[24]

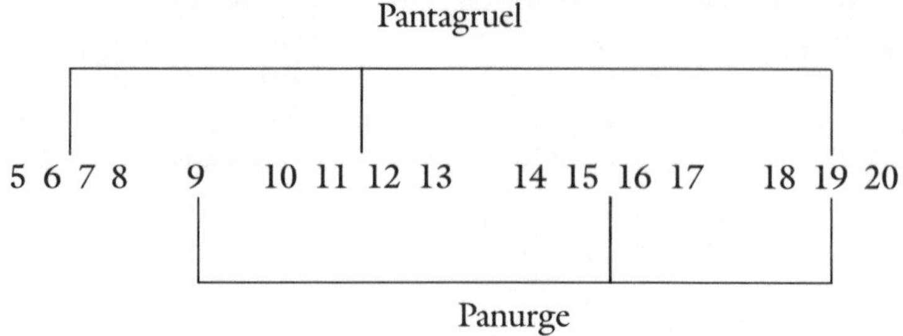

By the end of the episode of Thaumaste, the interdependence and true alliance of Pantagruel and Panurge have been consummated. The messianic hero and his unlikely *comes* are now ready to accomplish, together, the exploit that even Pantagruel could not have accomplished alone.

5

ANARCHE IN UTOPIA: THE POLITICAL DIMENSION

Epic is by nature political. From the *Iliad* and the *Aeneid* to the *Chronicles* of Turpinus and *Mélusine,* epics traditionally deal with empire, with good and bad rulers, and with the wars by which political orders are established, propagated, defended, or transferred. And their purpose is always, to one degree or another, propagandistic. The *Pantagruel* is no exception to this general rule. Its epic action consists in a war between neighboring kingdoms that results in the eventual colonization of one by the other and the establishment of a kind of utopian empire. Its hero is not only a messianic type of Christ but also a prince, a warrior, and ultimately a "dominateur."

But by situating the action of the *Pantagruel* in the "ville des Amaurotes" in "Utopie" near the "royaulme de Achorie" (*P* 24:340),[1] Rabelais suggests from the outset that the politics of his epic will be highly unorthodox. Thomas More's *Utopia,* which was much read and appreciated by the humanists whom Rabelais most admired,[2] contains a systematic indictment of dynastic wars and of the political and economic system that makes them necessary. Book 1 in particular contains explicit diatribes not only against the entire chivalric order whose only reason for existence is to fight wars (pp. 62–64) but, in one of its best-known passages, against the imperialistic and self-consciously chivalric wars of aggression waged by the kings of France against the cities of its neighbor Italy (pp. 86–90).[3] And book 2 states that the Utopians loathe all war as something bestial and find nothing more inglorious than the glory sought in battle. They never go to war except to defend their own borders or those of their friends from an invading army or to deliver an oppressed people from a tyrant (pp. 198–200).[4] If we are to take the geography of the *Pantagruel* seriously, we must be prepared to find a radical departure from the politics of both classical and chivalric epic in Alcofrybas's book.

This is indeed the case. Contrary to what is generally asserted, More's *Utopia* is very much present in Rabelais's Utopian epic, with specific textual echoes resonating throughout. The war that Pantagruel is called upon to fight is not a typical epic struggle for political or even religious hegemony but a purely defensive war against the imperialistic aggressions of a neighboring kingdom. The Dipsodes, taking advantage of the death of the legitimate king of Utopie and of the temporary absence of his rightful heir, have transgressed their legal borders—"estoyent yssus de leurs limites"—and invaded the defenseless realm in an attempt to seize control of it by destroying its countryside and laying siege to its capital city: "et avoyent gasté un grand pays de Utopie, et tenoyent pour lors la grande ville des Amaurotes assiegée" (*P* 23:335). This is the kind of war for which Gargantua had instructed Pantagruel to prepare himself by learning "la chevalerie et les armes pour defendre ma maison, et nos amys secourir en tous leurs affaires contre les assaulx des mal faisans" (*P* 8:261). It is also the only kind of war that More's Utopians consider legitimate: "quo aut suos fines tueantur, aut amicorum terris, infusos hostes propulsent" (p. 200).[5] The very terms in which the epic war of the *Pantagruel* is presented are those of More's pacificist and anti-imperialistic satire.

The king who leads this imperialistic act of aggression, moreover, bears the Morean name of "Anarche." The alpha privative with which it begins is a hallmark of More's symbolic Greek names. The prince of Utopia, for example, bears the title "Ademus" (ἀ-δῆμος = without people).[6] And the "arche" of Anarche recalls the title given to local magistrates in Utopia—"phyl*arcus*" (φύλαρχος = leader of a tribe). But beyond the Utopian form of Anarche's name, its meaning reveals the Utopian—or rather anti-Utopian—identity of the invading king. The root of Anarche is not ἀρχός (leader), as in More's phylarcus, but ἀρχή (sovereignty, rule, or authority). And whereas the alpha privative in More's names suggests only nonexistence, as is fitting in a place called Utopia (οὐ-τοπία = not-place), in the name of Rabelais's usurper king it seems to suggest a much stronger kind of negation. Unlike the "A-demus" of *Utopia,* who is an imaginary prince because he is "without a real people," the "An-arche" of the *Pantagruel* is an *illegitimate* prince because he is a ruler "without sovereignty," "without rule," or "without the authority to rule" (ἀν-ἀρχή). He is, in short, an antiprince—the antithesis of what a good Utopian prince should be.

Anarche's name and deeds thus conspire to suggest that his role is to pose an anti-Utopian threat to the Utopian order of Rabelais's "Utopie." The epic war of which he is the prime mover is an act of imperialistic aggression designed, it would seem, to raise many of the same political issues already treated in More's well-known political satire.

But what is the relevance of these political issues to the rest of the

Pantagruel, and what is their place within its larger redemptive design? One answer is that Anarche's role is analogous to that of his general, Loup Garou, but operates on a slightly different plane. Whereas Loup Garou the Cain figure functions as a moral antitype to Pantagruel the Christ figure and restorer of caritas, King Anarche the antiprince functions as a political antitype to Pantagruel the ideal Utopian prince. Behind fratricide, in other words, and as a kind of large-scale double to it, stands the politics of imperialism, and behind the redemptive design of the *Pantagruel* a distinct but parallel political dimension whose flavor is decidedly Utopian.[7]

To determine the full implications of this analogy, we must first examine the more important political episodes of the epic. By so doing we shall discover that the political dimension of the *Pantagruel* is informed by a design as compelling and coherent as that of its moral dimension, and that this political design, like the redemptive design it parallels, conveys a polemical meaning of unexpected force.

Although the political dimension of the *Pantagruel* does not become prominent until the invasion of the Dipsodes in chapter 23, it is prepared well in advance: at the beginning, where Gargantua prophesies that his son will one day become the "dominateur des alterez" (*P* 2:231), again in Gargantua's letter, which enjoins Pantagruel to learn "la chevalerie et les armes" for the defense of Utopie (*P* 8:261), and yet again throughout the demonstration portion of the sapience cycle where the hero is assimilated to the wise and pacific philosopher-king Solomon. But the most systematic preparation is made through the unlikely intervention of Pantagruel's epic companion, Panurge. One of the most important and misunderstood functions of Panurge is in fact to introduce the political dimension of the *Pantagruel*, to reveal its Utopian ethos through his initial contrast to Pantagruel, and eventually to participate directly in the political design of the epic by supplementing the qualities of the hero with certain indispensable Utopian qualities of his own.

This aspect of Panurge, and the political orientation of the entire epic, are most clearly set forth in the two chapters that immediately follow Pantagruel's emergence as a "new Solomon" in the episode of Baisecul and Humevesne. These are the chapters in which the newly met Panurge narrates the adventures that have led him to the sorry state in which Pantagruel finds him (chapter 14) and proposes a "maniere bien nouvelle de bastir les murailles de Paris" (chapter 15).

When the wandering Panurge is first met he is on his way home from Turkey where he was taken prisoner "lors qu'on alla à Metelin en la male heure" (*P* 9:270) and whence he has only recently managed to escape (*P* 14). He is returning, in short, from a Crusade against the Infidel. In direct contrast to the purely defensive war against a foreign invader to which Pantagruel will be called, the war in which Panurge has just participated is a war of aggression waged against a foreign power on foreign soil. It is precisely the kind of war that is forbidden to the Utopians and precisely the kind of attack against which Pantagruel will have to defend his native land. Panurge's "croysade" (*P* 17:309) is thus a mirror image and antithetical counterpart to Pantagruel's "epic" war.

The diametrical opposition between these two wars is reinforced by striking parallels between chapter 14, in which Panurge "racompte la maniere comment il eschappa de la main des Turcqs" (*P* 14 title:287), and chapter 29, in which Pantagruel defeats Loup Garou and his giant henchmen. According to Panurge's own account of his foreign adventures, he was about to be roasted and eaten by his Turkish captors when he uttered a prayer to God, asking for deliverance through divine intervention. This prayer is an exact counterpart to Pantagruel's famous prayer uttered in the last moments before his decisive duel with Loup Garou. The two prayers are spoken in similar circumstances: Loup Garou rushes toward Pantagruel, "la gueulle ouverte" (*P* 29:362), ready to devour him and threatening to chop him up "comme chair à pastez" (364), exactly as the Turks had been preparing to devour Panurge, roasting him on a spit "tout lardé comme un connil" (*P* 14:289). The two prayers resemble each other by their precise diction as well. The narrator's words in chapter 29:

> *Ainsi* doncques, *comme il* [Loup Garou] approuchoit en grande fierté, Pantagruel, jectant ses yeulx au ciel, *se recommanda à Dieu de bien bon cueur,* faisant voeu tel comme s'ensuyt: "*Seigneur Dieu,* qui *tousjours* as esté mon protecteur et mon servateur, tu vois la *destresse* en laquelle je suis maintenant. . . . S'il te plaist à ceste heure *me estre en ayde,* comme *en toy seul est ma totale confiance et espoir,* je te fais veu" [*P* 29:361, emphasis mine]

are virtually identical to Panurge's in chapter 14:

> "*Ainsi comme ilz* [the Turks] me roustissoyent, je *me recommandoys à la grace divine,* ayant en memoyre le bon sainct Laurent et *tousjours esperoys en Dieu* qu'il me delivreroit de ce torment. . . . Ainsi que *me recommandoys bien de bon cueur à Dieu,* cryant: '*Seigneur Dieu, ayde moy!* Seigneur Dieu, saulve moy! Seigneur Dieu, oste moy de *ce*

> *torment* auquel ces traistres chiens me tiennent.'" [*P* 14:289, emphasis mine]

Both prayers, moreover, are answered in a similar manner—Panurge's "bien estrangement" by "le vouloir divin, ou bien de quelque bon Mercure," which makes his roaster fall asleep; Pantagruel's by "une voix du ciel" and the fulfillment of its promise. The two prayers thus correspond to each other in the circumstances of their utterance, in purpose and content, in effect, and even in the smallest details of diction.

But a few crucial differences between these otherwise nearly identical passages are revealing. Panurge's superstition and relative faithlessness are obvious from the fact that he includes Saint Lawrence in his prayer and hesitates between divine will and "quelque bon Mercure," while Pantagruel places his "totale confiance et espoir" in God alone ("en toy seul"). Even more important is what each prayer reveals about the purpose of the two wars. Panurge ends his supplication with a specific "recommendation": "Seigneur Dieu, oste moy de ce torment auquel ces traistres chiens me detiennent *pour la maintenance de ta loy!*" (*P* 14:289, emphasis mine). Pantagruel, in direct contrast, devotes the central portion of his prayer to long protestations that he has *not* undertaken this war for the purpose of maintaining God's law, since God himself has forbidden Christians to do so:

> Rien icy ne me amene, sinon zele naturel, ainsi comme tu as octroyé es humains de garder et defendre soy, leurs femmes, enfans, pays et famille, *en cas que ne seroit ton negoce propre, qui est la foy; car en tel affaire tu ne veulx coadjuteur,* sinon de confession catholicque et service de ta parolle, *et nous a defendu toutes armes et defences,* car tu es le Tout Puissant, qui, en ton affaire propre, et où ta cause propre est tirée en action, te peulx defendre trop plus qu'on ne sçauroit estimer, toy qui a mille milliers de centaines de millions de legions d'anges, duquel le moindre peut occire tous les humains, et tourner le ciel et la terre à son plaisir, comme jadys bien apparut en l'armée de Sennacherib. [*P* 29:361, emphasis mine]

The purpose for which Panurge joined the war against the Turks is thus the one that Pantagruel, in undertaking his corresponding epic war against the Dipsodes, explicitly rejects as illegitimate. War is authorized for physical defense only, not for the propagation of faith. Crusades, like imperialistic wars, are strictly forbidden. Pantagruel drives this crucial point home at the end of his prayer by vowing, if only he is successful in the civil defense of his realm, to spread the true faith in the only permissible way—namely, through what he has already called "confession catholicque et service [1532: ministere] de ta parolle": "Je feray prescher ton sainct Evangile purement, simplement et entierement, si que les abus . . . seront d'entour moy exterminez" (*P* 29:361).

The point of this contrast between parallel episodes is corroborated by distinct Utopian and Erasmian echoes that resonate throughout Pantagruel's prayer. More's Utopians, it will be recalled, are forbidden not only to fight except in defense against aggression and tyranny but also to exercise any compulsion in matters of religion. All religions are tolerated in Utopia, even the recently imported sect called Christianity. Everyone has a right to choose his religion and even to proselytize, provided he do so "peacefully and modestly, by rational argument" alone. Anyone who uses force or even disparages other religions in his attempt to promote his own is sentenced to exile or enslavement, as the unfortunate experience of an overzealous Christian preacher in Utopia illustrates. The reasons for this strict law are that religious quarrels serve only to destroy peace; that God, being infinitely great, may well have desired to be worshipped in a variety of ways; and that it is both foolish and arrogant for any mortal to impose his own beliefs in such matters by means of threats and violence.[8] Pantagruel's prayer reflects all of these Utopian laws and customs. He wages war for the sake of neither empire nor religion but simply to defend his family and subjects. As for the propagation of his faith, he explicitly rejects war as a means to that end in favor of "peaceful and modest" words of persuasion—that is, the "pure, simple, and complete" dissemination of the Word. The contrast with Panurge's Crusade in faraway Mytilene "pour la maintenance de ta loy" could hardly be more absolute.

Another aspect of this contrast is illuminated by Erasmus. In the eloquent pacifist sermon that concludes the *Institutio principis christiani,* Erasmus develops the familiar theme that "tota Christi Philosophia dedocet bellum," that "tota undique Christi doctrina cum bello pugnat," to arrive at the observation that in the process of fighting wars Christians almost invariably degenerate into non-Christians—that is, into warriors like the unredeemed Hebrews of the Old Testament, or even worse. "I do not think," he concludes,

> that war should be taken up lightly even against the Turks, especially since the dominion of Christ was born, propagated, and established in such a radically different manner. Perhaps that dominion ought not to be defended by means other than those by which it was born and propagated. We see the Christian people continually plundered for the sake of wars of this kind, but nothing else is accomplished. Now if it is indeed for faith that we are fighting, faith was strength-

> ened and made known by the suffering of martyrs, not by armies of soldiers. If on the contrary it is for empire, wealth, and possessions that we are fighting, we must consider very carefully whether our undertaking is really a Christian one, or even whether, as usually happens to those who wage wars of this kind, we do not degenerate into Turks sooner than we make the Turks into Christians. Let us first make sure that we ourselves are true Christians and then, if it should still seem appropriate, let us attack the Turks.[9]

The theme of Pantagruel's prayer, and even some of its diction, are clearly discernible in this passage. Faith, according to both Erasmus and Pantagruel, is God's "business" and is not to be defended by the arms of men: "jam si *fidei negotium* agitur . . . non militum copiis aucta illustrataque est"; "en cas que ne seroit ton *negoce* propre, qui est la *foy;* car en tel affaire . . . nous a defendu toutes armes et defences" (emphasis mine).

Erasmus's text seems to go even further than Rabelais's in stating that holy wars are not only illegitimate means to a good end but most often merely pretexts for the pursuit of an end that is bad—not the defense of the Christian faith but the unchristian extension of worldly *imperium, opes,* and *possessiones.* Crusades against the Turks, in particular, are nothing more than imperialistic wars of aggression in disguise. Instead of turning Turks into Christians, they turn Christians into Turks.[10]

But this, it would seem, is precisely the point of the contrast between the parallel wars fought by Panurge and Pantagruel. The holy war fought by Panurge is illegitimate on three counts: as a war of aggression against a distant enemy, as an inappropriate means to the end of "maintaining God's law," and as a pope's stratagem for increasing secular power and wealth. Pantagruel's epic war, on the other hand, is a nonimperialistic and perfectly Utopian war against hostile invasion from without, intended to propagate neither faith nor empire but to liberate his besieged people from the oppressions of a usurping tyrant and to reestablish peace. It is clear from Panurge's account of his exploits in Mytilene, moreover, that in fighting the Turks he indeed degenerated into something worse than a Turk. Whereas the Turks took a quasi-Christian pity on the charred escapee ("eurent pitié de moy naturellement"), throwing buckets of water on him to refresh him "joyeusement" and comforting him by giving him something to eat and drink (*P* 14:292), the "Christian" Panurge, in direct contrast, rejoiced and exulted in the complete destruction of their city—a destruction that he had caused and that had come about only because the Turks had paused to comfort him instead of saving their buildings: "Je . . . vys toute la ville bruslant, dont je fuz tant aise que je me cuydé conchier de joye. . . . Ainsi . . . que je regardoys en grand liesse ce beau feu, me gabelant et disant: 'Ha, pauvres pulses, ha, pauvres souris, vous aurez maulvais hyver, le feu est en vostre paillier!'" (*P* 14:293). By his own account, then, Panurge was not at all a Christian soldier but a veritable Turk to the Turks. His behavior in war exemplifies the kind that Pantagruel's final act of redemption is destined to correct, and his holy war the kind that Pantagruel's Utopian epic war is destined to abolish forever.

For the sixteenth-century reader the Turks represented an undeniably imperialistic force and the single greatest external threat to Europe and to Christendom. In 1453 they had finished off what remained of the Byzantine Empire by taking Constantinople and had subsequently assured their domination of the eastern Mediterranean by seizing control of Hungary and all of the Balkans, Syria, Palestine, Egypt, and much of Arabia and North Africa under the expansionist rules of Mehmed II, Bayezid II, Selim I, and Suleiman. When the *Pantagruel* was first published, they seemed on the point of invading Europe as well, having laid siege to Vienna as recently as 1529 and having mounted a second campaign against Austria in 1532. For all that, however, the Turks are deliberately shown *not* to be the typological Enemy of the pacific Utopians. The *Pantagruel* deliberately directs its epic action away from the non-Christian Ottomans, whom the Crusader Panurge had gone off to fight "en la male heure" (*P* 9:270), and redirects it against the neighboring Dipsodes, the "alterez" whose insatiable thirst for *imperium* moves them to invade a neighboring, peace-loving realm. Pantagruel's political antitype is not the infidel Suleiman, who threatens the Christian faith from without (either as a real-life sultan or as an epic heir to Saladin), but Anarche, the anti-prince, the "Turk" among us who destroys Christian peace from within the confines of Christendom.[11]

In this respect the *Pantagruel* indeed subverts the political ethos of traditional epic—both the political imperialism of classical works like the *Aeneid* and the theocratic imperialism of medieval epics like the *Chanson de Roland*—to make way for the radically anti-imperialistic, pacificist politics of More's *Utopia* and Erasmus's idea of Christendom. Alcofrybas's epic New Testament is in effect an anti-epic, which adopts the structures and conventions of epic only to turn the politics of epic upside down to glorify not Empire but anti-imperialism.

After serving to define the political ethos of the *Pantagruel* through a deliberate contrast between his own past and the epic destiny of Pantagruel, Panurge is made to contribute positively to that ethos, even proving to be an indispensable ally in Pantagruel's anti-epic defense of Utopie. The episode that establishes Panurge's importance in this regard is the one in which he describes his notorious "maniere bien nouvelle de bastir les murailles de Paris" (*P* 15 title:294). In spite of its flagrant obscenity and apparent misogyny, this well-known episode is among the most consistently "political" chapters of the epic. It introduces what will become the most important question of political and military strategy confronted by the Pantagruelians in the execution of their entelechial epic war.

The entire chapter centers upon a question of what we would today call defense policy. Panurge's derisive comment about the dilapidated fortifications of Paris poses from the outset the problem of the French capital's vulnerability to military attack. It is important to observe that this remark is introduced by a virtual confession of cowardice on the part of Panurge, who pointedly refuses to wear a sword or to defend himself from assault except by running away (*P* 15:294–95). In this context, Panurge's observation about fortifications is thus motivated by a concern for his own personal safety. Being a coward who refuses to take responsibility for his own defense, Panurge would prefer that the city in which he presently resides have a wall behind which he might hide in case of attack.

Pantagruel answers his companion's self-interested observation by quoting the famous saying of a king of Sparta as it is recorded by Plutarch in the *Apophthegmata laconica* and translated by Erasmus in his own edition of the *Apophthegmata*, to the effect that the best defenses of a city are not its walls but the courage and military preparedness of its citizens:

> "O mon amy, dist Pantagruel, sçaitz tu bien ce que dist Agesilaee, quand on luy demanda pourquoy la grande cité de Lacedemone n'estoit ceincte de murailles? Car, monstrant les habitans et citoyens de la ville, tant bien expers en discipline militaire et tant fors et bien armez: 'Voicy (dist il) les murailles de la cité', signifiant qu'*il n'est muraille que de os* et que les villes et citez ne sçauroyent avoir muraille plus seure et plus forte que la *vertu* des citoyens et habitans.[12]
>
> "Ainsi ceste ville est si forte par la multitude du peuple belliqueux qui est dedans, qu'ilz ne se soucient de faire aultres murailles." [*P* 15:295, emphasis mine]

Whatever irony these lines may contain concerning the military preparedness or the bellicosity of the Parisians, they clearly contain an indirect reproach to Panurge. Agesilaus's noble Lacedaemonian fortitude is at the antipodes of Panurge's abject cowardice. At the same time, these lines reflect a perfectly Utopian attitude toward warfare. The pacific inhabitants of More's Utopia do not like to fight any more than Panurge does. But in spite of their abomination of war (or rather because of it) they all, women as well as men, "assiduously and regularly exercise themselves in military training, so as not to be unfit for war if the need to fight should arise."[13] More's point—and Pantagruel's, it would seem—is that, walls or no walls, defense is the responsibility of princes and citizens like Pantagruel and Panurge. It is in accordance with this principle that Gargantua advised his son to learn "la chevalerie et les armes" to assure the defense of his realm (*P* 8:261) and that Pantagruel will come to the defense of the besieged capital of his own realm in the epic climax of the *Pantagruel*.

But Panurge persists in his desire for some less hazardous form of defense. "Voire mais," he replies, "si faict il bon avoir quelque visaige de pierre quand on est envahy de ses ennemys" (295). It is to this end that he offers his well-known proposal for the "new kind of wall" that could defend the capital of France at less cost than new fortifications of stone. His proposal is a direct, burlesque counterpart to Pantagruel's Spartan idea of national defense. In place of Agesilaus's figurative, metonymic "wall of citizens" he proposes a grotesquely literal, synecdochic wall in which the "bones" of the city's manly inhabitants—"il n'est muraille que de *os*"—are replaced with the less noble parts of the city's less noble inhabitants, the "*callibistrys* des femmes de ce pays" and the "*bracquemars enroiddys* qui habitent par les braguettes claustrales [1532: *vitz* qu'on couppa en ceste ville es pouvres Italiens]" (*P* 15:296 and var.; Saulnier *P* 11:84, emphasis mine). The sole purpose behind this proposal for an anatomical wall is the disparagement and depreciation of the moral wall proposed by Pantagruel. If Panurge's wall is shocking it is not as an affront to the female sex, as superficial and anachronistic readings would have us believe, but as a willful degradation of a Spartan and Utopian ideal, in which the citizens' valor and courage—their "vertu" as Pantagruel says, quoting the "virtus" of Erasmus's apophthegma—are shown to count for less than their cunts and pricks.

For all its derisiveness and grotesque physicality, Panurge's burlesque counterproposal nevertheless continues to address the question of national defense directly, for his anti-Spartan walls have a metaphorical, strategic value as well as a parodic one, as Alcofrybas will take pains to show later in the epic. When Panurge learns that King Anarche's invading army has been accompanied by 150,000 prostitutes of all nationalities (including some "parisiannes"), he is concerned less with the pressing problem of how the minuscule band of Pantagruelians can prevail against the hundreds of thousands of soldiers in Anarche's army than with how he alone might "braquemarder toutes les putains qui y sont . . . qu'il n'en eschappe pas une que je ne taboure en forme commune" (*P* 26:348). This untimely scruple leads Carpalim, Eusthenes, and Epistemon to embroider on the same theme until Pantagruel must intervene to remind his friends that so much whoring would only deplete their strength and cause their defeat in the disproportionate battle to come: "J'ay grand peur que, devant qu'il soit nuyct, ne vous voye en estat que ne aurez grande envie d'arresser, et qu'on vous chevauchera à grand coup de picque et de lance" (349). Their venereal exploits, in other words, would preclude the martial exploits required by present circumstances, dooming them to defeat.

This apparently gratuitous digression at the beginning of the war with the Dipsodes provides a useful gloss on the episode under consideration here. It shows that the wall of cunts and pricks imagined by Panurge could indeed serve to defend a city no less effectively than the wall of bones proposed by Pantagruel, for instead of resisting the enemy with arms it could divert and exhaust him with sex and would have the added advantage, as Panurge points out, of afflicting him with syphilis as well (*P* 15:296). If Panurge cannot hide behind walls of stone, he would rather be shielded from military attack by the prowess of the city's virtueless citizens than by the valor of its virtuous ones. Like the earlier episode of Panurge's ill-starred Turkish adventure, the episode of Panurge's obscene proposal for new walls thus presents him as the political opposite of the hero he is henceforth destined to accompany and assist.

But the "walls of Paris" episode ends by suggesting a slightly different political relationship between hero and companion—a more complex, synergistic one that will become crucial in the rest of the epic. When Panurge goes on to suggest a solution to the "inconvenient" that such a wall would attract flies, his proposal first seems to degenerate completely into the gratuitous obscenity of *fabliaux*. Yet the crude fable he offers as a "bel exemple" of deflying contains unmistakable political overtones and contributes directly to the military and political subject of the chapter. Several details suggest as much, even on a superficial reading. First, the idea that flies might prove to be a problem, which strikes us as merely grotesque and entirely gratuitous today, may have suggested to Rabelais's readers a very real "inconvenient" in terms of national defense, because "mouche" in the sixteenth century had the common meaning of "spy" as well as "fly." Sex and espionage being so closely allied in international relations even today, it is easy to appreciate Panurge's scruple: a city defended by a "wall" of male and female prostitutes would also have to defend itself against the spies that would not fail to infiltrate their ranks. What is needed is a kind of counterintelligence agency consisting of

"quehues de renards, ou bons gros vietz d'azes de Provence" (*P* 15:296): "Ainsi fauldroit garder ces murailles des mousches et mettre esmoucheteurs à gaiges" (299).

A second telling detail is that Panurge's fable is set in "la forest de Bievre" (*P* 15:297)—that is, the forest of Fontainebleau, the favorite hunting ground of the kings of France. Thus it is situated squarely on political ground and in the royal domain, so to speak. Third, one of the characters of the fable makes a pointed allusion to an "esmoucheteur à gaiges" of "Don Pietro de Castille" (*P* 15:298). This Pedro el Cruel, king of Castille and León from 1350 to 1369, was involved from 1356 until his death in a long civil war against forces loyal to his bastard half-brother, Enrique of Trastámara. On more than one occasion Pedro had to defend his capital against foreign attack; in the end he was defeated by the French allies of his brother led by du Guesclin and was assassinated by his brother's own hand. This passing allusion thus clearly ties the fable not only to the subject of the fortification and defense of cities but to the two principal themes of the *Pantagruel*: personal struggles between brothers and power struggles between neighboring kingdoms—that is, fratricide and imperialistic war.

Most important, however, is the subject of the fable, which involves cooperation between a lion and a fox. Lions and foxes are of course common figures in fable literature from Aesop to the *Roman de Renart,* where they represent strength and wiles, respectively. But together they form a pair that was familiar to the Renaissance only from a commonplace of classical political theory. In a well-known passage of *De officiis* Cicero states that injustice in war is of two kinds: injustice by force and injustice by subterfuge. Both kinds are "bestial" and therefore unworthy of man—the former being more appropriate to a *lion* than a man, the latter more appropriate to a *fox*—but the second kind is especially hateful because it is hypocritical: "Cum autem duobus modis, id est aut *vi* aut *fraude,* fiat iniuria, *fraus quasi vulpeculae, vis leonis* videtur; utrumque homine alienissimum, sed fraus odio digna maiore. Totius autem iniustitiae nulla capitalior quam eorum, qui tum, cum maxime fallunt, id agunt, ut viri boni esse videantur" (1.13.41, emphasis mine).

A few years before Rabelais wrote the *Pantagruel*, Machiavelli had taken up this well-known analysis in the *Principe* to transform force and fraud into positive, or at least necessary, attributes of the prince. According to Machiavelli, ancient poets imagined that Achilles was brought up by Chiron the Centaur because they wished to signify that the prince must be educated by a composite creature that is half-beast, half-man and thereby learn how to make use of both natures. As for the bestial nature in himself, the prince must know how to play the parts of both the fox and the lion, because the lion cannot defend himself from traps and the fox cannot defend himself from wolves: "Sendo dunque uno principe necessitato sapere bene usare la *bestia,* debbe di quelle pigliare la *golpe* e il *lione;* perché il lione non si defende da' lacci, la golpe non si defende da' lupi. Bisogna adunque essere *golpe* a conoscere e lacci, e *lione* a sbigottire e lupi" (chapter 18, "Quomodo fides a principibus sit servanda," emphasis mine). All of this is to recommend that the prince have no scruples about "keeping faith" but practice deception in the manner of Pope Alexander VI whenever necessary to hold on to his power.[14]

While these passages are all pertinent to the meaning of Panurge's fable, their ultimate source is more pertinent still. As every Renaissance reader must have known, the commonplace of the lion and the fox originated in a famous saying of Lysander, the Spartan general in the Peloponnesian War. Criticized for his unscrupulous duplicity in political dealings and for resorting to deceit and ruse in his military undertakings, Lysander, a descendant of the lion-skin-clad Hercules, answered that when the lion skin does not suffice, one must sew a fox skin to it, implying that force in a political and military leader must be supplemented by ruse. The story is found in Plutarch's life of Lysander, which Amyot was soon to translate in the following way:

> Mais ceulx qui aimoient une ronde simplicité et ouverte magnanimité es meurs d'un gouverneur et capitaine general, quand ilz venoient à comparer Lysander à Callicratidas, le trouvoient *fin et cauteleux,* qui faisoit la plus part de ses faicts de guerre par *tromperie et surprise* plus tost qu'autrement, . . . en se mocquant de ceulx qui disoient, que les descendans de Hercules ne devoient point faire la guerre par ruzes ne cautelles: "Car quand la *peau de lion* n'y peult fournir, disoit il, il y fault couldre aussi celle du *regnard.*" [emphasis mine][15]

The interest of this ultimate source of Panurge's fable is that Lysander's witticism about lions and foxes, being a fine laconic saying, is recorded as such in the same *Apophthegmata laconica* of Plutarch-Erasmus that has already provided Pantagruel with Agesilaus's remark on Spartan walls. In telling his obscene fable Panurge is simply answering one laconic apophthegma with an obscene elaboration on another.

Once we have realized this, it becomes evident that the fable of the lion and the fox, like the anatomical wall on which it is offered as a commentary, is not an irrelevant and irreverent digression but a direct and pertinent reply to Pantagruel's remarks on military defense. Pantagruel has challenged Panurge's cowardice by quoting the Lacedaemonian wisdom of the Spartan king Agesilaus:

> Rursus alii cuidam percontanti, quam ob causam Sparta non cingeretur moenibus? ostendit cives armatos, "Hi," inquiens, "sunt Spartanae civitatis moenia": significans Respublicas nullo munimento tutiores esse, quam *virtute* civium. [emphasis mine]

Panurge counters this challenge first by parodying and degrading the metaphor of a "muraille d'os," which Pantagruel added to Agesilaus's metaphor of the wall of "cives armati," and then by alluding to a contrary piece of Lacedaemonian wisdom from the Spartan general Lysander:

> Ad eos vero qui ipsi probro dabant, quod pleraque *dolo ac fraude* gereret, non palam *virtute* conficeret, hac parte Hercule generis auctore indignus, ridens, dixit: "Ubi quod vellet non assequeretur *leonis* exuvium, ibi *vulpinum* applicandum esse": sentiens quod honestis rationibus non posset effici, id *fraude dolisque* perficiendum. [emphasis mine][16]

To an authorized classical expression of the need for courage and military preparedness, he answers with a no less authorized classical expression of the necessity of supplementing valor with wiles. Pantagruel would imitate Agesilaus in defending the city through "virtus" alone, by means of walls of bones. Panurge, who is like Lysander in proceeding by "dolus" and "fraus" rather than by "virtus," would imitate Lysander in supplementing Pantagruel's fortitude with guile, defending the city by means of walls of a more ignoble kind, which he would maintain, moreover, by means of "belles quehues de renards"—that is, by allying the fox's skin of "fraus" and "doli" to the lion's skin of "honestae rationes." Subterfuge, he is suggesting, can play as important a role as "vertu" in defending the commonwealth and must be allied to it.

It would seem that Panurge's ulterior motive in telling his tale is to suggest that he, as a fox, can be a useful and even indispensable ally to the regal and lionlike Pantagruel. This, in any case, is how Pantagruel understands the story, for his first reaction upon hearing its conclusion is to dress the teller in his livery: "Vrayement, dist Pantagruel, tu es gentil compaignon; je te veulx habiller de ma livrée" (*P* 15:299).[17] Henceforth, it would seem, the relationship between the hero and his epic companion will be modeled on that between the lion and the fox. And indeed in the episode of Thaumaste the wily Panurge will soon come to the aid of the noble Pantagruel in much the same way that the fox comes to the aid of the lion in Panurge's fable, as we have seen in the previous chapter.

But it is primarily as a political and military ally that Panurge is presenting his relationship and his potential usefulness to Pantagruel here—not only as a fox to a lion but as a Lysander to an Agesilaus as well. For we must recall that Lysander and Agesilaus were not just any two ancients who happened to be both Lacedaemonian and laconic but were contemporary patriots whose careers were inextricably bound together. Lysander was Agesilaus's political and military ally—the friend who helped him become king of Sparta and his general in the Peloponnesian War. He was, in Plutarch's word, Agesilaus's συναγωνιστής, his "fellow-combatant," his "coadjutor" (*Life of Lysander* 22.5). Lysander was also Agesilaus's sometime rival for political and military preferment. This complex relationship is identical to the one we find between Panurge and Pantagruel. In setting his own Lysander-inspired tale of the fox and the lion against Pantagruel's Agesilaus-inspired image of walls of bone, the epic companion Panurge is suggesting, indirectly but unmistakably, that he can be useful to the hero in specifically political and military ways, as the wily fox is to the virtuous lion of political allegory, and more specifically as the vulpine Lysander once was to the leonine Agesilaus.

Compelling confirmation of this reading is to be found within the source of Panurge's fable. In the passage from Plutarch's *Life of Lysander* quoted above, Lysander is characterized, in Amyot's version, as "fin et cauteleux." These epithets fit Panurge perfectly. But the fit is more striking still in the original Greek text, which Rabelais and his chosen readers certainly knew. There, the words translated by Amyot as "fin et cauteleux" are . . . "πανοῦργος καὶ σοφιστής," "*panurge*" and "*sophist.*" It is as though Rabelais's Panurge had emerged—fully armed, so to speak—from Plutarch's short characterization of Lysander. Lysander *is,* quite literally, "panurge," and Panurge the sophist *is* a kind of transposed Lysander. After the New Testament (2 Cor 12.16, 1 Cor 3.19, Lk 20.23; see chapter 4), Plutarch is thus the most important source of Panurge's name and of his essence. Panurge is not only a moral being but a *political* being, and his relationship to Pantagruel operates on both planes. We saw in the preceding chapter that as a moral being he is ambivalent, both opposed and allied to Pantagruel's messianic caritas. Here we may see that as a political being, too, he is equally ambivalent, both opposed and allied to Pantagruel's epic virtus.

The particular relationship implied in Panurge's fable and throughout the entire "walls" episode indeed proves to be most significant on the political, "epic" plane. As Panurge suggests, Pantagruel succeeds in defending the besieged capital of Utopie from foreign attack not on his own but only by conjoining his (and Agesilaus's) leonine "vertu" with Panurge's (and Lysander's) vulpine wiles.

When the small band of Pantagruelians first lands on the shores of Utopie and is attacked by 660 mounted horsemen, Pantagruel proposes to resist them alone by force: "Enfans, retirez vous en la navire," he says. "Voyez cy de noz ennemys qui accourent, mais je vous les tueray icy comme bestes, et feussent ilz dix foys autant" (*P* 25:343). But it is Panurge, not Pantagruel, who defeats the assailants effortlessly, thanks to a ruse by means of which he, Epistemon, Eusthenes, and Carpalim lure the enemy into a fatal trap by pretending to surrender (*P* 25:343–44). Impressed by the effectiveness of this stratagem, Pantagruel lavishes praise on his companions' "industrie" (344) and erects a memorial trophy whose inscription commemorates the victory as a triumph of wits over superior strength. Four unarmed men, it proclaims, were able to defeat 660 mounted, armed, and powerful scoundrels because they were armed not with armor but with "bon sens." The lesson it draws is precisely the lesson of Panurge's fable—that is, that ruse is superior to strength in war:

> Prenez y tous, roys, ducz, rocz et pions,
> Enseignement que *engin* mieulx vault que *force*.
> [*P* 27:350, emphasis mine]

The first "king" and "general" to put this lesson into practice is none other than Pantagruel himself. When it comes time to attack Anarche's vastly superior army, the hero does not lead a valorous head-on attack but deliberately misleads the Dipsodes with what today's princes and generals would call "disinformation," claiming to await reinforcements consisting of a fighting force far greater than Anarche's—1,800,000 troops as opposed to Anarche's 272,000, in addition to 7,000 giants larger than Pantagruel as opposed to Anarche's 300 giants smaller than Pantagruel—"en quoy *faignoit* Pantagruel avoir armée sur mer" (*P* 28:354 and 26:347, emphasis mine). To this untruth he adds a trick of another kind, a box of thirst-inducing drugs offered as a test of the Dipsodes' ability to resist his (nonexistent) superior forces. The purpose of this double ruse is to trick the enemy into frantic, last-minute preparations that will result in inebriation and somnolence, thus allowing Pantagruel and his army of four to attack them unawares during the night and thus to accomplish by wiles what they could not possibly hope to accomplish by force alone. "Enfans," he explains to his small band of followers, "J'ay donné entendre à ce prisonnier que nous avons armée sur mer, ensemble que nous ne leur donnerons l'assault que jusques à demain sus le midy, à celle fin que eulx, doubtant la grande venue de gens, ceste nuyct se occupent à mettre en ordre et soy remparer; mais ce pendent mon intention est que nous chargeons sur eulx environ l'heure du premier somme" (*P* 28:355).

The ruse succeeds, allowing Carpalim to enter the besieged capital of Utopie and dispatch all its armed inhabitants to the aid of Pantagruel, thence to enter the camp of the Dipsodes to set fire to their tents and artillery and send them with a stentorian cry scurrying out into the field (*P* 28:357–58). With the enemy in disarray, its weapons destroyed, and the balance of opposing forces somewhat restored thanks to reinforcements from the Utopians, the war can now be forced to a relatively bloodless end by the single combat between Pantagruel and Loup Garou.

The importance of this resolution is that the disproportionate conflict between Utopians and Dipsodes, which seemed certain to end in catastrophe, is concluded without a single fatality among the Utopians. Nor would there have been an additional fatality among the Dipsodes if a ruse of Panurge's own devising—a drug given to Pantagruel in imitation of the one Pantagruel had given to the Dipsodes—had not made Pantagruel piss so profusely in the enemy camp that he drowned them all (*P* 28:358). Without Panurge's rivalry in ruse, the only fatalities of the entire war would have been 659 of Anarche's 660 ambushing horsemen and all 300 of his mercenary, Cyclopic giants. Both of these groups, it will be noted, are killed strictly in self-defense: the first when they strike without warning at the small band of unarmed Pantagruelians, 660 to 4, the second when they break faith by coming to the aid of the defeated Loup Garou, 299 to 1. The former are vanquished thanks to Panurge's ruse, the latter thanks to Pantagruel's valor.

This unorthodox epic conclusion brings us back, once again, to More's *Utopia*. The most distinctive aspect of warfare in the commonwealth described by Hythlodaeus is that the Utopians, though exercised in the arts of war, prefer to fight by ruse rather than by force. In contrast to the Europeans, they are actually ashamed of a military victory won by force and bloodshed ("cruentae victoriae non piget modo eos, sed pudet quoque") and take glory only in victories won by stratagem and cunning ("arte doloque"). They consider that they have acted according to true valor and virtue whenever they prevail by means of the one faculty that sets them above brute beasts—the strength of their wits ("ingenii viribus"), the wit and intelligence ("ingenio, et ratione") with which man alone is endowed (book 2, "De re militari," 202).[18] In accordance with this principle of avoiding unnecessary bloodshed at all costs they try either by force or by ruse to kill the general of an opposing army ("hunc aperte invadunt, hunc ex insidiis adoriuntur") but to spare the enemy troops, preferring to take them prisoner or even let them escape rather than kill them or risk their own (210–12). Only when they have won a victory in this manner, by wiles rather than by force and with as little bloodshed as possible, do they celebrate a public triumph and erect a trophy as for a strenuous exploit ("triumphumque . . . publicitus agunt, et velut re strenue gesta, tropheum erigunt," 202).

In these details we recognize both the strategy and the ethos of the epic battle of the *Pantagruel*, from the hero's trophy erected in honor of his companions' "bon sens" and "engin" (compare More's "ingenio, et ratione") to the hero's own ruse that allows him to kill the opposing general but to spare both the enemy troops and his own people.[19] The Pantagruelians' military victory over the invading Dipsodes is the effect of a perfectly Utopian brand of warfare in which Pantagruel's own Spartan preparedness and fortitude are opportunely supplemented by Panurge's Lysandrian wiles. In this crucial respect the hero and his *comes* are indeed like the lion and the fox of Panurge's fable. Neither fortitude nor ruse alone could prevail against the superior forces of the Dipsodes. Together they not only prevail but, once the first surprise attack is foiled, succeed in liberating the oppressed Utopians without causing a drop of Utopian blood to be spilled. Thanks to the highly unorthodox collaboration between the noble, leonine hero and his ignoble, vulpine sidekick, the military exploit with which the epic climaxes is the very antithesis of the bloody massacres by which epic wars are traditionally won. Once again we find that the *Pantagruel* is perfectly a Utopian anti-epic.[20]

The epic war of the *Pantagruel* ends with the joyous liberation not only of the besieged capital of Utopie (*P* 31:374) but of the entire kingdom of Dipsodie, whose inhabitants, now rid of their illegitimate King Anarche, receive Pantagruel and his band of Utopian colonists with open arms: "Tout le monde en estoit joyeux, et incontinent se rendirent à luy, et, de leur franc vouloir, luy apporterent les clefz de toutes le villes où il alloit" (*P* 32:377). Only the recalcitrant Almyrodes (ἁλμυρός = briny, brackish, bitter) refuse liberation and must be reduced by force. Once this mopping-up operation is complete and the last traces of unredeemable bitterness have been removed, a universal peace and joy reign supreme in the anti-epic world of the *Pantagruel*. With this pacification of the Dipsodes and "renouvellement du temps de Saturne" (*P* 31:374), the Utopian Prince of Peace has at last become the entelechial "dominateur des alterez" he was destined to be.

The compelling rationality of this epic conclusion has been somewhat obscured for modern readers by what first appears to be an independent and virtually irrelevant episode inserted between the "desconfite gigantale" (*P* 30:365) and "victoire merveilleuse" (*P* 31:374), related in chapter 29, and the actual colonization of Dipsodie, described in chapter 32. But this intervening episode—the much-glossed account of the death and resurrection of Epistemon in chapter 30—is only an apparent digression, for like every other episode of the *Pantagruel* it finds a natural place in the overall design of the epic and in fact contributes an indispensable key to its political meaning.

Commentators of chapter 30 were once concerned almost exclusively with Epistemon's return to life and with the interpretation of what Abel Lefranc took to be a parody of miracles wrought by Christ—most notably, the resuscitation of the daughter of Jairus (Mt 9.18–26, Mk 5.21–43, Lk 8.40–56) and the raising of Lazarus (Jn 11.1–44).[21] Seen in its larger context, however, Epistemon's resurrection appears far less important as an act in itself than as a device allowing for a firsthand account of a descent into hell. Such descents are a familiar convention of classical epic. The illustrious precedents of *Odyssey* 11 and especially *Aeneid* 6 make it all but impossible for a classicizing epic not to include such an episode. From a purely generic point of view, then, it is not surprising to find a visit to hell in the *Pantagruel*. The epic pretensions of the work virtually require it.

Two aspects of this descent are, however, highly unorthodox. One is its placement and function within the overall design of the work. In Homer and Vergil the descent into Hades is placed just before the midpoint, at a point where the hero is still far from completing his prescribed role. The primary function of these descents is to reveal to the disheartened or anxious hero what his telos is and what he must do to attain it. Odysseus consults with the shade of Teiresias to learn what obstacles he will encounter on his way home to Ithaca, what difficulties he will find once he arrives there, and what he must do to overcome them (*Odyssey* 11.90–137). Similarly, Aeneas consults the shade of Anchises for the encouragement of a privileged, proleptic glimpse at the entire history of the glorious empire that he is destined to found and for advice on how to avoid or to bear the tribulations that await him in Latium (*Aeneid* 6.752–892).

In the *Pantagruel*, on the contrary, the descent into hell appears at the *end*, at the very moment the hero is completing his prescribed role of "dominateur des alterez" and the design of the epic is being fully consummated. It serves not to reveal the ultimate telos toward which the epic is moving or the means by which it will be reached, but to mark the moment of its attainment and reveal its larger significance. It functions as a simultaneous, rather than a proleptic, gloss on the political meaning of the *Pantagruel*.

A second anomaly is that the descent is undertaken not by the hero himself but by one of his lesser companions. There is no precedent in epic literature for such a substitution.

The explanation for both of these departures from a well-established norm is intimately related to the anti-epic function of the episode within the larger political design of the *Pantagruel*. Aside from the generic considerations that account for its presence, Rabelais's version of the descent into Hades owes more to philosophical sources than to epic ones. Epistemon's death, resurrection, and eyewitness report of an afterlife are drawn not from the *Odyssey* or the *Aeneid* but from Plato's *Republic,* which concludes with Socrates' fable of a warrior who was slain in battle and revived ten days later to tell what he had seen and learned during his sojourn in the underworld (10.614b–621d). The actual details reported by Epistemon are adapted directly from Lucian's satirical reworking of the *Republic* in the *Menippus* and the *Downward Journey.*

Unlike Homer and Vergil, Plato and Lucian are concerned not with empire but with equity and justice. Whereas Odysseus and Aeneas behold great military and political leaders in all their past or future glory—Agamemnon, Achilles, and Ajax in *Odyssey* 11.385–566; the ancient founders of Troy as well as the entire succession of kings, consuls, and emperors from Silvius to Julius Caesar who are to forge the new Roman *imperium* in *Aeneid* 6.637–55 and 752–853—Er and Menippus observe many of those same heroes exchanging, by will or by force, their former exalted estate for a humbler one. In the underworld of the *Republic* Ajax chooses to return to life as a lion, Agamemnon as an eagle, Odysseus as an ordinary private citizen (10.620a–d). In the underworld of the *Menippus* Philip of Macedon works as a poor cobbler, and the various kings and satraps of the world—the "Xerxeses, Dariuses and Polycrateses"—beg for a living at the crossroads (17).

It is precisely this deliberate, moralizing inversion of the epic underworld that characterizes the descent into hell in Alcofrybas's epic. In place of the *Odyssey*'s heroes of the Trojan War and (more to the point) in place of the *Aeneid*'s pompous pageant of heroes of the great empire to come, Epistemon witnesses a seemingly endless sequence of heroes whose "estat," like that of the characters observed by Er and Menippus, "est changé en estrange façon" (*P* 30:367).[22] Many of these are the most familiar heroes of classical and medieval imperial epics, including the Greek heroes of the *Iliad* seen by Odysseus in the underworld of the *Odyssey* (Achilles, Agamemnon, and Nestor) and most of the future heroes of Rome seen by Aeneas in the underworld of the *Aeneid* (Romulus, Numa, Ancus, Tarquin, Camillus, Scipio Africanus, Fabius Cunctator, Marcellus, Octavian, and Caesar). Their number even includes Ulysses and Aeneas themselves, the heroes of the *Odyssey* and the *Aeneid* who made those famous descents to the underworld before Epistemon. To all of these are added the heroes of latter day epics of conquest and dominion—Arthur and the knights of the Round Table, Lancelot, Valentin and Orson, Giglan and Gauvain, Huon de Bordeaux, Jean de Paris, Perceforest, Ogier le Danois, the four sons of Aymon.

Intermingled with these heroes of the great imperial epics we find a hodgepodge of emperors, kings, consuls, satraps, generals, and propagandists of the most powerful empires of history—Assyrian (Semiramis), Persian (Cyrus, Cambyses, Darius, Xerxes, Ataxerxes), Athenian, (Themistocles, Demosthenes), Macedonian (Alexander), Seleucid (Antiochus), Ptolemaic (Cleopatra), Byzantine (Justinian), Carthaginian (Dido, Hasdrubal, Hannibal), and of course most conspicuously, Roman (Romulus, Numa, Camillus, Tarquin, Lucretia, Marcellus, Fabius, Scipio Africanus, Sulla, Lucullus, Piso, Cicero, Pompey, Caesar, Brutus, Cassius, Octavian, Livia, Drusus, Nero, Nerva, Trajan, Antoninus, Commodus, Pertinax).[23]

To these are added a handful of popes whose power was excessively, sometimes almost exclusively, secular, political, and imperialistic—Urban II (1088–99), promoter of the first Crusade against the Turks in the Holy Land; Nicholas III (1277–80), who spent his short reign promoting his own family to power, expanding the papal state, and opposing the claims of both the Holy Roman Emperor and Saint Louis's brother, Charles of Anjou, to the kingdom of Sicily; Boniface VIII (1294–1303), the continuator of Nicholas's interventionist policies in Sicily and the great political opponent of Philippe le Bel in the Gallican crisis of the turn of the thirteenth century, sometime ally of the Holy Roman Emperor against the interests of the French king, author of the hated *Liber sextus* of the Decretals and of the bull *Unam sanctam,* which asserted the superiority of the pope's spiritual power over the emperor's secular power;[24] Calixtus III (1455–58), the simoniac Borgia whose sole passion as pope was the organization of Crusades to reconquer Constantinople from the Turks; Sixtus IV (1471–84), the simoniac della Rovere who meddled unceasingly in political affairs not only by sending a fleet against the Turks in Smyrna but by encouraging wars among Christian princes as well, inducing Ferdinand of Naples to wage war on the Medici in Florence, aiding and abetting Venice in its attacks against Ferrara, and opposing Louis XI over the Pragmatic Sanction of Bourges; Alexander VI (1492–1503), the notoriously Machiavellian and simoniac nephew of Calixtus III who pursued a policy of war against both Turks and Christians, joining forces with Milan, Venice, and the Holy Roman Emperor, for example, to expel Charles VIII from Italy; and of course Julius II (1503–13), the despised warrior-pope who set all the princes of Christendom to war against one another, and himself wore a morion more often than the tiara, joining the League of Cambrai against Venice to reclaim from it the Papal States lost by the Borgias, then forming the Holy League with Venice, Spain, and England to wage war against his former ally Louis XII and drive him from Italy.[25]

What all the damned of Alcofrybas's hell have in common is excessive and abusive political or military power—that is, illegitimate ἀρχή and *imperium*. All have served—as heroes, conquerors, or rulers—the cause of empire, expanding their dominions beyond legitimate borders to usurp the rule of neighboring or distant lands and extending their personal power beyond legitimate rule to tyranny. Epistemon points this out at the conclusion of his catalog by referring to them collectively as the "gros seigneurs en ce monde icy" and speaking of them as "coquins de royx" and "roys et papes de ce monde" (*P* 30:371–72). The narrator emphasizes the point further in the following chapter by calling them the "roys et riches de ce monde" (*P* 31:375).[26] And lest any doubt remain, Panurge glosses the entire episode with what amounts to a little diatribe against the politics of imperialism: "Ces diables de roys icy," he explains, "ne sont que veaulx, et ne sçavent ny ne valent rien, sinon à faire des maulx es pauvres subjectz, et à troubler tout le monde par guerre, pour leur inique et detestable plaisir" (*P* 31:376).

With this in mind we may begin to perceive more clearly the relevance of Epistemon's epic descent to the larger political design of the *Pantagruel*. All the "gros seigneurs" of his catalog—whether they be epic heroes or historical figures, popes or emperors, crusaders or infidels, men or women—have played political and military roles exactly analogous to the one played by King Anarche in the epic war of the *Pantagruel*. All were the agents of the kind of usurping imperialism that was condemned at the beginning of Alcofrybas's anti-epic in Panurge's Crusade against the Turks in Mytelene and that the hero himself resists at the end in his Utopian, anti-imperialist war against the Dipsodes. And conversely, King Anarche—"Monsieur du roy icy," as Panurge pointedly refers to him (*P* 30:373)—is one of the "diables de roys" whom Epistemon found suffering in hell. As such he is destined one day to join his brothers in tyranny below. This crucial point is driven home at the end of the episode when Panurge proposes to prepare the "pauvre roy Anarche" for life in the next world by teaching him a trade similar to the one practiced by the "gros seigneurs" in hell, so that he too will be able to earn his living when he is "par delà à tous les diables" (*P* 30:373). It is repeated even more explicitly in the following episode when Panurge, mindful of the way the "roys et riches de ce monde" are treated "par les Champs Elisées," makes Anarche into a poor peddler of green sauce and delivers his speech against the depredations of "ces diables de roys icy," claiming that "Monsieur du Roy de troys cuittes" was never so fortunate "que de n'estre plus roy" (*P* 31:375–76). Anarche is thus the last in a long line of epic and historical "heroes," and the Achilleses, Aeneases, Alexanders, Dariuses, and Caesars of this world are all "Anarches"—that is, tyrants and usurpers, antiprinces with no legitimate ἀρχή.

And so the *Pantagruel* remains an anti-epic to the end. Having narrated Pantagruel's victory in what first appears to be merely a burlesque of an ordinary epic battle, Rabelais reveals the revolutionary meaning of that victory through the moral philosophers' version of a descent into Hades. In this place traditionally reserved for a review of past or future heroes of epic conquest and empire, he offers a categorical condemnation of the ethos on which conquest and empire are predicated and the literal damnation of the heroes and practitioners of that ethos. He even goes so far as to identify the vanquished villain of the *Pantagruel* with all the greatest heroes of ancient and medieval epic, from the *Iliad* and *Aeneid* to the crusader epics of the Carolingian cycle. What Alcofrybas's hero has conquered at the end of his Utopian gesta is in fact the very idea of Hero, Empire, and Epic. The *Pantagruel*, it seems, is not simply an anti-epic but quite literally an epic to end all epics.

There is of course a large measure of literary play in Rabelais's burlesque inversion of the norms and the ethos of classical epics, and modern readers are particularly sensitive to the appeal of this kind of play. But we must remind ourselves that for Rabelais's intended readers more than literature was at stake. Like the serious epics it parodies, Alcofrybas's anti-epic is designed in large part to function as political propaganda. By inverting the norms and the ethos of the *Aeneid,* in particular, it deliberately subverts Caesar Augustus's politics of empire, which the *Aeneid* is designed, at least ostensibly, to promote and glorify.[27]

The general lines of this propaganda have now become clear enough. As opposed to classical and medieval epics, Alcofrybas's anti-epic condemns empires and imperialistic wars of all kinds, whether they be religious or territorial. In their place he proposes the anti-imperialistic pacificism of Utopia, which refuses territorial expansion and domination over other sovereign states and rejects all wars except those required to repel an imperialistic invasion of its own borders. Thus at the beginning of the epic Panurge is shown to be wrong in participating in the last Crusade against the Turks, and at the end we find the heroes of the first Crusade—Urban II and Godefroy de Bouillon—consigned to hell as damnable "diables de roys" and warmongers. The truly epic battle of the *Pantagruel*, in contrast, is fought not for empire but against empire. Its only object is the liberation of a sovereign capital that is besieged by the illegitimate, imperialistic antiprince Anarche, much in the same way that Troy was besieged by Agamemnon and Achilles, or Latium by Aeneas. Throughout the epic, meanwhile, from the episode of the walls of Paris to that of the war against the Dipsodes, we find a consistent apology for the most unheroic, Utopian kinds of ruse in the waging of an unavoidable defensive war against a more conventional—and therefore illegitimate—"epic hero."

The implications of this vision for a Europe in which emerging nations were consolidating their territories and disputing borders, and in which princes were contending with one another for hegemony and even for the title of emperor, are obvious. Far from promoting the imperial pretensions of any one state or prince against another, as epics traditionally do, the *Pantagruel* condemns the very ethos of empire, and with it the wars undertaken in the name of empire by *all* princes, whether they be named Charles V, Henry VIII, or even François I.

Beyond this general condemnation of imperialism, however, the *Pantagruel* was probably intended to have a more specific relevance for France. Unlike Picrochole of the *Gargantua,* Anarche is too general a type to be identified with an enemy of France like Charles V. And at the time the *Pantagruel* was first published the kings of France, no less than the Holy Roman Emperor, had recently and flagrantly violated the legal boundaries of sovereign states and waged war against neighboring peoples to make good their dubious imperialistic claims to foreign territories. Had François I learned the lesson of the disastrous Italian Wars? Given the state of political affairs in 1532 it seems likely that, despite the terms of the Treaties of Madrid and Cambrai (signed in 1526 and 1529, respectively), he had not, and that the *Pantagruel* was designed, at least in part, to make sure that he did.

Two small details would seem to confirm this assumption. One is the presence, in the original edition of the work, not only of the legendary heroes of Carolingian epics but also of the more or less historical founders of a specifically French empire—Pharamond, "le roy Pépin," Charlemagne, and "les douze pers de France"—among the various imperialists damned in hell (*P* 30:368–70 var.; Saulnier 20:161–63). In its first form the *Pantagruel* thus explicitly condemned the imperialistic pretensions of the kings of France along with those of every other state.

The other revealing detail is a more subtle one that survived through the definitive edition of the epic. At the beginning of the strictly heroic portion of the *Pantagruel*, at the moment when the hero arrives home to defend Utopie against Anarche's unjust invasion, Alcofrybas specifies that Utopie is located "jouxte le royaulme de Achorie" (*P* 24:340). This ostensibly superfluous detail from the geography of the *Utopia* is a deliberate allusion to the most memorably anti-imperialistic, *anti-French* passage of More's work. The Achorii ("without place" or "without land") are a people whose king dredges up an old marriage alliance to claim sovereignty over a neighboring state. On the strength of that dubious claim he invades the kingdom and succeeds in annexing it to his own. But annexation leads only to more wars abroad as well as to sedition, corruption, and financial ruin at home. In the face of such great disasters the Achorians force their king to choose between his two kingdoms, which he finally does, to the benefit of all.

Hythlodaeus mentions the Achorii and their anti-imperialistic "decreta" not as part of his general description of Utopia in book 2 but in the course of what is commonly called the "Dialogue of Counsel" in book 1, as the specific example he would use, if he were a counselor to the king of France, to persuade the monarch of that country to abandon his ill-advised claims to Milan, Naples, and Venice and to concentrate instead on loving his own subjects and making his ancestral kingdom a more prosperous and flourishing place.[28] To any reader of More, therefore, an allusion to "Achorie" would inevitably recall the subject of French imperialism in Italy and the humanists' condemnation of it. Appearing where it does in Alcofrybas's narrative, such an allusion can only point to the obvious similarities between Anarche's invasion of Utopie and the invasions of Italy by Charles VIII, Louis XII, and François I.

Contrary to Abel Lefranc's well-known thesis according to which Rabelais was a loyal propagandist for the policies of François I,[29] it would seem that in his first work, at least, Rabelais is playing the role not of apologist but of Hythlodaean counselor, dissuading François from further "Anarchism" undertaken in the name of empire and instructing the

Very Christian King in the proper role of the Christian prince, much as Erasmus had undertaken to do, through very different means, for the future Holy Roman Emperor in the *Institutio principis christiani*.

Whatever particular political implications the *Pantagruel* may have had for the French reader of 1532, its anti-imperialistic stance is clearly more than a political "message" appended willy-nilly to an otherwise self-sufficient epic. As we have seen, it infuses the whole work as a coherent political design. Having examined this political design in some detail we must return once again to the question of its relation to the moral, redemptive design of the *Pantagruel*.

At the beginning of this chapter I observed that Anarche's unprovoked, imperialistic war of aggression against his peaceful Utopian neighbors appears to be the collective, political manifestation of the same anticaritas that Loup Garou embodies on the individual, moral plane. It would indeed seem that in invading Utopie Anarche plays out on an international, epic scale the fratricide of Abel by Cain that Loup Garou reenacts in his single combat with Pantagruel, and that in defeating Anarche and bringing about a golden age of peace and joy in both Utopie and Dipsodie Pantagruel extends to the political realm the reign of brotherly love signaled by his ultimate triumph over Loup Garou. But it is the fusion of these moral and political planes, and the perfect integration of the anti-epic into the overall redemptive design of the *Pantagruel*, that lend to the work its fullest meaning.

Even before examining this fusion more closely we may perhaps catch a glimpse at its meaning in two works published shortly after the *Pantagruel*, both of which are considerably less oblique in their expression. One is the *Gargantua* which, as I have already noted, is in many ways a straightforward rewriting of the richer and more allusive *Pantagruel*. At the height of the Picrocholine war, in an episode that corresponds exactly to the duel in the *Pantagruel*, the good King Grandgousier admonishes his prisoner Toucquedillon with the following homily:

> Le temps n'est plus d'ainsi *conquester les royaulmes* avecques dommaige de son *prochain frere christian*. Ceste imitation des anciens Hercules, Alexandres, Hannibalz, Scipions, Cesars et aultres telz, est contraire à la *profession de l'Evangile,* par lequel nous est commandé guarder, saulver, regir et administrer chascun ses pays et terres, non hostilement envahir les aultres, et, ce que les Sarazins et Barbares jadis appelloient prouesses, maintenant nous appellons briguanderies et mechansetez. Mieulx eust il [Picrochole] faict soy contenir en sa maison, royallement la gouvernant, que insulter en la mienne,

> hostillement la pillant; car par bien la gouverner l'eust augmentée, par me piller sera destruict. [*G* 46:171, emphasis mine]

The other is an evangelical parody of almanacs written at about the same time as the *Gargantua,* in late 1534 or early 1535. Here Rabelais's "prediction" of the events of the coming year consists of the following "conditionale":

> Si les roys, princes et communités christianes ont en reverence la divine parole de Dieu et selon icelle gouvernent soy et leurs sujets, nous ne veismes de nostre aage année plus salubre es corps, plus paisible es asmes, plus fertile en biens, que sera cette-cy: et voirons la face du ciel, la vesture de la terre et le maintien du peuple, joyeux, gay, plaisant et benin, plus que ne fut depuis cinquante ans en ça. [*Almanach pour l'an 1535,* Jourda 2.523]

Both of these passages state explicitly what a fusion of the moral and political dimensions in the *Pantagruel* would seem to suggest—namely, that the New Order of political stability, tranquility, and *pax universalis* will come about not with the triumph of one empire over another but with the triumph of the New Commandment within each. The only true empire will be the peaceful one in which the princes of Christendom, like the private citizens they govern, are bound together by brotherly love.[30]

Keeping in mind these intimations of an evangelized political utopia, let us now consider more carefully how the redemptive and political designs are fused at the end of the *Pantagruel*, in the hope of understanding somewhat better the bizarre conclusion of Alcofrybas's epic New Testament, and the meaning of the New Order established in Utopie by the messianic anti-epic hero, the more-than-Solomonic Prince of Peace, Pantagruel.

6

THE NEW ORDER IN UTOPIA AND PANTAGRUEL'S TWO BODIES

Having killed Loup Garou in single combat and liberated both Utopie and Dipsodie from domination by the usurper king Anarche, Pantagruel has fulfilled his double role of messianic redeemer of Cain's original sin of brother against brother and of ideal Christian prince and Solomonic peacemaker in a larger conflict of kingdom against kingdom. The new Utopian reign of both brotherly love and international harmony can now begin.

But what, precisely, is the nature of this joyful New Order? Unlike the *Gargantua,* which ends with a lengthy, idealized description of the evangelized court of François I in the guise of the utopian antimonastery Thélème, the *Pantagruel* offers little in the way of concrete details. Typically, it merely hints obliquely at what the *Gargantua* will spell out more explicitly. Three highly allusive passages placed at critical points near the end of the epic nevertheless suggest the distinct outlines of a clear and coherent New Order.

The first of these is the evangelical prayer uttered by Pantagruel at the crucial turning point of the epic, in the last moments before his decisive duel with Loup Garou. As we noted in the preceding chapter, Pantagruel draws a clear distinction here between civil defense and crusades. In matters of war, the separation between religious and secular orders—between faith and politics, religion and government, church and state, one might even say between New Testament and epic—is absolute. But the same separation does not hold for the coming time of peace. On the contrary, the prayer points unmistakably to a future order in which these separate domains will be inseparably joined.

In petitioning God for aid in the defense of the civic order Pantagruel promises, in return for such aid and once the present military threat is removed, to defend the faith also, but only after political order is restored and only through the legitimate means of evangelization, by a "confession catholicque et service de ta parolle": "S'il te plaist à ceste heure me estre en ayde, . . . je te fais veu que par toutes contrées tant de ce pays de Utopie que d'ailleurs, où j'auray puissance et auctorité, je feray prescher ton sainct Evangile purement, simplement et entierement, si que les abus d'un tas de papelars et faulx prophetes, qui ont par constitutions humaines et inventions depravées envenimé tout le monde, seront d'entour moy exterminez" (*P* 29:361).[1] Because God accepts this vow as the condition on which he will grant Pantagruel's petition for aid in the present, we know that the heroic restoration of the political order is bound, by divine contract as it were, to be followed by an evangelical restoration of the religious order as well, in which heresies will be rooted out and the true faith fully restored. The two renovations will take place separately and by virtually contrary means, but each is a necessary condition of the other, and both *must* be accomplished in Pantagruel's redeemed Utopie. The future glimpsed in the prayer is thus a New Order in which both the political and religious orders will be renovated and fused in a divinely sanctioned Utopian rule.

These clear intimations concerning the New Order are thrown into striking relief by the words with which God sanctions them: "Alors fut ouye une voix du ciel, disant: '*Hoc fac et vinces*'; c'est à dire: 'Fais ainsi, et tu auras victoire'" (*P* 29:361–62). As M. A. Screech observed long ago (*Evangélisme,* 27–28 and 87–88), the phrase "Hoc fac et vinces" is a conflation of two separate phrases: Christ's words quoted in the Gospel of Luke—"Hoc fac et vives" (Lk 10.28)—and the well-known motto of Constantine's labarum—"In hoc signo vinces." The importance of this fact for our purposes is that the conflated phrases are among the most highly charged formulations associated with new political and religious orders.

Implicit in the formula "in hoc signo vinces" is one of the most crucial turning points in the political history of the West: the decisive, divinely assisted battle for empire by the first Christian emperor and the resulting Christianization of the universal empire. According to the canonic tradition authorized by Eusebius, Constantine was marching on Rome in 312 to deliver it from the usurping, impious tyrant Maxentius. Recognizing the need for assistance from some higher power he began praying to the God of the Christians, "entreating and beseeching Him to reveal to him who He might be and to stretch forth His right hand for the coming events." The next moment he saw, blazing in the sky over the sun, the sign of the cross and the inscription "in hoc signo vinces" (τούτῳ νίκα).

Constantine had this sign emblazoned on his banners and "with this sign" and the divine assistance to which it attests defeated Maxentius just outside Rome at the Mulvius Bridge, liberated Rome, and went on to become Augustus in the West and later sole emperor of the entire Roman Empire. In these roles he ended the official policy of persecutions against the Christians established by Diocletian, replaced paganism with Christianity as the official religion of the empire, and presided over the eradication of heresy at the Council of Nicaea in 325.[2]

These circumstances and their connotations of imperial conversion are of course perfectly consonant with Pantagruel's political, epic role as Christian prince. Like Constantine, Pantagruel is the Christian soldier destined to remove a usurping tyrant from the seat of imperial power and to liberate and reform the state as its divinely illuminated, divinely sanctioned head. He, like Constantine, receives providential assurance from heaven that he will prevail—"vinces"—in the decisive battle that will put him in power and change the course of imperial history. And as his last words have just shown he, like Constantine, is bound to accomplish a vast project of imperial *renovatio* and conversion by establishing the true Christian faith in place of a hostile, false one and by "exterminating" all heretical "abus" within the liberated empire.[3] Except for Constantine's traditional brand of unregenerate imperialism, for which we might expect to find him in Epistemon's Hades alongside Aeneas, Caesar, and Pope Julius II, the first Christian emperor is a perfect analogue for Pantagruel in his role of epic hero, and his Christianized empire a political archetype for the New Order of the *Pantagruel*.

But Constantine's Christian empire is only half of the vision implied by God's answer to Pantagruel's prayer. While "in hoc signo vinces" suggests a primarily political perspective on Pantagruel's New Order, the phrase with which it is conflated puts the same New Order in a primarily evangelical light. The words "hoc fac et vives" come from Luke's version of the giving of the Great Commandment. Like Matthew and Mark, Luke has a scribe "tempt" Jesus by asking him a perfidious question about the "first" or "great" Commandment, reformulated here as a question of means to eternal life: "Magister, quid faciendo vitam aeternam possidebo?" But whereas the other gospelists have Jesus confound his temptor with an irrefragable answer, Luke has Jesus turn the question back on his temptor. "Hoc fac et vives" is Jesus' reply to the scribe who, in answering his own question, has proven himself capable of regeneration and shown himself to be half converted already:[4] "And behold a lawyer stood up to put him to the test, saying, 'Teacher, what shall I do to inherit eternal life?' He said to him, 'What is written in the law? How do you read?' And he answered, 'You shall love the Lord your God with all your heart, and with all your soul, and with all your strength, and with all your mind; and your neighbor as yourself.' And he said to him, 'You have answered right; do this, and you will live [*Hoc fac et vives*]'" (Lk 10.25–28).

The context recalled by the phrase "hoc fac et vives" could hardly be more relevant to the question of a New Order in the *Pantagruel*. The "hoc" in question is the one Great Commandment of the New Law, which will fulfill and replace the Old Law as soon as Jesus' imminent redemptive sacrifice is completed. The second article of this Great Commandment, the most immediate antecedent of hoc, is the ethical foundation on which the Church—that is, the entire edifice of a redeemed, regenerate Christian community—is constructed: "You shall love your neighbor as yourself." And as we saw in chapter 2, this hoc is the point on which the epic design of the *Pantagruel* turns. The implications of the phrase "hoc fac et" are thus unmistakable and entirely appropriate to the work as a whole: the New Order to come will be the church of reconciled brothers, bound together by caritas.

Hoc fac et vinces. Fused in the single phrase pronounced by a numinous voice in answer to Pantagruel's promise of political and religious renovation, Christ's words to Constantine and to the lawyer confirm the double nature not only of the redemptive exploit that the messianic hero is about to perform but of the New Order that will result from it. Together they connote a perfect fusion of a renewed political order and a renewed religious order, in which Empire is purged of imperialism and converted into a truly Christian assembly (ἐκκλησία), in which Church is purged of theology and converted into a new social order governed by the rule of the New Law, and in which both are melded into an ideal community founded on brotherly love where church and state, faith and politics, are no longer distinguishable as separate orders because each is fulfilled and perfected in the other. It is as though that perfect future political order known as the kingdom of God were to be fully realized here on earth in Pantagruel's new messianic kingdom in Utopie.

The implications of this short passage preceding Pantagruel's redemptive exploit are fully borne out by the longer passage following the exploit—the episode of Epistemon's descent into Hades, in which all the emperors and empires of history, and even the idea of epic imperialism, are vigorously condemned.

The principle on which this anti-imperialist Hades is predicated is one of simple inversion: the "Anarchist" tyrants of history are punished simply by changing places with their former victims. Thus each of the bellicose "roys et papes de ce monde" (*P* 30:372) is reduced to the station of the weakest and humblest of his former subjects and made to practice a useful trade—making sandals or nails or glass, selling mustard or salt, tilling the soil or harvesting or milling wheat, tending vines or guarding cattle, and so forth. Conversely, the most abject of citizens, along with the philosophers and poets who in life opposed the "roys et papes de ce monde," are elevated to the station of kings, popes, and emperors, in which roles they become the agents of divine (or at least poetic) justice by subjecting their former oppressors to the tyranny and oppression that had been inflicted on them in the world. Thus the dog-philosopher Diogenes, who once mocked Alexander's worldly greatness, assumes the purple and the scepter of imperium to humiliate and beat the former emperor; the poor man's Stoic, Epictetus, who was once banished from Rome by Domitian, now lives in luxury and lords it over the Persian emperor Cyrus the Great; the impecunious scalawag Pathelin gives Julius II a taste of what it is like to be cheated and beaten; Jean Lemaire, the Gallican enemy of the papacy, plays pope to the former popes by making them grovel at his feet for indulgences; the poor fugitive from justice Villon, whose famous ballades illustrate how even "papes, roys, filz de roys / Et conceus en ventres de roynes / Sont ensevelis mors et frois" (*Testament* 413–15) and how Fortune has reduced to dust Priam, Hannibal, Scipio, Caesar, Pompey, Jason, Alexander (*Poésies diverses* 12), similarly plays cruel emperor to Xerxes; and the coward "franc archier de Baignolet" holds the life of the fearless warrior Perceforest in his hands. In all these cases cited by Epistemon, the tables are simply turned on the imperialistic rulers of the world. "Ceulx qui avoient esté gros seigneurs en ce monde icy, guaingnoyent leur pauvre meschante et paillarde vie là bas. Au contraire, les philosophes et ceulx qui avoient esté indigens en ce monde, de par de là estoient gros seigneurs en leur tour" (371).

This systematic inversion of estates is not found in the principal Lucianic source of Alcofrybas's Hades. In the *Menippus* we find a similar degradation of the rich and powerful but no corresponding elevation of the poor and powerless. All who have sinned are simply punished together, "kings, slaves, satraps, day-laborers, rich men, beggars." Former station counts for nothing, except that workers are tortured only half as much as lords and given a little rest between torments (*Menippus* 14). Even among the righteous, the only advantage of poor wisemen like

Socrates and Diogenes over wealthy tyrants like Sardanapalus and Midas is that they have lost nothing in death and so make sport of the lamentations of those who have lost much (*Menippus* 18).

The principle of inversion governing the episode is not at all Lucianic or even classical but uniquely and characteristically evangelical. The synoptic Gospels abound in examples of the exalted being humbled and the humbled being exalted. In virtually every case, moreover, these examples describe the new life to come in the next world. The only exceptions to this rule are Mary, who in the "Magnificat" praises God for having "regarded the low estate [*humilitas*] of his handmaiden" and done "great things" (*magna*) for her so that "henceforth all generations will call [her] blessed" (Lk 1.48–49), and Christ himself, whose life and being embody the principle: the son of God and the messiah promised by the prophets, he was nevertheless born in the most miserable of circumstances to the most obscure of parents in the most godforsaken corner of the Roman Empire. Ridiculed throughout his life by right-thinking citizens and eventually condemned to die the wretched and ignominious death of a criminal, he rose after his death to sit at God's right hand and preside eternally over the saved in heaven. Or as Paul put it: "He humbled himself [*humiliavit semetipsum*] and became obedient unto death, even death on a cross. Therefore God has highly exalted him [*exaltavit illum*] and bestowed on him the name which is above every name" (Phil 2.8–9).

With these two notable exceptions, the examples of an evangelical inversion of high and low appear throughout the Gospels not as reality in the present but as Christ's promise of a new and better life in the future. Jesus proclaims unequivocally that the "poor" and the "poor in spirit" are blessed because "theirs is the kingdom of heaven," and that the "meek" are blessed because "they shall inherit the earth" (Mt 5.3 and 5 [4], Lk 6.20), whereas it will be more difficult for the rich to enter the kingdom of God than for a camel to pass through the eye of a needle (Mt 19.23–24, Mk 10.23–25, Lk 18.24–25). And in countless exempla and proverbs he states that after death the tables will be turned on the rich and powerful. His fable of the rich man and the leprous beggar Lazarus is only the most obvious example of many (Lk 16.19–31). Elsewhere he warns that the rich shall be poor and the poor shall be rich (Mt 19.23–29, Mk 10.23–30, Lk 18.24–30; compare Jas 2.5); that the great shall be small and the smallest and least shall be greatest (Mt 18.1–3, Lk 9.46–48); that the first shall be last and the last shall be first (Mt 19.30 and 20.16, Mk 9.35 [34] and 10.31, Lk 13.30). Repeatedly and insistently he comes back to the same theme: "Whoever exalts himself will be humbled, and whoever humbles himself will be exalted"—"*omnis qui se exaltat, humiliabitur, et qui se humiliat, exaltabitur*" (Lk 14.11 and 18.14, Mt 23.12; compare Mt 18.4, 1 Pet 5.5–6).

Furthermore, whenever this theme of a future inversion occurs in the Gospels, questions of empire and political order are never far away. The God who exalted his humble handmaiden Mary is the one who "has put down the mighty from their thrones [*deposuit potentes de sede*] and exalted those of low degree [*exaltavit humiles*]" (Lk 1.52). The Jesus who was condemned to death by the representatives of the greatest empire in the history of the world constantly refers to the antithetical, new order of the future as the "kingdom" of heaven and the "kingdom" of God. And the ubiquitous idea that the exalted shall be humbled and the humble exalted is given its fullest expression in the contrast between the political rule of secular princes and the messianic role of Jesus in the world. Just as Jesus is about to enter Jerusalem for the last time, his apostles begin to quarrel about who will have the highest place in the new life to come. To these twelve who are charged with the task of spreading the Gospel and preparing the kingdom of God, Jesus warns: "You know that the *rulers of the Gentiles lord it over them,* and *their great men exercise authority over them.* It shall not be so among you; but whoever would be great among you must be your servant, and whoever would be first among you must be your slave; even as the Son of man came not to be served but to serve, and to give his life as a ransom for many" (Mt 20.25–28; compare Mk 10.42–45 and Lk 22.25–27, emphasis mine).

It is this evangelical vision of an upside-down kingdom of heaven that we find incorporated and literalized in the comic Hades of the *Pantagruel.* Alcofrybas's Alexander and Diogenes are little more than comic classical counterparts to Jesus' rich man and Lazarus. And the epic imperialists of Epistemon's catalog of the damned are those "potentes" of the world who have been brought low and made to cede their former station to the exalted "humiles" of the world. They are the "principes gentium" (Mt 20.25), the "reges gentium" (Lk 22.25), who in life lorded it over their subjects ("dominantur eorum") and exercised their authority over them ("potestatem exercent in eos"), were masters and occupied the first place, but are now dominated in turn, are the slaves of all, and occupy the last place. In this fundamental respect the burlesque, anti-epic Hades of Alcofrybas's epic New Testament is entirely consistent with the new political order of the kingdom of God as it is tirelessly evoked in the New Testament by the Christian messiah himself.[5]

The relevance of this crucial fact to the question of the New Order of the *Pantagruel* is this: that at the conclusion of his messianic epic gesta

Pantagruel deliberately undertakes to realize *here and now* the upside-down order of the kingdom of god to come. He does so, once again, with the assistance of his unlikely disciple Panurge.

From the beginning of the epic both the hero and his *comes* have shown a tendency to invert the hierarchies of the present order. This inclination in Pantagruel is illustrated by the parallel episodes of the Limousin schoolboy (*P* 6) and Panurge (*P* 9).[6] In spite of obvious similarities between them, the *écolier* is, in one crucial respect, Panurge's opposite. He is a hick, a country bumpkin, a prestigeless provincial—a "Lymosin, pour tout potaige"—who wants to conceal his humble origins and pass for Parisian ("contrefaire le Parisian") by mimicking the affected and pretentious language he has heard in the capital. He believes he has succeeded and is obviously delighted with the result: "tout jolliet . . . il cuide pindariser, et luy semble bien qu'il est quelque grand orateur en françoys, parce qu'il dedaigne l'usance commun de parler" (*P* 6:244 and 246). In short, he is a *humilis qui se exaltat,* and it is for this—not for his affected language as such, which is only a symptom of this far more grievous sin—that Pantagruel humiliates him by forcing him to speak his own most ignoble dialect and to shit in his fine Parisian pants. *Omnis qui se exaltat, humiliabitur.*

Panurge, on the contrary, is "beau de stature et elegant en tous lineamens du corps" and would appear to be born of some "riche et noble lignée" but has been reduced to a most wretched condition, "pitoyablement navré," "mal en ordre," "reduict en penurie et indigence" (*P* 9:263). He is a high-born noble whom fortune has brought low, *humiliavit,* and it is this wretched humiliation that moves Pantagruel to elevate him to the station of royal companion.[7] *Qui se humiliat, exaltabitur.* Together the parallel episodes condemn self-exaltation, condone humility, and clearly show Pantagruel as a systematic inverter of high and low estates, exalting the humble and humbling the proud. Even as he is being educated for his predestined redemptive exploit, the hero begins the process of evangelical inversion that is to be consummated in the kingdom of heaven at the end.

We have already seen in chapter 4 that an essential part of Panurge's role also consists in overturning the hierarchies of the existing social order, albeit in a far more destructive and negative way. He champions the cause of rejected lovers and used-up whores and delights in debasing the rich, the powerful, and the haughty, as exemplified by the overdressed, pharisaical Parisian lady. Panurge's tricks may be degraded simulacra of Pantagruel's more noble exploits, and the spirit behind them may be quite different (vindictive rather than righteously indignant), but their essential mechanism is the same. And once conscripted into Pantagruel's service, the mischievous trickster becomes a crucial ally in his master's evangelical program of inversion, as his role in confounding the "glorieux" cleric Thaumaste with obscene gestures shows.

It therefore comes as no surprise when at the end of the epic Panurge the great debaser first gets the idea of preparing Anarche for the fate that awaits him in Hades. Upon hearing Epistemon's report of the way the "gros seigneurs en ce monde icy" are treated in the next world, he inquires: "De quel mestier ferons nous Monsieur du roy icy, affin qu'il soit ja tout expert en l'art quand il sera de par delà à tous les diables?" (*P* 30:373). Later, recalling how the "roys et riches de ce monde . . . gaignoient pour lors leur vie à vilz et salles mestiers" (*P* 31:375), he dresses the king in rags, trains him in the abject art of peddling green sauce, and marries him to an old prostitute. In reducing a king to beggary and marrying a whore to a king Panurge merely plays his habitual role, for such have been his "meurs et condictions" from the very beginning (see *P* 16 and 17).

But Pantagruel gives special sanction to the prank—"Vrayement," he replies to Panurge's first inquiry, "c'est bien advisé à toy. Or, fais en à ton plaisir; je te le donne" (*P* 30:373), and on seeing the transformed king "prenoit à tout plaisir" (*P* 31:376)—and in so doing endows it with a far greater significance. Throughout the episode Rabelais has insisted with unusual emphasis on the distinction between "here" and "there," between "this world" and the next:

> Ceulx qui avoient esté gros seigneurs en ce monde icy, guaignoyent leur pauvre meschante et paillarde vie là bas. . . . Ceulx qui avoient esté indigens en ce monde, de par là estoient gros seigneurs [*P* 30:371]. . . . Mais les aultres coquins de royx qui sont là bas. . . . Tous ces pauvres roys et papes de ce monde [372]. . . . Comme vous voyez que font les coquins en ce monde. . . . De quel mestier ferons nous Monsieur du roy icy, affin qu'il soit ja expert en l'art quand il sera de par delà à tous les diables? [373]. . . . Comment estoient traictez les roys et riches de ce monde par les Champs Elisées [*P* 31:375]. . . . Ces diables de roys ici. [376]

By allowing Panurge to prepare Anarche for this future in Hades by treating him here and now as he would ordinarily be treated only then and there, Pantagruel abolishes the distinction between "here" and "there," "then" and "now," and anticipates *in this world* the upside-down order of the next. Henceforth kings will be humbled and the humble exalted not in the future world promised by Christ but in the Utopie liberated and renewed by the messianic hero Pantagruel.[8]

The New Order of Utopie is thus much like the more explicit new order of the Abbaye de Thélème at the end of the *Gargantua* in that an ungodly order is made godly by a simple process of inversion. By replacing monasticism with its antithesis Gargantua produces a utopia that resembles nothing so much as the idealized court of François I. Similarly, by inverting the imperialistic political order of this world Pantagruel reproduces the kingdom of heaven on earth. Compared to Thélème this oblique intimation of a New Order may appear to the modern reader too discreet to be taken seriously. To the sixteenth-century reader familiar with the biblical topos on which it is predicated, Pantagruel's New Order would have been, on the contrary, obvious and unambiguous. For unlike the inversion of the *Gargantua,* which is presented as heuristic (what would we get if we turned a monastery upside-down?) and whose result is a delightfully ironic surprise, the inversion of the *Pantagruel* is one of the most familiar and fundamental commonplaces of Christianity, and its result well known in advance. The kingdom of God is by Christ's own definition the inverse of the kingdom of man. By inverting the kingdom of man—first in the defeat of the idea of empire and then in the transformation of a king into a peddlar—Pantagruel in one highly charged gesture replaces fratricidal Empire with its evangelical opposite. The New Order in Utopie is indeed a kingdom of God on earth.

We began this investigation into the design of Rabelais's first Christian humanist epic with the general observation, supported by the prologue, that the *Pantagruel* Christianizes Vergil by fusing the epic structure of the *Aeneid* with the messianic structure of the New Testament. Having arrived at this final vision of a New Order in Utopie we may begin to understand the full implications of that fusion. The *Aeneid* glorifies the providential origins of the Roman Empire, presented as the last and greatest of all empires and a utopian state in which all inhabitants of the civilized world will one day flourish in peace and prosperity. The *Pantagruel*, as we have seen, glorifies the providential origins of an anti-imperialistic kingdom of God on earth in which all men will be reintegrated into the universal brotherhood of Christ. In so doing it not only Christianizes but actually inverts the pagan utopia of the *Aeneid*.

With this inversion in mind we must recall that the empire glorified in Vergil's epic is like the calamitous world redeemed by Pantagruel in that it, too, was founded on an original fratricide. Having traced the boundaries of the future city of Rome and begun construction of its walls, Romulus established the autonomy of the site by murdering his brother, Remus (Livy 1.6.4–1.7.3). The very name "Rome" commemorates that founding fratricide, and the Roman historical imagination never forgot it. In the *Epodes* Horace portrays civil strife in Rome as a consequence of the fratricidal origins of the empire:

> Sic est: acerba fata Romanos agunt
> Scelusque *fraternae necis,*
> Ut immerentis fluxit in terram Remi
> Sacer nepotibus cruor.
> [*Epodes* 7.17–20, emphasis mine]

> So it is: a harsh fate drives the Romans on, and the crime of a brother's murder, since the blood of innocent Remus soaked the earth, a curse to his brother's descendants.

Lucan similarly recalls those origins at the beginning of the *Pharsalia (De bello civili* 1.95)—"Fraterno primi maduerunt sanguine muri" ("the first walls dripped with a brother's blood")—and again, indirectly, just before the fateful encounter between Pompey and Caesar at Pharsalus:

> Vulturis ut primum laevo fundata volatu
> Romulus infami conplevit moenia luco,
> Usque ad Thessalicas servisses, Roma, ruinas.
> [*De bello civili* 7.437–39]

> So that from the time Romulus first founded the walls augured by the leftward flight of a vulture and populated them with bandits living in an ill-famed grove, up to the Thessalian disaster, Rome, you would be a slave.

More to the point, Jupiter, at the beginning of the *Aeneid,* concludes his prophecy of future Roman glory by evoking the coming *pax Romana* under universal Roman Empire as the moment of reconciliation between Remus and Romulus:

> Aspera tum positis mitescent saecula bellis;
> Cana Fides et Vesta, *Remo cum fratre Quirinus*
> *Iura dabunt;* dirae ferro et compagibus artis
> Claudentur Belli portae; Furor impius intus
> Saeva sedens super arma et centum vinctus aënis
> Post tergum nodis fremet horridus ore cruento.
> [*Aeneid* 1.291–96, emphasis mine]

> Then harsh times will become milder and wars will cease; white-haired Trust and Vesta and Quirinus along with his brother Remus

> will administer justice; the horrible doors of War will be sealed shut with steel; impius Rage, seated upon cruel arms and bound with a hundred bronze chains behind his back, wild, his mouth bloody, will quake.

To the Christian imagination the murder of Remus by Romulus could not help but recall the murder of Abel by Cain, a similarity made even more striking by the fact that Cain built the first city in sacred history (Gen 4.17). Augustine seized on these parallels to relate the two stories typologically, making Cain the founder of the "earthly city" of which Rome was the culmination and capital, and furthermore to represent the city that Cain founded on fratricide as the exemplum or archetype of the city that Romulus founded on fratricide:

> Primus itaque fuit terrenae civitatis conditor fratricida [Cain]. . . . Unde mirandum non est quod tanto post in ea civitate condenda quae fuerat huius terrenae civitatis, de qua loquimur, caput futura et tam multis gentibus regnatura huic primo exemplo et, ut Graeci appellant, ἀρχετύπῳ quaedam sui generis imago respondit. Nam et illic, sicut ipsum facinus quidam poeta commemoravit illorum, "Fraterno primi maduerunt sanguine muri." Sic enim condita est Roma quando occisum Remum a fratre Romulo Romana testatur historia. [*De civ. dei* 15.5]

> The first founder of the earthly city was thus the fratricide Cain. . . . It is therefore no wonder that much later, in the founding of Rome—the city that was to become the capital of the earthly city of which we are speaking and was to rule over so many peoples—we find an image or reflection, as it were, of that first exemplum, or "archetype" as the Greeks call it. For in that founding, there occurred the same crime, which one of their poets recalls in the following terms: "the first walls dripped with a brother's blood." For thus was Rome founded, when Romulus murdered his brother Remus, as Roman history attests.

The importance of this tradition for the design of the *Pantagruel* is obvious. We know that the establishment of an anti-imperialist, evangelical utopia at the end of Alcofrybas's anti-epic is made possible by Pantagruel's typological reversal of the first fratricide in sacred history. But if that first fratricide is itself typologically linked to the founding fratricide in Roman history, then the exploit by which Pantagruel prepares the way for his New Order obliterates not only Cain's murder of his brother, Abel, but also Romulus's murder of his brother, Remus—that is, not only the principle of anticaritas but the act on which the pagan utopia of universal empire was founded. The utopian church-state established at the end of the *Pantagruel* thus appears simultaneously to invert empire and to overturn the earthly city of which Rome is the emblem. In the place of Empire, in other words, Pantagruel substitutes a secularized City of God.[9]

Whether viewed from the perspective of the Gospels or from the perspective of epic, Alcofrybas's epic New Testament thus leads to the same conclusion: by unfounding and inverting Empire, the *Pantagruel* transforms the pagan epic telos into a kingdom of God on earth.

The *Pantagruel* is a highly complex work, but not in the generally accepted sense that its parts are autonomous or that its different meanings are inconsistent and even contradictory. On the contrary, every part of Rabelais's first epic is governed by a simple, coherent, overarching design that infuses the whole, and each part, with meanings more controlled but infinitely richer than any that could be inferred from the parts considered independently. These meanings may be multiple, but far from competing with one another or conspiring to create interpretive aporias, they form a harmonious complex of self-consistent, mutually reinforcing strands. Like the Bible, like the *Aeneid,* like any other serious work of literature as it was understood in the early sixteenth century, the *Pantagruel* signifies on a number of different planes at once—literal, typological, exemplary, topical; religious, moral, political; sacred, profane; comical, serious. The book cannot be reduced to any one of these, but neither does any one conflict with any other. All operate in harmony, lending a density and richness to the work, a kind of simple complexity to which modern readers have grown unaccustomed and insensitive.

But if all this is true, what are we to make of the ending of this great messianic epic? A commonplace of criticism holds that Rabelais's books end anticlimactically and inconclusively. At first glance this seems especially true of the *Pantagruel*, the last two chapters of which appear to abandon the overarching design of the epic in favor of bathetic popular representations of Pantagruel's body—first in the narrator's voyage into the hero's mouth and again in the strange cure of the hero's digestive disorders.[10] It is for precisely such disappointed epic promises, it would seem, that Horace coined the phrase "en queue de poisson": "ut turpiter atrum / desinat in piscem mulier formosa superne" (*AP* 3–4).

Without denying the comic effect of such an unexpected conclusion, we must reject the commonly held view that it is irrelevant to the preceding narrative. On the contrary, chapters 32 and 33 clinch the design of the *Pantagruel* while confirming the intimations of a New Order contained in chapters 29 through 31. In the context of an epic design that we have found to be both evangelical and political, representations of the giant Pantagruel's body would not evoke some (dubious) popular preoccupation with what Mikhail Bakhtin called the grotesque image of the body and the "lower bodily stratum,"[11] but would inevitably recall the most familiar, canonical metaphors for political and ecclesiological organization—those of the state as the "body politic" of the king, and of the Church as the mystical "body of Christ." These metaphors and their rich associations were inescapable for a sixteenth-century reader. Classical, biblical, juridical, and contemporary poetic literature abounds in allusions to them, and the institutions of late medieval France were consciously created in their image.

The idea of the "body politic" originates, for all practical purposes, in the allegory of the revolt of the members against the stomach, used by Menenius Agrippa in the early days of the Roman Republic to dissuade the plebs from civil war against the patrician senate. Indignant that the stomach should receive without toil the food they work so hard to send it, the other members of the body conspire to refuse the idle stomach their services. As a result, not only the stomach but the whole body, and with it each rebellious member, becomes weak and feeble. Thus it appears that the stomach, too, plays an important role, distributing back to all the other members the nourishment it derives from the food they furnish it. The speech appears in Livy (2.32.9–12) and is variously recorded by Dionysius of Halicarnasus in his *Roman Antiquities* (6.86), Plutarch in his *Life of Coriolanus* (6.2–4), and Dio Cassius in his *Roman History* (4.17.10–13). Cicero used the metaphor in a similar way to argue that if individuals seek their own good at the expense of others the entire social order will be destroyed (*De officiis* 3.5.22), and Seneca to argue that society cannot be safe except through the mutual protection and love of its individual parts (*De ira* 2.31.7).

In juridical writing of the Middle Ages the corporate idea of the state ceased to be a mere metaphor to become a virtual legal reality. By the mid-thirteenth century, and increasingly throughout the later Middle Ages, the monarchies of Christendom—and particularly that of France—were analyzed in ever more realistic terms as "bodies politic" of which the three estates were the members and the king was, by juridical definition, the "head." This definition was consistently propounded by jurists from Lucas de Penna through Jean Gerson to Claude de Seyssel and beyond. At the same time, the evolving notion of the "king's two bodies" tended to identify the kingdom as the king's political "body," and thus with the king himself. From Seneca's statement that the republic was Nero's body ("tu animus rei publicae tuae es, illa corpus tuum" [*De clementia* 1.5.1]) and Gratian's doctrine that the bishop is in the church and the church in the bishop (*Decretum* C.7, q.1, c.7), jurists derived the notion that the king and his kingdom are, on a certain level, one and the same: "Princeps est in republica et respublica in principe," as Matthaeus de Afflictis put it in the early sixteenth century, following a long line of jurists beginning around 1300. Thus the king had a kind of double corporational status. He was both a *part* of the kingdom and the corporate representation of the *whole* kingdom. In his body natural he was the head of the kingdom as of the "body politic"; but in his supernatural body he *was* kingdom, the *corpus reipublicae mysticum* being his collective, political body. Or as the jurists put it: "Princeps caput reipublicae, et res publica eius corpus."[12]

The ecclesiological use of the corporate metaphor originates in Paul's adaptation of Menenius Agrippa's fable. Repeatedly in Romans, 1 Corinthians, Ephesians, and Colossians, Paul represents the Church as the "body of Christ" and the individual members of the Church as members of that mystical body of which Christ is the head:

> For as in one body we have many members, and all the members do not have the same function, so we, though many, are one body in Christ, and individually members one of another. [Rom 12.4–5]
>
> Do you not know that your bodies are members of Christ? . . . For just as the body is one and has many members, and all the members of the body, though many, are one body, so it is with Christ. For by one Spirit we were all baptized into one body. . . . Now you are the body of Christ and individually members of it. [1 Cor 6.15, 12.12–13 and 27]
>
> [God] has put all things under his [Christ's] feet and has made him the head over all things for the church, which is his body. . . . We are to grow up in every way into him who is the head, into Christ, from whom the whole body, joined and knit together by every joint with which it is supplied, when each part is working properly, makes bodily growth and upbuilds itself in love. [Eph 1.22–23, 4.15–16]
>
> [Christ] is the head of the body, the church. . . . [Christ's] body, that is the church . . . holding fast to the Head, from whom the whole body, nourished and knit together through its joints and ligaments, grows with a growth that is from God. [Col 1.18 and 24,

2.19; compare Eph 2.16, 3.4–6, 4.12, 5.23 and 29–30; Col 1.24, 2.9–10, 3.15, and so on]

Paul's metaphor had a vigorous history throughout the Middle Ages from the Greek and Latin fathers on, surviving intact even as a more hierarchical notion of the Church as an institution came to be represented as a body whose head was the pope (witness the notorious bull *Unam sanctam* of Boniface VIII). As the doctrines of real presence and transubstantiation evolved, Christ, like the prince, came to have two bodies—a body natural physically present in the Eucharist, and a mystical body consisting in the community of all Christians. Like the prince, then, Christ was both a part and the whole of the mystical body of the Church. Individually he was the head of the *corpus Ecclesiae mysticum,* but at the same time the Church was his collective, mystical body.[13]

The familiarity of the corporate metaphor in Rabelais's day, in both its political and ecclesiological applications, is evident from its ubiquity in nontechnical literature throughout the sixteenth century. Thus Thomas More could describe the good king and his people as a body held together by love:

> Totum est unus homo regnum, idque cohaeret amore.
>   Rex caput est, populus caetera membra facit.
> Rex quot habet cives (dolet ergo perdere quenquam)
>   Tot numerat parteis corporis ipse sui.
> Exponit populus sese pro rege, putatque
>   Quilibet hunc proprii corporis esse caput.
>
> [*Epigrammata* 112]

> The whole kingdom is one man, and is held together by love. The king is the head, the people are the other members. The king counts his citizens as so many parts of his own body, and therefore grieves to lose a single one. The people expose themselves to danger for the king, whom each one considers the head of his own body.

and Agrippa d'Aubigné could condemn the persecutions of Henri III against the Protestants because

> Le peuple estant le corps et les membres du Roy,
> Le Roy est chef du peuple, et c'est aussi pourquoy
> La teste est frenetique et pleine de manie
> Qui ne garde son sang pour conserver sa vie
> Et le chef n'est plus chef quand il prend ses esbats
> A coupper de son corps les jambes et les bras.
>
> [*Les tragiques* 2.467–72]

Similarly, Erasmus could appeal for caritas among Christians and peace among Christian princes because Christians are by definition members of the same body:

> He is my flesh, he is my brother in Christ. Whatever is done to the member, does it not effect the whole body and consequently the head too? We are all members of one another. [*Enchiridion,* canon 6]

> We call it parricide if a brother kills his brother. But the Christian is more closely related to the Christian than any sibling to his sibling. . . . How absurd that those who share one house, the Church, and who as members of the same body glory in their common head, Christ, should hardly refrain from waging war against one another. . . . Christ called one precept his own, namely caritas. [*Adagia* 4.1.1 ("Dulce bellum inexpertis")][14]

As these examples show, the corporate metaphor suggests a larger unity made up of diverse but interdependent parts, all held together by a shared interest in the common good. The moral of the fable told by Menenius Agrippa is that all the members of a hierarchical political order contribute something essential to the commonweal. That of Paul's adaptation is that although individuals may differ (for example, Gentiles and Jews) and may receive different gifts (for example, prophecy and service), each is dependent on all others, and even the humblest is essential to the well-being of all:

> For just as the body is one and has many members, and all the members of the body, though many, are one body, so it is with Christ. For by one Spirit we were all baptized into one body—Jews or Greeks, slaves or free—and all were made to drink of one Spirit. For the body does not consist of one member but of many. If the foot should say, "Because I am not a hand, I do not belong to the body," that would not make it any less a part of the body. And if the ear should say, "Because I am not an eye, I do not belong to the body," that would not make it any less a part of the body. If the whole body were an eye, where would be the hearing? If the whole body were an ear, where would be the sense of smell? But as it is, God arranged the organs in the body, each one of them, as he chose. If all were a single organ, where would the body be? As it is there are many parts, yet one body. The eye cannot say to the hand, "I have no need of you," nor again the head to the feet, "I have no need of you." On the contrary, the parts of the body which seem to be weaker are

> indispensable, and those parts of the body which we think less honorable we invest with the greater honor, and our unpresentable parts are treated with greater modesty, which our more presentable parts do not require. But God has so adjusted the body, giving the greater honor to the inferior part, that there may be no discord in the body, but that the members may have the same care for one another. If one member suffers, all suffer together; if one member is honored, all rejoice together. [1 Cor 12.12–25; compare Rom 12.4–8]

The community evoked through the corporate metaphor is thus one of inclusion, tolerance, and mutual aid, in which even the humblest member is perfectly integrated and plays an indispensable role. The force that binds the diverse parts, moreover, is "concordia civium" in the case of the body politic (Livy 2.32.7 and 33.1; compare Seneca, *De ira* 2.31.7), "dilectio" and "caritas fraternitatis" in the case of the body of Christ (Rom 12.9–10; compare 1 Cor 13.1–13, Eph 4.2 and 16, Col 3.14). These being the forces that prevail with Pantagruel's victory over Anarche and Loup Garou, the relevance of the corporate idea of State and Church to Pantagruel's New Order in Utopie is self-evident.[15]

But let us consider more carefully the medieval elaboration of the metaphor and its particular relevance to the concluding chapters of the *Pantagruel*. Pantagruel has functioned from the beginning of the epic as both a type of Christ and an ideal Christian prince. Having completed his double redemptive role he has emerged at the end as the founder and head of a new rule that is both a Church and a State, a kind of kingdom of heaven on earth. When in the general context of this overall design Alcofrybas turns his attention to the physical body of his hero—first to Pantagruel's head in chapter 32 and then to his stomach in chapter 33—it is difficult to imagine that a sixteenth-century reader would not have associated these unexpected descriptions with the familiar ideas of the *corpus reipublicae mysticum* and the *corpus Ecclesiae mysticum*. To the degree that these associations are realized, the final chapters of the *Pantagruel*, far from degenerating into bathos or some otherwise undocumented form of popular imagination, appear to offer the most conventional, accessible, and immediately comprehensible representation of the new political and evangelical community of which Pantagruel, as a Christ and a prince, will be both the head and the corporate, mystical incarnation.[16]

The episode of Alcofrybas's Lucianic visit to the world inside Pantagruel's mouth contains clear indications that Pantagruel's body is indeed both a body of Christ and a body politic. As Pantagruel sets off to reduce the Almyrodes and establish his new colony in the promised land of Dipsodie, he and his band are caught in a sudden downpour. The hero bids his cohorts "qu'ilz se missent en ordre et qu'il les vouloit couvrir." Obeying this call to order the Utopian colonists "se mirent en bon ordre et bien serrez, et Pantagruel tira sa langue seulement à demy, et les en couvrit comme une geline faict ses poulletz" (*P* 32:378). This last comparison, as we noted in chapter 1, identifies Pantagruel one last time with Christ, who in Matthew similarly compares himself to a hen covering her chicks with her wings. What we must not fail to notice now is that in making this comparison Christ was referring specifically to his desire to form a new Church—a "congregation," or "episynagogue"—of the recalcitrant members of an old church. Speaking to the scribes and Pharisees in the temple he says: "O Jerusalem, Jerusalem, . . . how often would I have gathered your children together as a hen gathers her brood under her wings, and you would not!" ("Quoties volui *congregare* [ἐπισυναγαγεῖν] filios tuos, quemadmodum gallina *congregat* [ἐπισυνάγει] pullos suos sub alas?") (Mt 23.37, emphasis mine; compare Lk 13.34). Covered by Pantagruel as a brood by their mother hen, the Utopian colonists are represented as constituting a new Church under the wing, as it were, of the Christ-like prince Pantagruel.

At this point Alcofrybas takes us inside the body of the messianic protector. What he finds there is a vast country—"de grans rochiers, . . . de grands prez, de grandes forestz, de fortes et grosses villes" (*P* 32:378)—which, to his great surprise and ours, is an exact replica of the kingdom of France. The first cities that he encounters are "non moins grandes que *Lyon ou Poictiers*"; two others, Laryngues and Pharingues, are "grosses villes telles que *Rouen et Nantes,* riches et bien marchandes" (378–79, emphasis mine). Between the first pair and the second is Aspharge, "belle, bien forte et en bel air," which would appear by its position to correspond to Paris. Elsewhere Alcofrybas finds the grounds of an early Renaissance château reminiscent of Amboise, Fontainebleau, and the future Abbaye de Thélème: "Là trouvay les plus beaulx lieux du monde, beaulx grands jeux de paulme, belles galeries, belles praries, force vignes et une infinité de cassines à la mode Italicque, par les champs pleins de delices" (380). On the other side of the mountains (Piedmont? the Milanais?) he is robbed by brigands, and in a sleepy "bourgade à la devallée" (Geneva?) he finds an isolated *pays de Cocagne*. At the end of his travels Alcofrybas draws a final parallel between the land of the "Gorgias" and the kingdom of France. Having learned that "les gens de delà estoient mal vivans et brigans de nature" he reflects that "ainsi comme nous avons les contrées de deçà et delà les montz, aussi ont ilz deçà et delà les dentz; mais il fait beaucoup meilleur deçà et y a meilleur air" (380).

As the prince of Utopie and the "roy des Dipsodes," Pantagruel in his body natural constitutes the head of a new body politic, while in his own body politic he incorporates the realm of which he is king. By a powerful conflation of these two representations of kingship Pantagruel is shown, at the very moment he is completing his conquest of Dipsodie, to contain within his head the body politic of which he is the head. But this body politic is not Utopie or Dipsodie, as we might expect. It is France. And what is extraordinary about this France, as Erich Auerbach pointed out long ago, is that it is not at all extraordinary. This is not a strange new world or a utopia but the ordinary land familiar to Rabelais's readers from everyday experience—a France in which peasants must work hard to earn a living, citizens are subject to terrible epidemics, and travelers to neighboring countries risk attack by brigands.

In this paradox lies a crucial aspect of the meaning of the *Pantagruel*. Pantagruel is an ideal figure. He represents the absolute perfection of the perfectly Christ-like Christian prince and inhabits a utopian world where caritas can conquer fratricide once and for all, where Empire can be replaced by a never-ending kingdom of heaven on earth. All this is merely literature, a utopian fiction, a Christian humanist's dream. Yet by making Pantagruel embody the real world of everyday France in the penultimate chapter of his narrative, Rabelais transforms his book into something quite different from the escapist wish fulfillment it might otherwise have been and suggests a plausible link between the ideal world of his fiction and the imperfect world that he and his readers inhabit. More than a neat epic conflict between transcendent, abstract forces, the *Pantagruel* proposes a kind of Platonic ideal pertinent to the contingent world of human affairs and toward which actual governments—and France in particular—must tend.

The precise relation between these ideal and real worlds is suggested not only by the inclusion of a real body politic inside the head of an ideal Christian prince but by a pointed allusion in the same episode to Plato's parable of the cave. In the course of his conversation with a peasant planting cabbage Alcofrybas exclaims, "Jesus . . . il y a icy un nouveau monde?" to which the peasant answers, "Certes . . . il n'est mie nouveau; mais l'on dist bien que, hors d'icy y a une terre neufve où ilz ont et soleil et lune, et tout plein de belles besoignes; mais cestuy cy est plus ancien" (*P* 32:379). The peasant's reference to another world "hors d'icy" where there is a sun and a moon suggests that the episode has less to do with the relation between the Old World and the recently discovered New World than with the relation between the shadowy world of appearances and becoming *inside* the cave and the bright, sunlit world of Ideas and being *outside*[17] (compare *Republic* 7.514a–517c).

We must recall here that Plato's parable of the cave is offered as a means of determining the best kind of ruler for the well-run state. The ideal to which Socrates leads Glaucon is the philosopher-king, whose mind has been "converted" to the higher realm of being where he apprehends by pure intellection the ideas of the beautiful, the just, and the good and is then required to return to the cave where he rules in such a way as to assure the common good of all by harmonizing the citizens into a community of mutual aid and benevolence (*Republic* 7.517c–521b, esp. 519e–520a). Having beheld the good in the world above, the philosopher-king must use it as a model or a pattern (παράδειγμα) for ordering the state below (540a).

If we may take Alcofrybas's allusion to Plato's cave seriously, we must conclude that France—the shadowy realm represented inside the "cave" of Pantagruel's mouth—will be well ruled only when one of us ascends to the sunny world of Utopie outside, beholds firsthand the Idea of the Christian prince in Pantagruel and the Idea of perfect government in the New Order in Utopie, and then returns to order our contingent world in the image of the ideal one above. Alcofrybas has of course made that ascent himself and provided us with the means to follow him, for the same chronicler who has described our world for the Utopians in his *Histoire des Gorgias* (*P* 32:381) has also, having recently returned from Utopie to his "païs de vache" (*P* prol:219), described their world for us in his *Horribles et espoventables faictz et prouesses du tresrenommé Pantagruel, Roy des Dipsodes.* In that book—the book we have just read—our own philosopher-kings will find the παράδειγμα for right rule in France. It is the ideal Church-State of which Pantagruel, as Christ and prince, is head.

The next chapter suggests a similar link between the real world of France and the fictional world of Utopie through its treatment of another aspect of Pantagruel's body. Here "le bon Pantagruel" falls ill and can neither eat nor drink because he is "prins de l'estomach" (*P* 33:382). It seems almost grotesquely anticlimactic to find Alcofrybas devoting the final chapter of his epic New Testament to a temporary case of constipation and "pisse chaulde" in his Christ-like hero. But we must recall that one of the most common uses of the corporate metaphor had always been the representation of imperfections in the state as a disease in some limb or member of the body politic, and particularly as a localized "distemper"—that is, an imbalance in the four humors that make up the body (see Hale, p. 15). Plato, for example, developed the analogy in both the *Republic*

(4.425e–426d) and the *Laws* (1.628c–d), and in Rabelais's day Claude de Seyssel, in discussing the rise and fall of states, similarly compared the "corps mystiques" to "corps matériels humains"

> lesquels (pour autant qu'ils sont créés et composés de quatre éléments et humeurs contraires), jaçoit que par aucun temps se puissent entretenir et conserver en vie (à savoir tant que lesdites humeurs s'accordent), toutesfois est impossible qu'à la longue l'un ne surmonte les autres et par ce moyen que la masse ne revienne à sa première matière par la dissolution de ladite compaigne; car par ordre de nature, tous lesdits éléments et humeurs, après qu'ils sont assemblés, ont augmentation, état et diminution, advenant laquelle est besoin aider à la nature et secourir celui membre et celle humeur qui se trouvent les plus faibles: mais il advient que, quand l'on cuide aider à l'un, l'on nuit à l'autre.
>
> Tout ainsi advient aux corps mystiques de la société humaine; car, après qu'ils sont assemblés par une civile et politique union, ils vont par quelque temps en accroissant et multipliant, après demeurant en leur état quelque autre temps, puis—pour autant qu'ils sont composés de plusieurs entendements et volontés discordantes et répugnantes—commencent à décliner et finalement viennent à néant. [*De la monarchie* 1.3]

According to this common use of the corporate metaphor, identifying and correcting the troubles of the state is a matter of diagnosing and curing the ills—and particularly the distemper—of the body politic.[18]

If we approach the final chapter of the *Pantagruel* with this in mind we will note first that the digression on the hero's secondary ailment of "pisse chaulde" contains, once again, the comical hint of a relation between Pantagruel's body and the realm of France. After taking the diuretic drugs prescribed by his doctors, Pantagruel "piss[e] son malheur" in hot urine that has remained in the hot springs of spas in France and Italy (*P* 33:382). The physical geography of France and her neighbor is thus associated directly not only with Pantagruel's head (chapter 32) but with his bladder as well.

But the cure for Pantagruel's principal ailment suggests something perhaps more serious. To loosen Pantagruel's bowels, his physicians dispatch workers into his stomach where they seek out the "humeurs corrumpues" and proceed to break up and remove the "montjoye d'ordure" that has been blocking his system (384). Whether Pantagruel's stomach is to be identified with the wealthy and powerful "senate," as it is in Menenius Agrippa's fable,[19] or with corrupt institutions like the Sorbonne, as a comic interpolation of 1534 suggests—the workers descend "en un goulphre horrible, puant et infect plus que . . . le punays lac de Sorbone, duquel escript Strabo" (384)—it seems reasonable to suppose that the conventional notion of a diseased body politic is at play here. To the degree that it is, we must understand Pantagruel's cure as the purge of a class, an estate, or an institution that has somehow failed to perform its proper function within the community, with the result that the whole community has begun to suffer.[20]

Seen in this light the concluding chapter appears to reinforce the implications of the penultimate chapter. The anti-imperialist, evangelical New Order toward which the *Pantagruel* points is not a reality but a literally Utopian ideal. Transposed from "No place" to France—and the hot springs of the realm are there to remind us of the link—it is bound to be vitiated by the distempers that characterize everything in this contingent world of becoming. Like the Church described by Augustine, it will be a necessarily imperfect body, in spite of the absolute perfection of its head (see note 18). As such, it will require human correction, not in its head but in its body and limbs. Only by means of such direct human intervention, and a purge of corrupt institutions, can "Pantagruel" be "guery et reduict à sa premiere convalescence" (384).

What is remarkable about these two concluding chapters is that they conspire to suggest the need for action on the part of the Christian citizen-reader. If the *Pantagruel* is open-ended and anticlimactic, it is not because it ends *en queue de poisson* but because its otherwise perfectly coherent epic design refuses to close in upon its own utopian vision in an esthetically satisfying—and therefore morally disengaging—way. Instead, it deliberately projects its vision of a perfect, self-sufficient New Order out into the imperfect, contingent world inhabited by the reader in an esthetically unsettling—and therefore morally provocative—way. The design of the *Pantagruel* thus remains perfectly coherent to the very end. It will appear flawed only if we fail to understand that its ultimate purpose is a call to action in a nonfictional world where the story is not yet—and indeed never can be—finished. "This is the ideal telos toward which we all must strive," it says in conclusion. "Now, fellow citizens and brothers in Christ, let the work begin."

EPILOGUE

STYLE, POPULAR CULTURE, AND THE CHRISTIAN HUMANIST DESIGN OF THE *PANTAGRUEL*

Like all serious readings of Rabelais, this one invites a serious objection. Why, one must ask, would Rabelais have chosen to express such high-minded political, religious, and moral meanings through a language and style ostensibly so inappropriate? It would seem that the comic, boisterous, even obscene forms of expression would belie, if not sabotage outright, any seriousness of purpose we might have discovered in them.

So great is the apparent incongruity between low manner and high matter in Rabelais's books that until recently readers generally felt constrained to choose between the two, either ignoring the husk of language in their attentiveness to the kernel of meaning or abandoning the hermeneutic pursuit in their attention to language and style. From the mid-1950s to the mid-1970s there even raged a critical battle between intellectual historians, or "Rabelaisants," for whom Rabelais's books were so many bones to chew on and tough nuts to crack, and literary critics, or "stylists," for whom those same books were verbal icons whose riches lay not hidden within but exposed to all on the surface of the text. More recently readers have recognized that both manner and matter, form and content, are essential to Rabelais's books. Yet there persists a certain tension, if not a deliberate contradiction between the two, and attempts to explain the relation between them inevitably tend to favor one over the other. It would seem either that the effect of Rabelais's style is to destabilize meaning or that Rabelais's meaning must somehow domesticate the effects of his style.

Of all Rabelais's books the *Pantagruel* is the most problematic in this regard. Its popular tone and format, its vulgar style, its crude humor and obscenity, are so conspicuous and persistent as to make any attempt to find a "doctrine plus absconce"—not to mention "très haultz sacremens et mysteres horrificques"—behind its "mocqueries, folateries et menteries joyeuses" (*G* prol:6–8) appear slightly ridiculous from the outset. How then are we to defend the serious meanings we have found in Rabelais's first Christian humanist epic against the reasonable objection of the stylists that these meanings are incompatible with the popular, vulgar, funny medium through which they are expressed? Or is this study defensible only as a partial interpretation acceptable only to the Rabelaisants?

We might be tempted to begin by invoking the Horatian "utile dulci" topos and claim that Rabelais's comic textual surface is justified as a kind of sugar coating on a Christian humanist pill. The advantage of this argument is that it is authorized by Rabelais's own contemporaries. Hugues Salel's liminary dizain to Rabelais, first published in the 1534 edition of the *Pantagruel*, states the point explicitly:

> Si, pour mesler *profit* avec *doulceur,*
> On mect en pris un aucteur grandement,
> Prisé seras, de cela tien toy sceur;
> Je le congnois, car ton entendement
> En ce livret, soubz *plaisant* fondement,
> *L'utilité* a si très bien descripte,
> Qu'il m'est advis que voy un Democrite. . . .
> [Jourda 1.213, emphasis mine]

And Du Bellay consistently refers to Rabelais as "l'utiledoux" or the "doulx-utile" who helped to resuscitate the ancients in an epic war against Ignorance.[1] More significantly, the royal *privilège* for the *Tiers Livre* speaks of Rabelais's preceding volumes as "non moins utiles que delectables" and grants permission to print the *Tiers* because François I desires "les bonnes letres estre promeues par nostre Royaulme à l'utilité et erudition de noz subjectz" (*TL,* ed. Screech, 3, note).

But this argument, however valid in its own terms, is not at all satisfactory for our purposes. From the point of view of the stylists it merely begs the question by assuming that Rabelais's matter is somehow more important than his manner. And in any case it provides further sanction for viewing textual surface as something distinct and separate from content, and essentially unrelated to it. If low style and popular culture are autonomous aspects of the text, extraneous and irreducible to any serious meaning, then they certainly merit study as ends in themselves rather than as problematic means to some other end. The only satisfactory defense of our reading of the *Pantagruel* is one that would demonstrate that its surface is *not* distinct, separable, and essentially unrelated to its content; further, that its low style and popular culture are entirely compatible with the particular meanings we have found in it; and further still, that they are actually essential, indispensable components perfectly integrated into the overall design of the work.

As a first step in this direction we must begin to think about this perennial problem of Rabelais criticism historically and try to understand that the inveterate distinction between what we perceive to be the high seriousness of Christian humanism, on the one hand, and the broad humor and obscenity of "popular culture," on the other, is a specious and anachronistic one extremely inappropriate to the study of Rabelais. It is specious because what we mistakenly call popular culture was in fact a *common* culture in the Renaissance, a universal culture that played an inescapable and intimate role in the daily existence of every person regardless of class, education, or profession. The educated elite of Rabelais's time were at least as familiar with the common culture into which they were born and in which they lived as they were with the high culture they acquired through the diligent study of ancient languages and literatures. To imagine otherwise would be as absurd as to think that twentieth-century professors of literature could be innocent of mass culture—far more absurd, in fact, because we moderns can easily avoid watching "Star Wars" and "Dallas" or listening to Michael Jackson if we so choose, even if we cannot ignore their existence, whereas sixteenth-century humanists could no more isolate themselves from the omnipresent forms and manifestations of their common culture than they could forget their native language.[2]

The distinction is anachronistic because throughout the later Middle Ages the serious and the comic, the high and the low, the sacred and the profane, were routinely married in ways that seem virtually incomprehensible to us today. As an illustration it may help to recall that for centuries cathedrals served not only as places of worship where priests celebrated the holiest of communions but also as community centers where merchants and artisans held guild meetings, as hangouts where teenagers cruised members of the opposite sex, and even as stables where livestock was sheltered during the night. Such comfortable proximity and interpenetration of what we now think of as two totally separate realms is characteristic of the culture in which and for which Rabelais wrote his first books. The separation of those realms, which began within Rabelais's lifetime with the Protestant Reformation and the Catholic Counter-Reformation, has made it extremely difficult for modern readers, starting with the generation following Rabelais's, to understand that high seriousness and low humor are not necessarily in conflict in Rabelais's books but can coexist easily within a perfectly integrated view of human experience.

Finally, the distinction is particularly inappropriate to the study of Rabelais because everything in his books points to a deliberate attempt to integrate even further the aspects of human experience that history, despite Rabelais's best efforts, was to consign to ever more distinct spheres. A detail that modern readers find particularly disconcerting—that the young Gargantua "fai[t] excretion des digestions naturelles" while listening to an exposition of the most obscure and difficult points of the day's Bible reading (*G* 23:88–89)—is only one of many that suggest a view in which high and low, serious and funny, sacred and profane, are to be viewed as something like the two sides of the same coin. To separate them is obviously to put asunder what Rabelais has so painstakingly joined, and in the process to destroy the integrity of his works.

In spite of what our most deeply rooted, unexamined post-Reformation attitudes would lead us to believe, then, we have no valid reason to assume that high purpose and low humor are necessarily incompatible in any of Rabelais's books. On the contrary, there is every reason to believe that Rabelais has deliberately juxtaposed and even fused them. This being the case, we would be entirely unjustified in treating them as separable, incommensurable aspects of Rabelais's books, much less in asserting, as both the Rabelaisants and the stylists used to do, that one is somehow more essential than the other.

But the most crucial questions still remain: What is the function of low style and common culture in the particular case of the *Pantagruel*, and what is their relation to the specific meanings we have found in it?

The answer to these questions will be obvious to anyone who has fully understood the design of Alcofrybas's epic New Testament as a Christian humanist epic. First as an epic, we have found that the *Pantagruel* is in a profound sense an *anti-epic* in which heroes, heroism, and the imperial ideal are overthrown and the lowly victims of heroic imperialism are given the place of honor in an entelechial utopian community. This fundamental aspect of the work's design is itself sufficient to account for both the peculiar style and the popular culture of the *Pantagruel*.

As for the latter, the *populus* is at the antipodes of the aristocratic caste of princes and knights from which the heroes of traditional epic are drawn. The inversion of epic thus requires that noble heroes be replaced by ignoble commoners and that dignity, protocol, and the chivalric code of epic be systematically demoted and replaced by their popular counterparts—that is, by the mores and manners of a common, popular culture. The "haulte dame de Paris" pissed on by dogs in heat (*P* 21–22) and Perceforest condemned to die at the stake by the "franc archier de Baignolet" for pissing on a picture of Saint Anthony's fire (*P* 30:373) are emblematic of this systematic demotion of the heroic and the noble in favor of the popular. In the *Pantagruel* epic is literally taken over by the people it traditionally excludes.

As for the style of this anti-epic, it is actually determined by the classical ideal of decorum. Just as the heroic subjects of true epics like the *Iliad* and the *Aeneid* require an elevated style, so a work like Rabelais's, which manipulates the norms and conventions of epic in such a way as to subvert the genre, overturn its ideology, and literally turn epic on its head, requires a style that is appropriate to the inversion, a low style normally reserved for low, popular genres like satiric comedy.

It is important to note how this perspective differs from the more conventional view of the *Pantagruel* as a simple burlesque of epic. The *Pantagruel* resembles burlesque in that its popular elements and low style deflate a noble genre. But in a burlesque such deflation is an end in itself and ordinarily serves no other purpose than to amuse sophisticated and jaded readers through inconsequential games with literature. In the *Pantagruel*, on the contrary, deflation of the epic is motivated by the profoundly anti-imperialist, evangelical ideology that infuses the entire work. Burlesque is only one of many mutually reinforcing devices contributing to a coherent design whose implications are at once theological, moral, and political. Here low style and elements of popular culture are not comic breaches of epic decorum irrelevant to questions of meaning but are actually *required* by the decorum of an authentic anti-epic and are crucial to its most fundamental meanings.

If we now turn to the specifically Christian humanist aspects of this evangelized anti-epic, the relevance of its low style and popular culture become even clearer. As we have seen, the telos of the epic is an evangelical community in which all men are reunited in a universal brotherhood based on caritas. "All men" in such a context does not mean all noblemen, all rich men, all powerful men, or all educated men. It means *all* men, including the dispossessed, the poor, the downtrodden, and the ignorant—the *vulgus,* in short. The existence of such an evangelical brotherhood depends on the complete breakdown of distinctions between highborn and lowborn, rich and poor, elite and popular. Brotherhood requires it. Caritas commands it: "If you really fulfill the royal law, according to the scripture, 'You shall love your neighbor as yourself,' you do well. But if you show partiality, you commit sin, and are convicted by the law as transgressors" (Jas 2.8–9). As a universal culture common to high and low alike, a culture that "shows no partiality," popular culture is the common denominator linking all Christ's brothers—humanists and illiterates alike—into one community. As such it may be properly understood as nothing less than the culture of the saved in this messianic anti-epic.

Rabelais makes this crucial point even more forcefully by predicating the New Order of his anti-epic on the evangelical principle that the first in this world will be the last in the kingdom of God, and vice versa. Who are these "first"? Who are these "last"? Lest we take too complacent and pharisaical a view of the familiar, pious verities of the beatitudes, Rabelais's epic reminds us that the "humble," the "meek," and the "poor in spirit" who are destined to inherit the earth and to be first in the kingdom of God are none other than those ill-bred, ill-mannered, uncouth, unwashed, vulgar masses from whom the first of this world—the highborn, well-dressed, well-spoken, church-going lords and ladies—strive to distinguish themselves.

The role of Panurge is crucial in this respect. Panurge is a nobleman who has fallen on hard times and freely mixes with the riffraff on the lowest rung of the social ladder. He is the character in whom virtually all the popular obscenity of the *Pantagruel* resides. But Panurge is also, by virtue of his conspicuously popular culture, an active agent in the inversion of estates that will lead eventually to Pantagruel's evangelical New Order. His obscenity, vulgar jokes, dirty tricks, all serve the single end of deflating the pretensions of the first in this world, humiliating those who have exalted themselves above their brothers, and promoting the last in this world who are scorned by their superiors as vulgar.

The humiliation inflicted by Panurge on the elegantly dressed "haulte dame de Paris" is, here again, emblematic. It is designed to reduce a haughty lady to the common humanity she shares (but tries to deny) with the used-up old whores whom Panurge promotes in her place. For it is these, not she, who according to Christ will "inherit the earth" and to whom the kingdom of God belongs. To set oneself apart from and above the dregs of society as the "haulte dame" does is not only to refuse entry into the universal brotherhood of Christ's Church but to destine oneself to hold the lowest place in the kingdom of God to come. Or to rephrase the same point in terms of the epic design of the *Pantagruel*, it is to exclude oneself from the entelechial New Order established in Utopie by the messianic redeemer of Cain's original sin. Seen in this light, popular culture is not only the common culture of the saved but actually a means to salvation in the *Pantagruel*. By humiliating the exalted in this world it allows for the possibility of exaltation in the next. Far from being extraneous to serious meanings or incompatible with the Christian humanist design of the work, it is inextricably bound up with the radically evangelical ideology of the work and plays a crucial, integral role in it.[3]

The style of the *Pantagruel* is similarly justified and even required by its Christian humanist design. Here we must recall that from its earliest beginnings Christianity insisted that its simple truths were offered to simple people and therefore required simple forms of expression. For this reason it rejected the rhetorical eloquence of Greek and Latin and the *genus grande* of the great in favor of the vulgar tongues and *genus humile* of the humble. Jesus acted on this principle by speaking not in an exquisite rhetorical style in the prestigious languages of culture and empire but in a simple style and common, homely metaphors in his own native Aramaic. Paul stated the point explicitly for the benefit of his Greek converts in Corinth:

> For Christ did not send me to baptize but to preach the gospel, and not with eloquent wisdom [*sapientia verbi*], lest the cross of Christ be emptied of its power. . . . When I came to you, [brothers], I did not come proclaiming to you the testimony of God in lofty words or wisdom [*sublimitate sermonis aut sapientiae*]. . . . My speech and my message were not in plausible words of wisdom [*persuasibilibus humanae sapientiae verbis*], but in demonstration of the Spirit and power. . . . And we impart this in words not taught by human wisdom [*doctis humanae sapientiae verbis*] but taught by the Spirit, interpreting the spiritual truths for those who possess the Spirit. [1 Cor 1.17 and 2.1, 4, 13]

The gospelists assumed the same principle in writing their Gospel narratives in the shabbiest street Greek, and Jerome respected it in making the Bible *Vulgata*—that is, translating it into the plain, common, vulgar Latin spoken by the simple vulgus of the Roman Empire.

We must recall too that this same Jerome began his career as a professor of rhetoric and that before he could become the translator of the *Vulgate* and a father of the Latin Church he had to unlearn the classical eloquence of which he was a master. The story of his conversion from high to humble style is well known. During an ascetic retreat from the world he found that he could not give up his beloved classical authors—and worse, that after reading Cicero he would find the language of the Old Testament prophets so crude and coarse as to be repellent. Sick to the point of death, he was taken up in the spirit to the seat of divine judgment where, commanded to state his condition, he said "a Christian." To this God answered, "You are a liar. You are a Ciceronian, not a Christian," and ordered him to be flogged. Christian and Ciceronian being strictly incompatible professions, Jerome had to choose between them. Only through the most arduous ascesis could he free himself from his unchristian attachment to classical eloquence.[4] Augustine was another professor of rhetoric who suffered from a similar attachment to high style. He tells in the *Confessions* how at an early age he could not bring himself to read the Bible because "it seemed to me too unworthy to be compared to the great worthiness of Cicero: for my pride disdained its lowliness and my wits were unable to penetrate its depths." Only much later would he learn that "something must not be taken as true just because it is said eloquently, nor as false just because it is said poorly."[5]

This same conflict between Cicero and Christ was very much alive in Rabelais's time and came directly into play in the contemporary debate over Ciceronianism. Whereas a Bembo refused to read the Epistles of Paul for fear of corrupting his pure Ciceronian style, an Erasmus argued that pure Ciceronianism was incapable of Christian discourse because Cicero knew neither Christianity nor the vocabulary and forms of expression necessary to speak about it. In the sixteenth century, as in the first and fourth centuries, eloquence and Christianity were uneasy allies at best. In their most extreme forms they were antagonistic and even mutually exclusive.

The Christianity of the *Pantagruel* is extreme in this regard. Being a profoundly evangelical work it is also a profoundly anti-Ciceronian work openly hostile to pure (that is, unmotivated) eloquence. Fancy talk, like fancy clothes, can too easily become a means of exalting oneself, of setting oneself apart from the vulgar crowd. It is for precisely such an abuse of eloquence that Pantagruel punishes the Limousin schoolboy. This self-aggrandizing brat affects an exalted, ornate, highly latinate language, not to enter into a community with his interlocutors but to set himself apart from them, to exclude them, to humiliate them. Pantagruel's response is not unlike God's response to Jerome. He threatens to flog him—"Tu escorche le latin; par sainct Jean, je te feray escorcher le renard, car je te escorcheray tout vif" (*P* 6:247)—and forces him to quit his affected eloquence for the popular dialect of his own people and, further, to confess his common humanity by shitting in his elegant pants. Having abused language for the same purpose that the haughty Parisian lady abuses clothing, the arrogant Limousin schoolboy is stripped of his pretensions by Pantagruel in the same way that the Parisian lady is stripped of hers by Panurge.

But it is in the language and style of the narrative itself, more than that of any character, that the *Pantagruel* may be said to take the Christian argument against Ciceronian eloquence to its farthest logical conclusion. In conformity with its design and the ideology that infuses it, Rabelais's work abandons the prestige and power of Latin for the common vernacular spoken by the vulgus and refuses the genus grande of the high and mighty in favor of the genus humile of the humble, the meek, and the poor in spirit.[6] Language and style thus play the same role in Rabelais's first book that popular culture does. This book speaks the language not of the Ciceronians but of the Christians—a lowly, vulgar vernacular as comprehensible to the humble and poor in spirit as to the refined and learned. Many of the hidden treasures in the book may be accessible only to humanists whose elite culture allows them to perceive classical and biblical echoes, allusions, and analogies invisible to the uninitiated. But the book as a whole lies open to all and may be understood on some level by virtually everyone; no one is excluded on the basis of language or acquired culture. In this respect Alcofrybas's epic New Testament is very much like the Bible itself which, to quote Augustine, is "incessu humilem, successu excelsam"—"humble at first approach and in its gait, lofty in its advance upward and in its end." "With the plainest of words and the humblest of styles it offers itself to all and engages the attention of the serious-minded, so as to include everyone in its large, common folds and through narrow openings pass a few on to [God]" (*Confessions* 3.5 and 6.5).[7]

This is an extremely important aspect of the *Pantagruel* too easily overlooked by the serious, high-minded Rabelaisants. The Christian humanism of this epic New Testament is not a fastidious, thin-lipped ideology from which the raucous style and tone of the book may be separated and disregarded as irrelevant. On the contrary, vulgar tongue, low style, and popular elements work together to create an all-inclusive community of readers parallel to the all-inclusive community of the redeemed represented within. Readers both high and low are bound together by the common experience of the book's convivial "Pantagruelism," just as the redeemed of Pantagruel's New Order are bound together by the common bond of caritas. Even in those funny, vulgar, rambunctious aspects that strike the modern reader as most recalcitrant to serious interpretation—especially in those aspects—the *Pantagruel* is a perfectly coherent and integrated evangelical work. Its matter and manner work together to bring about in the real world of its readers the joyful Christian brotherhood that the messianic hero Pantagruel has restored to a redeemed Utopie.

In spite of this extraordinarily catholic, evangelical design, the *Pantagruel* never really succeeded in its generous purpose. Many readers, beginning with Rabelais's contemporaries, have refused to enter into the liberal communion it seeks to establish and, mistaking or refusing the spirit in which it is offered, have condemned it as frivolous or even scandalous.

Rabelais responded to this reaction in the prologue to the *Gargantua* and continued to respond in the prologues to all his subsequent books. Addressing his readers for the first time since the publication of the *Pantagruel* two years earlier, Alcofrybas insists that in spite of what his readers may have concluded on the basis of silly titles, frivolous content, and insouciant tone, his books do contain something of great value, as he had already claimed in the prologue to the *Pantagruel*. Behind the "mocqueries, folateries et menteries joyeuses" that seem to have put some readers off (*G* prol:6) lie "de très haultz sacremens et mysteres horrificques, tant en ce que concerne nostre religion que aussi l'estat politicq et vie oeconomicque" (8). Readers need only a little diligence to seek these out and, far more important, a little tolerance to accept the book in the charitable, nonjudgmental spirit in which it is offered: "Vous, mes bons disciples, . . . lisans les joyeulx tiltres . . . jugez trop facillement ne estre au dedans traicté que mocqueries, folateries et menteries joyeuses . . . sans plus avant enquerir. . . . Mais par telle legiereté ne convient estimer les oeuvres des humains" (6). Rather than leap to judgment his readers must "interprete[r] tous mes faictz et mes dictz en la perfectissime partie" (9)—that is, they must read the books for a serious meaning *and* take their frivolousness in good part, not amiss, by putting the best possible interpretation on them. What this means is nothing less than practicing caritas while reading, interpreting, and judging, and thereby accepting inclusion in the larger, nonhierarchical community that Pantagruel has established in Utopie and that the *Pantagruel* seeks to establish with and among its readers—that popular, convivial, evangelical brotherhood to which the narrator and his less supercilious readers already belong: "A moy n'est que honneur et gloire d'estre dict et reputé bon gaultier et bon compaignon, et en ce nom suis bien venu en toutes bonnes compaignies de Pantagruelistes" (9).[8]

It is important to note that this appeal is addressed only to those serious, elite readers for whom low style and popular culture have proven an obstacle to understanding. Popular readers require no such apology—and in any case are not likely to be made more docile and more benevolent by a humanistic reference in the exordium to the authority of "Alcibiades, ou dialoge de Platon intitulé *Le Bancquet*" (5). Paradoxically, it is those readers best equipped by a fine humanistic education to understand the fullness and complexity of the *Pantagruel* who have mistaken most grievously the intention and the meaning of its design. Those who are incapable of deciphering the erudite allusions or of discerning the meticulously wrought design but who are naturally inclined simply to enjoy the humor and convivial tone of the book are far better readers, because they have received the book in the spirit in which it was offered.[9] They either belong already or have willingly joined the jocular, unpretentious community of "beuveurs illustres." Only the exalted, supercilious, unamused elite, it seems, have balked at full membership in a common brotherhood based on caritas.

For these readers the *Pantagruel* is indeed scandalous in the strictest sense of the word. Its low style and popular culture are literally *σκάνδαλα*, "stumbling blocks," small obstacles that make them fall. But the scandal of the *Pantagruel* is not quite what a Calvin or the Roman censors seem to have thought it was. It is none other than the scandal of Christianity itself. For in its origins Christianity was a profoundly scandalous religion that made a mockery of everything that wise, serious, and dignified people held to be most self-evident. That the messiah prophesied by all God's prophets, the descendant of David and king of the Jews, the savior of all mankind, should be a man of doubtful legitimacy born to obscure parents in the most abject of circumstances; that he should live a life of sordid poverty among fishermen, tax collectors, prostitutes, and other low life of Palestine; that he should not even know any Greek or Latin; that he should be condemned to death as a common criminal by the greatest, most just, and most cultured empire in history—these are manifestly preposterous ideas that no cultivated, right-thinking, self-respecting citizen, whether Jew or Gentile, could possibly accept.

The Gospels are filled with details intended to accentuate this scandalousness and frequently show its effect on decent, respectable citizens:

> And as he sat at table in the house, behold, many tax collectors and sinners came and sat down with Jesus and his disciples. And when the Pharisees saw this, they said to his disciples, "Why does your teacher eat with tax collectors and sinners?" But when he heard it, he said, "Those who are well have no need of a physician, but those who are sick. Go and learn what this means, 'I desire mercy, and not

> sacrifice.' For I came not to call the righteous, but sinners." [Mt 9.10–13; compare Mk 2.15–17, Lk 5.29–32]

And Paul spoke of the "scandal of the cross" (*σκάνδαλον τοῦ σταυροῦ*, *scandalum crucis*) and flaunted what he called the "silliness" (*μωρία*, *stultitia*) and the "scandal" (*σκάνδαλον*, *scandalum*) of a religion in which crucifixion is salvation, weakness is strength, foolishness wisdom, vileness nobility:

> Has not God made foolish the wisdom of the world? For since, in the wisdom of God, the world did not know God through wisdom, it pleased God through the folly of what we preach to save those who believe. For Jews demand signs and Greeks seek wisdom, but we preach Christ crucified, a *stumbling block* [σκάνδαλον] to Jews and *folly* [μωρία] to Gentiles, but to those who are called, both Jews and Greeks, Christ the power of God and the wisdom of God.
>
> For the foolishness of God is wiser than men, and the weakness of God is stronger than men. For consider your call, [brothers]: not many of you were wise according to [the flesh], not many were powerful, not many were of noble birth; but God chose what is foolish in the world to shame the wise, God chose what is weak in the world to shame the strong, God chose what is low and despised in the world, even things that are not, to bring to nothing things that are. [1 Cor 1.20–28, emphasis mine]

With its adoption as the official religion of the empire Christianity gained a legitimacy and decency quite alien to its original essence and over the course of twelve centuries degenerated into a respectable and even fastuous religion of latter-day scribes and Pharisees. It was precisely in order to restore to it a measure of its original scandalousness that Erasmus, emulating Paul, spoke so provocatively of Christ and his apostles as ugly, grotesque *Sileni:*

> Was not Christ an amazing Silenus? . . . If you were to consider only his outward appearance what could be more vile and more contemptible by common standards? His parents were obscure little people, his house was humble, he himself was poor and his disciples were a handful of poor devils taken not from the palaces of grandees, the yeshivas of Pharisees, or the schools of philosophers, but from toll booths and fishnets. As for the life he lived, so far from any pleasure it led through hunger, exhaustion, insults, and jeers to death on a cross. . . .
>
> The Apostles were Sileni of the same kind: poor, uneducated,

> illiterate, lowborn, disenfranchised, abject, exposed to the insults of all and sundry, ridiculed, hated, cursed, at once the public objects of the whole world's loathing and mockery. [*Adagia* 3.3.1, "Sileni Alcibiadis"][10]

From this point of view the apparent worthlessness of Scripture is perfectly suited to its subject: "Holy Scripture has it Sileni too. . . . To judge the parables in the Gospels by their outward shell, who would not conclude that they were the words of an idiot? But if you crack the nut you will certainly find a hidden and truly divine wisdom, and something very much like Christ himself" ("Sileni Alcibiadis").[11]

From the same point of view the apparent worthlessness of the *Pantagruel* is also perfectly suited to the radically evangelical subject of this epic New Testament. And if Rabelais chose Erasmus's "Sileni Alcibiadis" as the starting point for the defense of his book in the prologue to the *Gargantua,* it is undoubtedly for this reason. For the *Pantagruel* is silly and scandalous in the same way, and for the same reasons, that Christianity, the Bible, and Christ himself are silly and scandalous.

If we are offended by the vulgarity of this popular little chapbook, if we refuse to take it seriously because we consider that nothing so trivial, so funny, and so low could possibly be worthy of the attention of serious, right-thinking, high-minded people like ourselves, then by that very judgment we identify ourselves with the well-dressed lords and ladies who find Panurge so obnoxious and unsavory and with the scribes and Pharisees who were scandalized by Christ—those first in this world who will be last in the next. If, on the contrary, we freely abandon our pride, dignity, and sense of self-importance and accept the book in its true spirit, taking it in good part in spite of its vulgar appearance, style, and tone, then we have in that very process identified with those lowly friends of Panurge who are last in this world and first in the next, or better yet with that incarnation of caritas, the Christ-like Pantagruel, who in spite of his royalty and exquisite humanistic education loves the vulgar and unlovable Panurge as himself. In the first case we simultaneously demonstrate that we have not understood the design of the book and the full implications of the evangelical meaning to which it points; we declare that we do not love our brother as this epic New Testament and Christ himself command; and we refuse citizenship in Pantagruel's kingdom of God on earth. In the second we simultaneously put into practice the moral and theological imperative it contains; we begin to love the brothers from whom we have been estranged; and we accept membership in the ideal community in which even the lowest of men are our equals and precious members of the same body.

If Calvin, the Congregation of the Index, and so many other *agelastes* were scandalized by the patent silliness of the *Pantagruel* and its sequels, it is either because they were poor readers or because, from a radically evangelical perspective like Rabelais's, they were poor Christians. Either their hermeneutic skills were insufficient to penetrate the book's "mocqueries, folateries et matieres joyeuses" to its "doctrine plus absconce," or their caritas was insufficient to accept those same "mocqueries, folateries et matieres joyeuses" as true Sileni—that is, as the modern equivalent of Jesus and his vulgar Aramaic, Paul and his vulgar Greek, Jerome and his vulgar Latin—and as the language and culture of those last in this world who will be first in the kingdom of God. Offended by scandalous outward appearances, they have read and judged like Pharisees who demand decorum, like Jews who demand signs, and like Greeks who demand wisdom. They have been confounded and shamed by what is manifestly foolish in the world and are therefore fools in the eyes of God (1 Cor 1.20–28). They have tripped on the scandal of the Christian Silenus and fallen short of redemption and of Pantagruel's kingdom of God on earth. What is worse, in rejecting the Silenus of Alcofrybas's epic New Testament as a vile and ugly thing they have leapt to judgment and condemned their poor brother Alcofrybas, and in so doing have renewed Cain's original sin—the very sin that Pantagruel, and Rabelais himself, had so heroically sought to redeem.

Having failed to hasten the advent of Pantagruel's New Order among his readers, Rabelais rewrote his epic, this time abandoning the typological design and attenuating the vulgar style and popular elements that, judging from the prologue to the *Gargantua,* seem to have led so many of his first readers to mistake his intentions entirely. So complete is this recasting of the original design that the ideal evangelical community allusively adumbrated at the end of the *Pantagruel* as a popular, inclusive, saturnalian inversion of estates is described at the end of the *Gargantua* in laborious detail as an exclusive, polite, aristocratic court in which highborn, well-educated, exquisitely dressed ladies and lords of evangelical convictions live in peace, love, and fabulous luxury.

Whether this more explicit, less vulgar rewriting was any better understood or any more successful in its purpose than the *Pantagruel* is impossible to gauge. But when many years later Rabelais wrote a sequel to his first epic, he raised the level of his style even further and eliminated virtually all remaining traces of popular culture in an apparent attempt to remove all the stumbling blocks that had made so many elite readers fall. For in the meantime he had discovered another way to reach and redeem those humanistic readers for whom he never ceased to write—a completely new design for an entirely new kind of Christian humanist epic called *Le Tiers livre des faictz et dictz Heroïques du noble Pantagruel.*

NOTES

INTRODUCTION

1. For most readers this view is merely an unexamined, perhaps even an unconscious, assumption. For a few it has become an explicit article of faith. The most extreme view is perhaps that of Dorothy Coleman, who attempted to prove the thesis that Rabelais's books are "Menippean satires" in the strictest sense and asserted of the *Tiers Livre,* for example, that "within the framework provided by the beginning and end of the book, there is a piling-up of episodes. . . . Grotesque parodies mingle with serious episodes; other episodes could well have come earlier or later in the book; it is written with the same formlessness as . . . *Gargantua*" (*Rabelais,* pp. 83–84).

2. Although virtually all studies of Rabelais deal in some way with what we might call the "coherence" of his books—whether in Weltanschauung, ideology, narrative technique, comic technique, language, tone, etc.—only two to my knowledge have systematically investigated something resembling what I am calling "design" here, both dealing exclusively with the *Tiers Livre:* V. L. Saulnier's *Le dessein de Rabelais* (1957), reprinted in *Rabelais I* (1983), and Walter Kaiser's *Praisers of Folly* (1963). These extremely valuable studies point the way to a more appropriate approach to Rabelais, even if their interpretations do not always stand up under scrutiny. By contrast even the most useful and influential studies of Rabelais—those of Abel Lefranc and Lucien Febvre, M. A. Screech and Gérard Defaux, Mikhail Bakhtin and Michel Jeanneret, François Rigolot and Terence Cave—are, in spite of the light they shed on Rabelais's meaning and manner, characteristically fragmentary and inductive in their approach (i.e., "microscopic" in the neutral, purely Horatian sense).

3. One could reasonably object that perception of the whole cannot precede at least a provisional interpretation of the parts, and that it is precisely this impossibility that makes *poesis* fundamentally different from *pictura.* Because pictura is a spatial medium, we can easily perceive the overall design of a painting at a glance, even before identifying a single figure in it. But because poesis is to a considerable degree temporal, we must encounter each part of a poem serially before discerning the larger design that informs it.

Without denying the truth of this observation or wishing to simplify the complex dialectic known as the hermeneutic circle, I would answer only that the priority I am granting to design over detail is one not of perception but of perspective. The macroscopic approach would consist in arriving as quickly as possible and by any reliable means at a complete sense of a work's overarching design and then proceeding to solve local problems of interpretation in the manner that the design requires. Theoretical difficulties with such an approach are only theoretical. In the case of Rabelais's works, the overarching design is remarkably easy to discern, provided only that we cease to assume that none is there to be found.

4. It is of no consequence that the term *epic* was not yet in use in Rabelais's time, nor that the categories *epic* and *romance* had not yet been differentiated and defined by literary theorists, nor that the two modes were indistinguishable in many late medieval romance epics. Rabelais and his readers knew Vergil's epic intimately and considered it a model of the genre. They also knew the basic "rules" of the genre, not only from Horace's ubiquitous *Epistola ad Pisones* but also from Marco Girolamo Vida's detailed discussion of Vergilian epic in book 2 of the *De arte poetica* (dedicated in 1527 to the French dauphin François, son of François I). They even had direct access to the recently rediscovered (if not yet critically important) text of Aristotle's *Poetics,* which had been available in Giorgio Valla's Latin translation since 1498, in the Greek original since 1508, and in Alessandro de' Pazzi's soon-to-become standard bilingual edition since 1536 at the latest (dedicated in 1527, first printed in 1536). Even without the aid of critical labels and categories, Rabelais's readers were thus capable of identifying the *Pantagruel* and its sequels as something quite distinct from a *roman,* as different from *Mélusine* and the *Orlando furioso* as is the *Aeneid* from the *Aethiopica.*

On the availability of Aristotle's *Poetics* in Rabelais's time see Weinberg, *A History of Literary Criticism,* 1.349–423, and Cranz, *A Bibliography of Aristotle Editions.* On the eventual elaboration of a theoretical distinction between epic and romance, begun in the year following Rabelais's death with the quarrel between Giraldi and Pigna and continued to the end of the century through Tasso's quarrel with Ariosto, see Weinberg, 1.433–51 and 2.954–1073. For a parallel development in France, see Fumaroli, "Jacques Amyot and the Clerical Polemic Against the Chivalric Novel."

CHAPTER 1

ALCOFRYBAS'S EPIC NEW TESTAMENT

1. The phrase *roman de verve* was coined as early as 1946 by V. L. Saulnier in the introduction to his critical edition of the original (1532) *Pantagruel* (pp. xxiii–xxiv). It reflects an attitude toward Rabelais's first book that is still prevalent today. For a full catalog of similar judgments, see La Charité, *Recreation,* pp. 14–18.

2. In the first edition of the *Pantagruel* this important aspect of the book was emphasized even in its title, which attributes to the hero of these "horribles et espoventables faictz et prouesses" the purely entelechial epithet "Roy des Dipsodes" (*P* title:212).

3. This reference to Scripture in the original *Pantagruel* was retained in all subsequent editions through 1537 but replaced in the so-called definitive edition

with the colorless and insignificant adverb "gualantement." Such trivializing bowdlerization is typical of the 1542 corrections which, individually, often destroy the original meaning of a passage and, cumulatively, tend to obscure the point of the book. For this reason I shall quote primarily from the original text of the *Pantagruel* in the following discussion.

4. There is a tendency to read the words "sainct Jehan de l'Apocalypse" as a single nominal unit—"saint-John-of-the-Apocalypse"—as though they identified the "John" in question, like "John of Patmos." But the deliberate syntactical parallelism—"Ne croyez . . . que j'*en* parle comme les Juifz *de* la Loy. . . . J'*en* parle comme sainct Jehan *de* l'Apocalypse"—clearly indicates that Alcofrybas is claiming to speak not "*like* John of the Apoclypse" but rather "*as* saint John" speaks "*about* apocalypse," or "*about* revelation," as opposed to the way the Jews talk *about* the Law. A proper understanding of syntax here eliminates any need to explain what looks to modern readers like a confusion between Revelation and the Gospel of John.

Rabelais's eventual substitution of an elaborate pun—"un gaillard Onocrotale, voyre dy je, crotenotaire des martyrs amans, et crocquenotaire de amours"—for the words "sainct Jehan de l'Apocalypse" in the 1542 edition diminished considerably the original force of this passage (see note 3 above). But the contrast to the Jews and the direct quotation from John still allowed Rabelais's later readers to draw many of the inferences discussed below.

5. Cf. Jesus' reply in the temple to the Jews who are similarly unable to understand his words: "I know that you are descendants of Abraham; yet you seek to kill me, because my word finds no place in you. I speak of what I have seen with my Father [*quod vidi apud Patrem meum, loquor*], and you do what you have [seen with] your father" (Jn 8.37–38).

6. The entire passage quoted above (2 Cor 3.13–16, 18) reads in the Vulgate: "Et non sicut Moyses ponebat *velamen* super faciem suam, ut non intenderent filii Israel in faciem eius, quod evacuatur, sed obtusi sunt sensus eorum. Usque in hodiernum enim diem, idipsum *velamen* in lectione veteris testamenti manet *non revelatum* (quoniam in Christo evacuatur), sed usque in hodiernum diem, cum legitur Moyses, *velamen* positum est super cor eorum. Cum autem conversus fuerit ad Dominum, *auferetur velamen*. . . . Nos vero omnes, *revelata facie* gloriam Domini speculantes, in eandem imaginem transformamur a claritate in claritatem, tanquam a Domini Spiritu."

No such pun was possible in the original Greek because the words *reveal* (ἀποκαλύπτω) and *Revelation* ('Αποκάλυψις) are too different from *veil* (κάλυμμα) and *unveil* (ἀνακαλύπτω), even though their roots are etymologically related, as in English.

7. This stronger interpretation of the equation is explicitly authorized by Alcofrybas when he presents the matter of his new book as the analogue, or even the equivalent, of *what John and Christ saw:* "J'en parle comme sainct Jehan de l'Apocalypse. *Quod vidimus testamur.* C'est des horribles faictz et prouesses de Pantagruel, lequel j'ay servy à gaiges" (218–19). It is confirmed by the violent

imprecation with which Alcofrybas concludes his prologue, in imitation, it would seem, of the imprecation with which John concludes Revelation and the entire New Testament: "Pourtant . . . tout ainsi comme je me donne à cent mille panerées de beaulx diables, corps et ame, trippes et boyaulx, en cas que j'en mente en toute l'hystoire d'un seul mot, pareillement le feu sainct Antoine vous arde, . . . et comme Sodome et Gomorre puissiez tomber en soulphre, en feu et en abysme, en cas que vous ne croyez fermement tout ce que je vous racompteray en ceste presente *Chronicque!*" (219). Cf. "I warn every one who hears the words of the prophecy of this book: if any one adds to them, God will add to him the plagues described in this book, and if any one takes away from the words of the book of this prophecy, God will take away his share in the tree of life and in the holy city, which are described in this book" (Rev 22.18–19).

8. This final reference to Scripture in the epilogue of the original edition conspicuously echoed those of the prologue, thus framing the narrative of the *Pantagruel* with corresponding allusions to the New Testament: "Tout ainsi que texte de Bible ou du sainct Evangile [Saulnier, p. 3]. . . . Ce sont beaux textes d'evangilles en françoys [Saulnier 23:177]." It disappeared with all other such references in 1542, giving way to the trivial expression "belles besoignes," just as the first had given way to "gualantement."

9. This fact is all the more striking when we compare Rabelais's version with its Italian source (see Masuccio, pp. 368–69). All the basic elements are the same—the lover's departure for home, the golden ring, the inscription, the explanation of the rebus ("Di', amante falso, perché me hai abandonata?")—*except* the form of the inscription. In Masuccio's novella, and in all other versions of the anecdote except Rabelais's, the inscription reproduces Christ's dying words more or less as they are recorded in Matthew and Mark: "Lama zabatani." Rabelais's only innovation in taking over the tale was to substitute an Old Testament text in Hebrew for its New Testament counterpart. And this is precisely the detail that gives the episode its meaning in the larger context of the *Pantagruel*.

10. It is intriguing to note in this regard that Jacques Lefèvre d'Etaples explains the instruction to the choirmaster, "pro cervo matutino" ("for the hind of dawn") in the original Hebrew text of Psalm 22, as a reference to Christ's humanity and his arrest at dawn on the day of the Crucifixion. He does so by referring directly to the metaphor of the *cerva* in the Song of Songs, which he reads in the traditional way as a prophetic allegory of Christ and his Church: "Et spiritualis sponsa in amatoriis carminibus cervo dominum comparat cum dicit: 'similis est dilectus meus capreae, hinnuloque cervorum' [Song 2.9]" (*Quincuplex psalterium*, fol. 34).

CHAPTER 2

THE REDEMPTIVE DESIGN OF THE *PANTAGRUEL*

1. I quote here from the first editions of *Pantagruel* and *Gargantua*. Rabelais eventually eliminated the reference to the Gospel genealogies from the *Pantagruel*,

modifying the first sentence to read: ". . . car je voy que tous bons hystoriographes ainsi ont traicté leurs Chronicques, non seullement les Arabes, Barbares et Latins, mais aussi Gregoys, Gentilz, qui furent buveurs eternelz" (*P* 1:221). But a simultaneous attenuation of the text quoted above from the *Gargantua* only served to accentuate the original suggestion of a parallel with the *genealogia Christi:* ". . . exceptez celle du *Messias,* dont je ne parle . . ." (*G* 1:12, emphasis mine). I insist on these unequivocal allusions because M. A. Screech has consistently maintained that Pantagruel's genealogy is a harmless parody of strictly *Old* Testament genealogies (see note 20 below). It will become clear in what follows that this is a seriously misleading half-truth and that Alcofrybas means to be taken at his word.

2. Though widely available elsewhere, the text was probably best known even in the sixteenth century from Augustine's *De civitate dei,* where it appears in the following form: "Iudicii *signum: tellus sudore madescet.* / E caelo rex adveniet per saecla futurus, / Scilicet ut carnem praesens, ut iudicet orbem. / Unde Deum cernent incredulus atque fidelis / Celsum cum sanctis aevi iam termino in ipso" (*De civ. dei* 18.23, emphasis mine). Augustine makes much of this text, pointing out its uncanny signs of prophetic authenticity: that the total number of lines in the poem is twenty-seven, which is the trinitarian number three cubed; that the first letters of each line in the original Greek text spell the words "'Ιησοῦς Χρειστὸς Θεοῦ υἱὸς σωτήρ"; that the first letters of these words in turn spell the word "ἰχϑύς," and so forth.

In the liturgical use of this prophecy the line that interests us here, "Iudicii signum: tellus sudore madescet," is treated as a refrain that is repeated tirelessly after every two lines of text. The setting may be heard on the Boston Camerata's recording, "A Medieval Christmas" (Nonesuch H–71315).

Rabelais helps his reader recognize the echo of this line in his own text by having Alcofrybas launch into a digression on the saltiness of sea water that allows him to emphasize the idea of a "sweating" earth: "Le Philosophe raconte, en mouvant la question pour quoy c'est que l'eaue de la mer est salée, que . . . *la terre* fut tant eschaufée [by Phaeton's mishap] que il luy vint une *sueur* enorme, dont elle *sua* toute la mer, qui par ce est salée, car toute *sueur* est salée; ce que vous direz estre vray si vous voulez taster de la vostre propre, ou bien de celles des verollez quand on les faict *suer*" (*P* 2:229–30, emphasis mine). The enormous drops of water "plus salée que n'estoit l'eaue de la mer" exuded by the earth "comme quand quelque personne *sue* copieusement" are presented as a "quasi pareil cas."

3. The naming of Cain (Gen 4.1), Seth (Gen 4.25), Ishmael (Gen 16.11), Isaac (Gen 18.11–15, 21.6), Esau and Jacob (Gen 25.25–26), and Reuben and Simeon (Gen 29.32–33) is typical of the circumstantial naming of newborns in the Old Testament. The commemorative renaming of adults—e.g., Abraham (Gen 17.5) and Israel (Gen 32.28)—conforms to the same convention.

4. It is significant that in direct contrast to the messianic hero of the *Pantagruel,* the patriarchal hero of the *Gargantua,* being identified already in the *Pantagruel* as an Old Testament figure, is named in the purely circumstantial manner of Genesis. Like Cain, Seth, Reuben, and Simeon, Gargantua is named according to "la

premiere parolle de son pere à sa naissance ['Que grand tu as!'], à l'imitation et exemple des anciens Hebreux" (*G* 7:33).

5. "Mespila arbor spinosa, fructu similitudine malorum, sed paulo breviori, unde et appellata, quod pilulae formulam habeant eius poma" (Isidore of Seville, *Etymologiae* 17.7.14). Vincent de Beauvais quotes Isidore verbatim (*Speculum naturale* 13.23 and 14.42). It is piquant to note that according to Pliny the puniest, most "degenerate" kind of medlar is called a "French medlar": "Malorumque pirorumque generi iure annumerentur mespila atque sorva. Mespilis tria genera: anthedon, setania; tertium degenerat, anthedoni tamen similius, quod Gallicum vocant. Setaniae maius pomum candidiusque, acini molliore ligno; ceteris minus pomum, sed odore praestantius et quod diutius servetur" (*HN* 15.22.84).

6. The original text qualifies this "enfleure" as "bien estrange" (Saulnier, p. 11). Although "estrange" still retained a strongly negative meaning in the sixteenth century—Tobler and Lommatzsch define it as "ausserordentlich, erstaunlich"; "hart, grausam"; Robert as "épouvantable, extrême"—the more neutral meaning of "unusual" had already become current. It would seem that the later correction to "très horrible" was meant to preclude any ambivalence. The swelling is to be understood as unambiguously dreadful.

7. The notion of the "good giant" on which amateur folklorists like Mikhail Bakhtin base their readings of Rabelais is a grotesque anachronism that leads to the most serious errors of interpretation. The tradition in which Rabelais wrote (unlike the tradition that derives from him) was consistent and unequivocal in maintaining that giants are by nature completely *evil*. The very idea of a good giant would have been so alien to Rabelais's readers as to appear profoundly paradoxical. Indeed, it is *as* a comical paradox, as a kind of walking oxymoron, that Rabelais introduces a hero who is a giant.

The only other exceptions to this universal rule of gigantology are, like Pantagruel, comic characters in burlesque romance epics: Pulci's *Morgante,* Folengo's *Baldus,* and the *Grandes Chronicques.* Moreover, the first of these paradoxically good giants, Pulci's Morgante, begins his career as a typically murderous brute and must be subdued and converted by Orlando before he can serve the hero as an epic companion (in which role he must kill other giants who are, naturally, thoroughly villainous). These comic precedents notwithstanding, there is not a single instance of a giant in the role of epic hero (as opposed to tamed companion) before the *Pantagruel.*

For the best treatment of this crucial point, as well as a brilliant and detailed treatment of patristic and medieval gigantology and its relevance to Rabelais's first two books, see Walter Stephens's invaluable new study, *Giants in Those Days: Folklore, Ancient History, and Nationalism.*

8. For the most vivid and gruesome descriptions of anthropophagy in giants, see *Odyssey* 9.287–98 and 458–60, *Aeneid* 3.616–38, and *Metamorphoses* 14.167–220 (Polyphemus); *Aeneid* 8.193–97 (Cacus); and *Orlando furioso* 15.43–45, 49–51 (Caligorante). Cf. also Boiardo's *Orlando innamorato* 1.8.25.

9. According to Genesis, the earth stained with Abel's blood became sterile and no longer yielded its fruits to Cain. To the fratricide God says: "Nunc igitur maledictus eris super terram, quae aperuit os suum, et suscepit sanguinem fratris tui de manu tua. Cum operatus fueris eam, non dabit tibi fructus suos" (Gen 4.11–12). According to Rabelais, on the contrary, "La terre embue du sang du juste fut . . . très fertile en tous fruictz."

There is no need to view this transformation of sterility into fertility as a positive rewriting of the Fall and thus as a light-hearted denial of sin and guilt, as some have recently attempted to do (see Jeanneret, *Des mets,* pp. 26–27, 100). Indeed three factors suggest that this is not an appropriate way to view the passage: (1) the contradiction is entirely consistent with other oxymoronic *impossibilia* in the chapter (e.g., "grosses mesles," a giant Pantagruel, a giant hero, "la sepmaine des troys jeudis," etc.); (2) it is authorized by Ovid's classical version of the Fall, of which Rabelais's version contains a textual echo (see below); and (3) it contributes in a forceful way to the chapter's deliberate and systematic conflation of the Fall and the first fratricide on which the meaning of the chapter and the entire book obviously depends. Alcofrybas's burlesque version of the Fall, considered on its own terms, is as coherent and self-consistent as the biblical version on which it is modeled, and it retains the same function within the epic that the Fall has within salvational history.

10. David Quint has rightly pointed out the eucharistic quality of a food that is swollen with the "blood of the just" (*Origin,* pp. 178–80). The medlars are indeed eucharists of a kind, but Rabelais will simply not allow us to read a positive value into them. On the contrary, everything in the chapter—from the description of the medlars as the fruit of the Fall to the fact that the medlars once ingested produce a Nimrod, a Goliath, and a Polyphemus—indicates that the grosses mesles are a negative counterpart to the eucharist and that partaking of them constitutes a participation not in Christ's Passion and Resurrection or in the community of Christ's Church but in Cain's murder of Abel.

This strictly "dyscharistic" value of the medlars is in fact consistent with the original use of the biblical phrase that Rabelais borrows to refer to Abel. Vituperating against the scribes, Pharisees, and hypocrites, Jesus utters the following curse: "that upon you may come all the righteous blood shed on earth [*sanguis iustus qui effusus est super terram*], from the blood of innocent Abel [*sanguis Abel iusti*] to the blood of Zechariah. . . . Truly, I say to you, all this will come upon this generation" (Mt 23.35–36). The "blood of the just" that has been "shed on the earth" indeed "comes upon" the cursed generation of Chalbroth when they eat Abel's blood in unholy communion at the moment of their "Fall."

11. For a complete account of this tradition see Stephens, *Giants,* pp. 76–84.

12. David Quint has observed that Rabelais's account is an inversion of Ovid's: "If the blood of the Ovidian giants begets a race of Cain, Rabelais's giants owe their existence to Cain's bloodshed" (*Origin,* p. 178). This remark is true, but applies as well to the traditional biblical explanation for the existence of giants, with which Rabelais is merely conflating elements of Ovid's narrative. An inverse

relation in Ovid is obviously less significant than a comparable relation in Genesis. The crucial point is that giants and Cain are intimately linked. In the *Pantagruel,* as in the Bible, that link is direct and causal.

13. "Quae fuit autem odii causa? Nimirum vitae dissimilitudo, quapropter et diversi generis erant, quanquam juxta corporis propagationem fratres erant germani. Uterque suum parentem exprimebat. Abel erat innocens, et ad benefaciendi studium accensus. Cain contra, fratris odio concepto, non de se corrigendo, sed de fratre trucidando cogitavit" (*Opera* 7.1152f).

14. Although *L'Enfer* was not published until 1539, Marot composed it in prison in 1526 and must certainly have circulated it in manuscript form shortly after his release.

15. As the century wore on and religious conflicts intensified, the symbolic value of Cain's fratricide became less moral and abstract, more political and polemical. Thus Agrippa d'Aubigné presents Cain and Abel as types of contemporary Catholic persecutors and Protestant martyrs: they are "le premier bourreau et le premier martyre" (*Les tragiques* 6.158).

16. Paul's Epistle to the Romans designates Adam as a "forma futuri," a "type of the one who was to come" (Rom 5.14) and concludes its typological analysis of the pattern of fall and redemption with the following synopsis: "Then as one man's trespass led to condemnation for all men, so one man's act of [justice] leads to [justification of life] for all men. For as by one man's disobedience many were made sinners, so by one man's obedience many will be made righteous" (Rom 5.18–19).

The typology of Rabelais's first chapter substitutes Cain for the "unus homo" who introduced sin and Pantagruel for the "unus homo" who rectifies that transgression and redeems its inheritors.

17. Rabelais's hero has frequently been understood as a liberating force, and his role has even been characterized as in some way redemptive. Stanley G. Eskin, for example, rightly considers Pantagruel's defeat of the invading Dipsodes as a "restorative act" that allows the return of "order, harmony, goodness, and perhaps innocence" ("Mythic Unity," pp. 548–49). Florence M. Weinberg discusses Pantagruel as a syncretic "logos figure" in whom elements of Bacchus and Christ are fused and whose war against the Dipsodes reenacts the conquest of India and, along with it, the triumph of Christianity (*The Wine and the Will,* pp. 45–50, 73–76, 101–06). And for Raymond C. La Charité Pantagruel's Christological role of "new savior," "redeemer," and "liberator" consists in righting the wrongs of a "world upside down" (*Recreation,* pp. 25–35, 57–59). La Charité's insights are of particular interest in the light of the typological scheme discussed here.

18. It has long been thought that Hurtaly derives from the rabbinic tradition of "הַפָּלִיט" (Happalit), "the escapee" or "saved one" (see Sainéan, vol. 2, pp. 34–36; Screech, *Rabelais,* pp. 45–47; and Stephens, pp. 89–90). Walter Stephens has recently challenged this opinion with great erudition, arguing that Rabelais is working here and throughout the *Pantagruel* within a framework provided by

Annius of Viterbo's counterfeit "Antiquities of Berosus Chaldaeus" (Stephens, pp. 239–48). But given the logic of the chapter and Hurtaly's function in it the question of sources would appear to be relatively inconsequential. Even if Rabelais had found no precedent for a survivor of the Flood he would have had to invent one because, as Alcofrybas's argument here shows, the redemptive design of the chapter and the book depends on the continuation of the messianic line.

19. The controversy is evident not only in the well-known discrepancy between Matthew and Luke (cf. Mt 1.3–16 and Lk 3.23–33) but in major inconsistencies between both of these genealogies and those of the Old Testament, particularly for the period immediately preceding and following the exile in Babylon (cf., for example, Mt 1.7–15 and 1 Chr 3.10–24).

20. See Screech, *Rabelaisian Marriage,* pp. 54–56; and *Rabelais,* pp. 41–42. Screech's interpretation is apparently a reaction against both Abel Lefranc's "atheist" interpretation, according to which the genealogy is one of several destructive parodies of the Gospels designed to debunk the entire Christian religion (Lefranc, ed., *Oeuvres,* vol. 3, pp. xlii–xliii, and *Rabelais,* pp. 180–81), and the "frivolous" interpretation of Lucien Febvre, according to which the genealogy is one of several harmless "gamineries" typical of late medieval monastic jokes about the New Testament (see *L'Incroyance,* pp. 144–47). It should be apparent by now that none of these conflicting readings of the genealogy does justice to Rabelais's meticulously ordered text.

21. The neatness of the order is purchased at the expense of considerable juggling with numbers. Matthew had to count both the beginning and end terms of the Abraham-to-David and captivity-to-Christ portions to arrive at the figure of fourteen generations, but he had to count only the end term (Jechoniah) of the David-to-captivity portion to arrive at the same number. In other words, he actually counted two generations (Abraham and Jechoniah) *twice.* Lefèvre d'Etaples devotes several dense pages of his commentaries on the four Gospels to this point, remarking that two of the groups of fourteen (*quaternadena,* or *tessaradecades*) are conjoined (*coniuncta*), while the remaining one is not (*disiunctum*). (See *Commentarii in quatuor evangelia,* fol. 3v.)

Medieval exegetes took Matthew's groupings, forced or not, very seriously. A major tradition reflected in the *Glossa ordinaria* and in the commentary of Nicholas of Lyra analyzes Matthew's three groups of fourteen as $3 \times (10 + 4)$, in which 3 signifies the Trinity, 10 the Old Law (ten articles of the Decalogue), and 4 the New Law (four Gospels of the New Testament), so that the "three groupings in Christ's genealogy mystically suggest the faith of the Holy Trinity harmoniously constructed by the doctrines of the Law and of Evangelical teaching" ("Tres distinctiones in generatione Christi mystice insinuant fidem sanctae trinitatis quam concorditer astruit doctrina legalis, et evangelicae institutionis"), or so that "by these numbers contained in the genealogy of Christ is mystically inscribed the fact that by observing the Decalogue in the faith of the trinity, Christ, who is the sun of justice by virtue of his spiritual illumination, rises in us" ("Per istos igitur numeros in genealogia Christi contentos mistice signatur quod per observationem decalogi in fide trinitatis Christus qui sol est justiciae per spiritualem illuminationem oritur in nobis" [*Textus Bibliae,* vol. 5, fols. 7 and 4v]).

If it was really for numerological reasons that Matthew fudged his data it is far more likely that his purpose was to force a suggestive correspondence between the number of generations between Abraham and Jesus (3 × 14) and the number of *mansiones* made by the children of Israel in their exodus from Egypt to the Promised Land (42). See Num 33.1–49 and note 23 below.

22. *Historia Francorum* 1.4, 7, 12, 15, 16. The first printed edition of Gregory's chronicle was that of Jodocus Badius, published in Paris twenty years before the *Pantagruel,* in 1512.

23. Because of Matthew's sleight of hand noted above (note 21), a count of the actual names in Mt 1 suggests that there were only forty rather than forty-two generations between Abraham and Christ and therefore that the number of generations from Adam to Christ is sixty rather than sixty-two. But here again the significance of numbers prevailed over their accuracy, and forty-two become the canonical number of generations between Abraham and Christ. Both Nicholas of Lyra and the *Glossa ordinaria* state as a matter of simple fact that "the three groups of fourteen make *forty-two* generations by which we arrived at Christ who was promised to us as a gift, just as the children of Israel arrived at the land promised to them by way of forty-two stations" ("Tres quaterdenae faciunt quadragintaduas generationes per quas pervenimus ad Christum qui promissus est nobis in praemium, sicut filii Israel per quadragintaduas mansiones venerunt ad terram sibi promissam" [*Textus Bibliae,* vol. 5, fol. 4v]). On this point too, the Christian humanist Lefèvre d'Etaples takes up the traditional count of forty-two and discusses it with utmost seriousness and respect, comparing its merits and significance with those of the actual count of forty.

24. A tradition in northern Renaissance painting provides a precedent of sorts for the kind of typological relation between redemption and the first fratricide we find suggested in the first chapter of the *Pantagruel.* In a *Nativity* (1452) by Petrus Christus now in the Groeninge Museum of Bruges, for example, the manger scene is framed by a gothic arch sculpted with reliefs representing, on the bottom, Adam on one side and Eve on the other; above them the sacrifice of Abel on one side and the sacrifice of Cain on the other; and at the apex of the arch, in the upper center of the painting directly above the spot where the infant Jesus lies on the floor flanked by Mary and Joseph, the scene of Cain's murder of Abel. By his position, the lowly baby Jesus is clearly represented as a counterpart and answer to the invidious, violent Cain.

In van Eyck's famous *Madonna of Canon George van der Paele* (1436) in the same museum, the right arm of Mary's throne is ornamented with a relief of Cain's murder of Abel (represented above a relief of Adam), and the left arm with a relief of Samson's killing of the lion (represented above a relief of Eve). The infant Jesus sits with his back to the image of Cain's murder and as he looks at the Canon his line of sight passes directly through the image of Samson. This positioning suggests that Jesus' soteriological role will consist in redeeming or reversing the effects of the first fratricide by slaying an allegorical beast while filled, like Samson, with the Spirit of the Lord (Jud 14.6).

25. Among these are the first encounter between Pantagruel and Panurge in *P* 9 and the lawsuit between Baisecul and Humevesne in *P* 10–14. These crucial episodes will be considered more fully in chapters 3 and 4.

26. These characteristics correspond to the three definitions of *altéré* given by Cotgrave: (1) "Altered, changed, varied, different from what it was; falsified, sophisticated"; (2) "drie, athirst, almost dried up"; (3) "extreamely passionat, exceedingly angred, or moved; in a chafe, in a fume." By understanding "altéré" only in the primary sense of "thirsty," readers have overlooked an important aspect of the Dipsodes that is explicit in their name. Like all Chalbroth's descendants, they are different from what they once were, changed, deformed, "falsified." Like all inheritors of Cain's sin, they are "exceedingly angred" and violent.

27. Whereas Homer generally uses such invocations to request information that lies beyond ordinary human ken or recall (e.g., *Iliad* 2.484–93), Vergil occasionally adapts the convention to highlight and set off a crucial episode. The following example, which seems to have inspired Rabelais, introduces the first full-fledged battle between Rutuli and Dardanians and marks the real beginning of the war for Latium: "Vos, o *Calliope,* precor, *aspirate* canenti, / Quas ibi tum ferro strages, quae funera Turnus / Ediderit, quem quisque virum demiserit Orco, / Et mecum ingentes oras evolvite belli" (*Aeneid* 9:525–28; cf. 7.37–45, emphasis mine).

28. Loup Garou's arrogance in this episode illustrates a proverbial attribute of giants: "gigantum arrogantia" (*Adagia* 3.10.93). Erasmus's commentary on the proverb describes Loup Garou's behavior exactly: "Dicebatur, ubi quis viribus suis fretus, temere, nulloque consilio res non tentandas moliretur. Tractum à notissima gigantum fabula. Proverbium admonet, inauspicato cedere, quaecunque citra consilium, adversus Deos, adversus pietatem, adversus jus et aequum, per vim instituuntur" (*Opera* 2.948d).

Other details in Loup Garou's description serve to associate him with classical giants and perhaps even with Cain. Armed with "enclumes Cyclopicques" (*P* 26:347) and a "masse toute d'acier . . . de Calibes" (*P* 29:360), he is described in terms that recall the subterranean Cyclopes of Vergil's epic: ". . . specus et *Cyclopum* exesa caminis / Antra Aetnaea tonant validique *incudibus* ictus / Auditi referunt gemitus striduntque cavernis / *Stricturae Chalybum* et fornacibus ignis anhelat" (*Aeneid* 8.419–21, emphasis mine; cf. 8.446). Rabelais's allusion to the Cyclopes as arms-forging blacksmiths may be motivated in part by the fact that Cain's descendant Tubalcain was the first blacksmith, the "forger of all instruments of bronze and iron" (Gen 4.22). Cain's line invented not only murder but the handmaid of murder, metallurgy.

29. "Ejus figuram diabolus portat, qui semper humano generi jugiter invidet, ac circuit Ecclesias fidelium ut mactet et perdat animas eorum" (Hugh of Saint Victor, *De bestiis et aliis rebus libri quatuor* 2.20, in *PL* 177.67). Although patristic

literature commonly allegorized the wolf in this way the *Latin Physiologus,* and consequently many vernacular bestiaries, do not mention the wolf at all. One exception is the bestiary of Pierre de Beauvais (c. 1217), whose entire chapter on the wolf (36) in the "short version" is a virtual translation of Hugh's chapter in *De bestiis.* Pierre's sentence corresponding to the one quoted above is the following: "Li leus senefie li deables car il a toutes eures envie seur l'umain lingnage et avironne les cogitations de feeus qu'il descive lour ames" (p. 89).

30. Galen and Aetius describe a kind of melancholy, or psychosis, called the "wolf-man disease" (λυκανϑρωπία), whose victims believe they have been transformed into wolves and behave accordingly. Pliny (*HN* 8.34) and Augustine (*De civ. dei* 18.17) record the popular belief that some men are physically transformed into real wolves, usually for a period of nine or ten years, during which they must resist their natural urge to eat human flesh if they are ever to regain their human form.

31. On "homo homini lupus" see Erasmus's *Adagia* 1.1.70 in *Opera* 2.55d. Later in the century Agrippa d'Aubigné was to use this well-known proverb in a similar way, adapting it to the standard Ovidian description of the Iron Age to evoke the anarchy and depredations of contemporary France: "L'homme est en proye à l'homme, un loup à son pareil; / Le pere estrangle au lict le fils, et le cercueil / Preparé par le fils sollicite le pere; / Le frere avant le temps herite de son frere" (*Les tragiques* 1.211–14; cf. *Met* 1.144–50).

32. ". . . ab ipso / Colligit os rabiem solitaeque cupidine caedis / Vertitur in pecudes et nunc quoque sanguine gaudet. / . . . Fit lupus et veteris servat vestigia formae. / Canities eadem est, eadem violentia vultus, / Idem oculi lucent, eadem feritatis imago est" (*Met* 1.233–35, 237–39).

There are other versions of the myth than the one recorded by Ovid (e.g., Apollodorus, *Bibliotheca* 3.8.1; Hyginus, *Fabulae* 176; and Pausanias, *Descriptio Graeciae* 8.2), but Ovid's was by far the most accessible and current throughout the Middle Ages and early Renaissance. It was also the one customarily reproduced in late medieval and early Renaissance mythographies and dictionaries. See for example Boccaccio's *Genealogia deorum* (4.66), Nicolas Perottus's *Cornucopiae, sive linguae latinae commentarii,* Ravisius Textor's *Officina,* Herman Torrentinus's *Elucidarius poeticus,* and Robert Estienne's *Dictionarium historicum ac poeticum.* Not until the mid-sixteenth century did lesser-known versions of the myth begin to be disseminated by more erudite mythographers like Giraldi (*De deis gentium* 2) and Comes (*Mythologiae* 9.9).

33. "Lychaon fuit quidam tyrannus nequissimus qui habebat mentem lupinam licet homo exterius appareret. Iste dum Iuppiter ad domum eius veniret occidit unum hominem et eius carnes ipsi obtulit ad comedendum, propter quam causam iratus Iuppiter eum mutavit in lupum. Et sic factus est lupus manifeste, qui lupus fuerat mentaliter et occulte" (Bersuire, fol. 18v).

34. On Petrus Lavinius, see J. B. Allen, *Friar,* pp. 52, 81–83; D. C. Allen, *Mysteriously Meant,* pp. 174–77; and Moss, *Ovid,* pp. 31–36. It is possible that Lavinius was the "Frere Lubin" later mocked in the prologue to *Gargantua* as a

"vray croque lardon" who contrived to show that "Ovide en ses *Metamorphoses*" was thinking of "les sacremens de l'Evangile" (*G* prol:8).

35. I do not mean to suggest, of course, that Rabelais took this kind of allegorizing seriously or that he expected his reader to do so. I mean simply that he adapted a familiar and highly suggestive type to his own purposes, making it serve in an extremely economical manner the design of a new and original work.

36. The events of *Pantagruel* 29 parallel those of Genesis 4 in several ways. For example, just as Cain murders Abel out of spite after Abel's sacrificial offering to God has been accepted and his own rejected, so Pantagruel's impious aggressor lunges toward him with gaping jaws immediately following the manifest acceptance of Pantagruel's vow to "[faire] prescher ton sainct Evangile purement, simplement et entierement" (361).

CHAPTER 3

THE EDUCATION OF THE CHRISTIAN PRINCE

1. "Princeps salutaris, ut erudite dictum est a Plutarcho, vivum quoddam est Dei simulacrum, qui simul et optimus est et potentissimus, cui bonitas hoc praestat, ut omnibus prodesse velit, potentia, ut quibus velit, possit quoque" (*Institutio principis christiani* 1, in *Opera* 4.569b). See Plutarch, *Ad principem ineruditem* 780e–f.

The idea of the prince as a simulacrum, image, or vicar of God, and conversely of God as an exemplar or archetype of the good prince, is found throughout Erasmus's works. See, for example, *Adagia* 1.3.1 ("Aut regem, aut fatuum nasci oportere"): "Denique *Dei* moderantis universa, salutaris Princeps *vivam imaginem* refert. Atque eo magnificentior est Princeps, quo propius ad *archetypi* sui formam accessit. . . . Contra qui pestilens est Princeps, is cacodaemonis simulacrum, ac vicem reddere videtur" (*Opera* 2.109b, emphasis mine).

2. "Theologia Christianorum tria praecipua quaedam in Deo ponit, summam *potentiam,* summam *sapientiam,* summam *bonitatem.* Hunc ternarium pro viribus absolvas oportet. Nam *potentia* sine *bonitate* mera Tyrannis est; sine *sapientia,* pernicies, non regnum. Primum igitur des operam, ut quandoquidem *potentiam* fortuna dedit, quam maximam *sapientiae* vim tibi compares, ut unus omnium optime quid expetendum, quidve fugiendum sit, perspicias, deinde ut quam maxime prodesse studeas omnibus, nam id est *bonitatis*" (*Institutio* 1, *Opera* 4.569d, emphasis mine).

We find this same trinitarian analysis in many of the texts in which Erasmus describes the ideal Christian prince as an image of God. Cf., for example, *Adagia* 3.3.1 ("Sileni Alcibiadis"): "At cum Principis praecipua bona sint tria, quibus Deum, qui vere solus est Rex, quodammodo repraesentat, *bonitas, sapientia, potentia,* num is Principi videtur amicus esse, qui duobus praecipuis bonis illum spoliet, *bonitate* et *sapientia,* solamque *potentiam* illi relinquat, et hanc non modo falsam, verum ne propriam quidem? Siquidem *potentia* nisi sit cum *sapientia bonitateque* conjuncta, Tyrannis est, non potentia" (*Opera* 2.775c, emphasis mine). Cf. also *Adagia* 1.3.1 ("Aut regem, aut fatuum nasci oportere"): "Deus [archetypus principis] nihil non perspicit, nihil non sentit, nullis corrumpitur affectibus [*sapientia*]. Ita potentissimus est [*potentia*], ut idem sit optimus. Omnibus bene facit, etiam indignis. Non punit nisi raro, idque coactus. Nobis administrat hunc mundum, non sibi. Hoc illi praemii loco est, si profuit [*bonitas*]" (*Opera* 2.109b).

3. "Principis animus ante omnia decretis ac sententiis erit instruendus, ut *ratione* sapiat, non *usu*. . . . *Praecepta* statim . . . instillanda sunt . . . *Exercitatio* . . . non perinde tuta est in Principe. . . . At grave fuerit affligi Rempublicam, dum Princeps discit administrare Rempublicam" (*Institutio* 1, *Opera* 4.568d and 580e–f, emphasis mine).

4. Although Pantagruel's bonitas is also evident by the end of the sapience cycle (see below, chapter 4), we must defer consideration of its acquisition until the following chapter. The coherence of Rabelais's book is so absolute, and its design so organic, as to defy a perfectly satisfactory plan of exposition.

5. Three such hypotheses have been advanced. One holds that because the original edition of the *Pantagruel* contained two chapters numbered "IX," the second of these (chapters 10–13 in the definitive edition) must have been composed later than the rest and inserted hastily into the book as it was being printed. (See Saulnier, ed., *Pantagruel,* pp. xxviii–xxix). A second hypothesis holds that chapter 8, not 9 bis, must be the late, interpolated one, because the Ciceronian style and high seriousness of Gargantua's letter seem so out of place in the context of the surrounding chapters. (See Béné, "Erasme et le chapitre VIII," and Françon, *Autour de la lettre,* p. 52). Yet a third hypothesis holds that neither 8 nor 9 bis, but rather the first of the two chapter 9s must be the interpolated one, because the first appearance of Panurge interrupts an otherwise coherent narration of Pantagruel's education (see Defaux, "Au coeur du *Pantagruel*").

What is common to all three hypotheses is that they start from the simple observation that two chapters of the 1532 edition are numbered "IX" and end by implying the need to correct the sequence of chapters. And yet Rabelais himself never altered the original sequence of chapters in later editions of his book. The only change he ever made was to correct the faulty numbering of the chapters—that is, to eliminate the single circumstance unanimously adduced by all modern readers in defense of their own "corrections" of sequence! More recently, readers have wisely abandoned such presumptuous license and sought to demonstrate the integrity of the work not as they think it ought to have been but as it actually is and was clearly intended to be. For fine examples of this more prudent approach see Bastiaensen, "La rencontre de Panurge," and La Charité, "Gargantua's Letter."

6. In the original 1532 edition of the *Pantagruel* the second of these two groups consisted of a single, disproportionately long chapter misnumbered "IX" (bis). It seems likely that in dividing this chapter into four shorter ones in later editions Rabelais may have been motivated at least in part by the desire to balance the two phases of the sapience cycle—acquisition and demonstration—so that

they would consist of equal numbers of chapters (four) as well as roughly equal numbers of pages.

It should be noted in passing that the two distinct phases of the sapience cycle are separated by the famous first meeting with Panurge (chapter 9). This episode, which has seemed out of place to some readers (see note 5), appears where it does for very good reasons, which will be discussed more fully in the next chapter. What must be clear already is that from a purely formal point of view, chapter 9 appears where it does in order to articulate the entire sapience cycle according to the following rational plan:

4	1	4
Acquisition of sapientia	Panurge	Demonstration of sapientia

7. In response to Pantagruel's question: "Et à quoy *passez vous le temps,* vous aultres messieurs estudiens, audict Paris?" the Limousin answers: "Nous transfretons la Sequane au dilucule et crepuscule; nous deambulons par les compites et quadrivies de l'urbe; nous despumons la verbocination latiale, et, comme verisimiles amorabonds, captons la benevolence de l'omnijuge, omniforme, et omnigene sexe feminin. Certaines diecules, nous invisons les lupanares et en ecstase venereique, inculcons nos veretres es penitissimes recesses des pudendes de ces meritricules amicabilissimes; puis cauponizons es tabernes meritoires . . . belles spatules vervecines, perforaminées de petrosil, et si, par forte fortune, y a rarité ou penurie de pecune en nos marsupies, et soyent exhaustes de metal ferruginé, pour l'escot nous dimittons nos codices et vestes oppignerées, prestolans les tabellaires à venir des Penates et Lares patriotiques" (*P* 6:244–25, emphasis mine).

This little speech is usually considered only from the point of view of language. Its style is indeed important, as we shall see in the next chapter, but even more important is what the speech *says.* On the most literal level it merely completes the review of "passetemps" in French universities (*P* 5) by showing that students at the University of Paris are no better, and are in fact a bit worse, than the wastrels already encountered in all the other universities of France.

8. This last detail is more significant than may first appear. The mere mention of "clystères" in the 1530s was sufficient to evoke the old guard of the Faculty of Medicine, since Symphorien Champier had published in 1528 and 1532 a virulent, overzealously humanistic attack on the doctrinaire, "medieval" practitioners of Arab medicine entitled *Clysteriorum Campi,* "Champier's Fields of Clysters," a title that Rabelais added in 1542 to the list of books in the Library of Saint Victor (*P* 7:255). See Antonioli, *Rabelais,* pp. 40–50, 104, and 109.

9. Pantagruel's admiration for the text of the *Pandects* and his corresponding revulsion at the teaching of barbaric medieval glosses like those of Accursius are characteristic of the attitude of the legal humanists like Budé (whose revolutionary *Annotationes in Pandectas* had been published in 1508 and again as recently as 1526). Pantagruel thus shows a natural predisposition for the kind of humanistic law he will eventually come to study (*P* 8:261) and practice (*P* 10:273–74). It

should be noted that Accursius's glosses are derided a second time in this acquisition portion of the sapience cycle in a title added to the library of Saint Victor in 1534: "De bobelinandis Glosse Accursiane baguenaudis Repetitio enucidiluculidissima" (*P* 7:252).

10. Most of the real names appearing in the modest catalog (42 titles) of the first edition of the *Pantagruel* were those of the principal enemies of Erasmus: Ortuinus, Bricot, Mayr, Beda, Sutor. Most of those added in subsequent editions (139 titles by 1542) tend rather to be scholastic theologians or philosophers: Duns Scotus, Ockham, Brûlefer, Lulle, Gerson (though they also include three of Luther's principal adversaries in his criticisms of the institutions of the Church: Silvester of Prierio, Johan Eyck, Gaietan). This difference of emphasis helps us see more clearly that the original function of the catalog of Saint Victor was not so much to ridicule scholastic learning per se but to ridicule the scholastic enemies of humanism.

11. This bleak picture of the University is not entirely accurate, as the presence of an Alciati in the Faculty of Law at Bourges will suffice to recall. But the reality of French universities in the 1530s is irrelevant here. The crucial point is the way those universities are presented in the text and the negative role they play in the prince's education.

12. To point to the incongruity between the style of the letter and the character of its fictive author, Gargantua, as some have done in an attempt to read the letter satirically, is surely to read with an anachronistic notion of character and verisimilitude and to overlook the most important function of style in the *Pantagruel*—namely, to inflect meaning. Here style is designed not to reveal character, as it would in a realistic novel, but to function as a narrative signpost, in much the same way that it sometimes does in another modern epic, James Joyce's *Ulysses*.

13. The three professions and their hierarchy were traditionally related to Aristotle's tripartite division of "goods" in the *Nicomachean Ethics:* external goods, goods of the body, and goods of the soul, in order of increasing importance (1.8.2). Pantagruel will refer to this tradition in the *Tiers Livre* when he proposes that Panurge consult a representative of each of the three professions, in order of decreasing importance: "Tout ce que sommes et qu'avons consiste en trois choses, en *l'ame,* on *corps,* es *biens.* A la conservation de chascun des trois respectivement sont au jourd'huy destinées troys manieres de gens: les *theologiens* à l'ame, les *medicins* au corps, les *jurisconsultes* aux biens" (*TL* 29:526, emphasis mine). In actual practice law had become a more prestigious profession than medicine in the late Middle Ages, but Rabelais remains faithful to the traditional hierarchy.

14. For a fuller demonstration of the points that follow, see Duval, "The Medieval Curriculum."

15. Alcalá was the center at which Cardinal Ximenes's team had in 1517 completed their work on the famous Complutensian Polyglot Bible containing the original Hebrew, Aramaic, and Greek texts of the Bible along with interlinear Latin translations and the Latin version of the Vulgate. The academy at Louvain had been founded by Busleiden in 1517 for the purpose of teaching the "tres

linguae." As for the equivalent institution in Paris, two *lecteurs* of Greek (Pierre Danès and Jacques Toussain) and two lecteurs of Hebrew (Agathias Guidacerius and François Vatable) had been appointed two years before the publication of the *Pantagruel,* and a third lecteur of Hebrew (Paul Paradis) in 1531. The first lecteur of classical Latin, Barthélemy Latomus, was not to be appointed until two years after the *Pantagruel,* in 1534.

16. "Chaldean"—that is, Aramaic—is the fourth major biblical language that first became important in 1520, when the Complutensian Polyglot Bible was finally approved for sale, making available for the first time the "Chaldean" text of the Aramaic Targums along with the other original texts of the Bible. By the time the *Pantagruel* was first published, "Chaldean" seemed on the verge of joining the tres linguae as one of the canonic languages of humanism. See Erasmus's comment in *Adagia* 2.1.1 ("Festina lente"): "Intra paucos annos illud futurum polliceor studiosis, ut quicquid est bonorum auctorum in *quatuor linguis,* Latina, Graeca, Hebraica, *Chaldaica,* . . . id unius hujus [Aldus Manutius] opera, et plenum habeant et emendatum" (*Opera* 2.402e, emphasis mine); Robert Estienne's proper name index entitled *Hebraea, Chaldaea, Graeca, et Latina nomina . . . quae in Bibliis leguntur,* which figured in all the Latin Bibles edited by Estienne and was eventually published separately in 1537; Des Périers's index entitled *Table de tous les motz Ebrieux, Chaldees, Grecz, et Latins,* which figured in the Olivétan translation of the Bible; and Rabelais's own review of all the "langues instaurées" earlier in this same letter: "*Grecque,* sans laquelle c'est honte que une personne se die sçavant, *Hebraïcque, Caldaïcque, Latine*" (*P* 8:259, emphasis mine). Rabelais borrows ostentatiously from the "Chaldean" text of the Complutensian in his *Almanach pour l'an 1533,* where he quotes Psalm 64 "selon la lettre *chaldaïcque*" (Jourda 2.520).

Arabic was one of the two original languages of medicine (the other being Greek) and as such was of vital interest to medical humanists who wished to control the standard Latin translations of Avicenna and Averroes and to discover remedies for the new diseases that were ravaging Europe.

17. In addition to this typically humanist emphasis on style it is perhaps significant that the two classical authors singled out as the best models of style—Plato and Cicero—also happen to be moral philosophers. From the beginning one of the chief characteristics of humanism had been the deliberate marriage of Rhetoric and Philosophy, founded on the assumption that human truths (moral philosophy) and beauty of expression (eloquence) are inseparable aspects of one and the same thing and cannot be apprehended separately. Peter Ramus was soon to make both the reform of Rhetoric (purged of inventio and dispositio, which he relegated to Dialectic) and its relation with Philosophy a major issue in Paris. See *QL* prol:17–20.

18. On the question of authority in Renaissance medicine, see Antonioli, *Rabelais,* 40–54.

19. Cf. Rabelais's dedicatory epistle to his edition of Marliani's *Topographia antiquae Romae,* in which the author, writing as a doctor ("Franciscus Rabelaesus,

Medicus"), mentions his interest in the "plantae, animantia, et pharmaca" of Italy as a strictly professional one: "quod artis erat meae" (Jourda 2.527). Cf. also Juan Vives's remark about the transition from the study of "causae naturae" to the study of medicine in *De tradendis disciplinis:* "Qui ad artem Medicam transiturus est, vel commigratus verius, huic sunt exactissime vires naturaque pernoscendae fossilium omnium, quae sunt variorum generum, pigmentorum, lapidum, gemmarum, stirpium, animantium, humani corporis" (fol. 122r). The "transiturus est, vel commigratus verius" of this statement is a perfect gloss on Gargantua's insertion of natural science as a propaedeutic to Medicine in his program.

20. The "sophistes, Sorbillans, Sorbonagres, Sorbonigenes, Sorbonicoles, Sorboniformes, Sorbonisecques, Niborcisans, Borsonisans, Saniborsans" (*P* 19:318 var.)—that is, the scholastic theologians of the Faculty of Theology at Paris—form the most loathsome group in the *Pantagruel.* See Defaux, *Pantagruel et les sophistes.*

21. "Doctos esse vix paucis contigit: at nulli non licet esse Christianum, nulli non licet esse pium, addam audacter illud, *nulli non licet esse Theologum.* . . . Utinam fiat, ut . . . Christianis omnibus Euangelia et Apostolorum litterae ita sanctae habeantur, ut haec [human writings and institutions] prae illis non videantur esse sancta. Quid Alberto magno, quid Alexandro, quid Thomae, quid Aegidio, quid Ricardo, quid Occám alii velint tribuere, per me sane cuique liberum erit. . . . Sint illa quantumvis erudita, quantumvis subtilia, quantumvis, si velint, Seraphica, haec tamen certissima fateantur oportet. . . . Hunc auctorem nobis non schola Theologorum, sed ipse Pater coelestis, divinae vocis testimonio comprobavit. . . . O solidam auctoritatem, vereque (ut isti vocant) irrefragabilem. . . . Hic unicus est Doctor, hujus unius discipuli sitis. . . . Quid, quaeso, simile in Scoto? . . . quid simile in Thoma? . . . Cur tota pene aetas in hominum decretis, et inter se pugnantibus opinionibus conteritur? Jam vero sint illa sane, si libet, sublimium Theologorum: At in his certe sit futuri quondam *magni Theologi tirocinium*" (*Opera* 5.141f and 143a–44a, emphasis mine).

22. This being the case it is obviously not possible to accept the reading according to which Gargantua's encyclopedic program is a foolish rehash of the medieval *orbis doctrinarum.* Gargantua's encyclopedia is, on the contrary, an ironic, point-for-point humanistic *subversion* of the old encyclopedia.

23. The "anticurriculum" of Gargantua's letter helps us to see that Pantagruel's first gothic education was not only desultory but quite literally "prae-posterous," because the order in which it introduced the various disciplines of the old curriculum is actually the *reverse* of the canonical order reflected in the letter: first, *Theology* in its most contemptible medieval form (Pantagruel's visit to the Benedictine monastery at Maillezais outside Poitiers [*P* 5:240]); then *Medecine* at Montpellier (241); then *Law* at Montpellier, Bourges, and Orléans (241–43); and finally, "tous les *sept ars liberaulx*" at Paris (*P* 7:249, emphasis mine)!

24. There is no justification for taking the word *abysme* in a pejorative sense here, as some have attempted to do. The adjective ἄβυσσος originally had neither positive nor negative connotations but meant simply "bottomless, unfathomed,

boundless." As a noun it came to mean anything deep, especially the sea, the "great deep" of Genesis 1.2. Patristic writers tended to use the word positively, to describe the abyss of God's wisdom, for example, or of goodness, righteousness, the knowledge of God, the loving kindness of Christ, Scripture, etc. See Lampe, *A Patristic Greek Lexicon,* and Brault, "'Ung abysme de science,'" p. 626.

The expression "abysme de science" seems in fact to have been an idiomatic expression in Rabelais's day, meaning an "ocean of knowledge." See the lines quoted in Huguet's dictionary from Rabelais's friend Jean Bouchet: "On l'eust jugé à l'ouyr et le veoir / Une profunde *abisme de sçavoir*" (emphasis mine). Nothing in the history of the word suggests a contradiction between "abysme de science" and other expressions in the letter like "tout sçavoir liberal et honeste" (258), "toute perfection et sçavoir politique," and "manne celeste de bonne doctrine" (260). As for the latter, we find it used without irony by Erasmus: "Quid aptius arcanae legis scientiam adumbrare queat quam Manna? . . . Ad Manna quantum potest properandum caelestis sapientiae" (*Enchiridion* 2, *Opera* 5.6f and 8b).

25. This same opposition between two successive and antithetical educations will be made again, but much more explicitly, in the corresponding chapters of the *Gargantua* (*G* 14 vs. *G* 15 and especially *G* 21–22 vs. *G* 23–24). Here as elsewhere, the *Gargantua* loses in subtlety and irony what it gains in explicitness.

26. It has been argued that Pantagruel's engaging in "disputations" (cf. *P* 10:273) is a sign that his learning remains somehow gothic. Such a view is triply invalid. It is belied (1) by the antischolastic mechanism at work throughout the elaboration of Gargantua's curriculum, discussed above, (2) by the antischolastic function of the disputations within the sapience cycle, discussed below, and (3) by the fact that "disputations" were not at all a distinctly scholastic practice but, on the contrary, a classical one (witness Cicero's *Tusculanae disputationes*), which the Scholastics had corrupted but which the humanists restored, imitated, and embraced as the most appropriate means of arriving at philosophical truth (witness Christoforo Landino's *Disputationes Camaldulenses*).

On this last point, see Leonardo Bruni's *Dialogus de tribus vatibus florentinis* (itself a perfect model of a classicizing disputation), in which no less a humanist than Coluccio Salutati makes repeated and passionate appeals for a revival of the classical practice of the *disputatio* as an antidote to the gothic "perturbation" of all disciplines—e.g., "in hoc uno . . . vos hebescere neque utilitati vestrae satis consulere video, quod *disputandi* usum exercitationemque negligitis: qua ego quidem re nescio an quicquam ad studia vestra reperiatur utilius. Nam quid est, per deos immortales, quod ad res subtiles cognoscendas atque discutiendas plus valere possit quam *disputatio?* . . . Est autem exercitatio studiorum nostrorum collocutio, perquisitio, agitatioque earum rerum quae in studiis nostris versantur: quam ego uno verbo *disputationem* appello" (pp. 46–48 and 66, emphasis mine).

27. The famous *galimatias* of the episode is not a satire of legalese, as it is sometimes said to be, because it represents not the technical language of legal professionals as the episode of Judge Bridoye in the *Tiers Livre* will do but the

testimony of two private citizens—"deux gros seigneurs" (*P* 10:272). The title of chapter 11 is explicit in this regard: "Comment les seigneurs de Baisecul et Humevesne plaidoient devant Pantagruel *sans advocatz*" (*P* 11 title:276, emphasis mine). And indeed, except for the presence of certain burlesque words of popular origin, the lexicon of the three speeches is almost entirely ordinary and the syntax consistently perspicuous. The difficulty of the speeches is purely a semantic one arising from the kind of radical non sequitur called "coq-à-l'âne." See the excellent analysis of Rigolot in *Les langages de Rabelais,* pp. 41–48 ("Horizontalité et verticalité linguistiques s'ignorent ou se contredisent dans une palinodie simultanée," p. 46).

The resulting meaninglessness functions not satirically, therefore, but *strategically,* to confirm—comically but very effectively—the already-stated difficulty of the case, and to force the reader to acknowledge its difficulty by placing him in the same position vis-à-vis the case as those experts who "n'y entendoi[en]t que le hault alemant" (*P* 10:272). A similar strategy involving the reader often lies behind Rabelais's recourse to strange or incomprehensible languages, as we shall see in the case of Panurge's glossolalia in chapter 9 (see below, chapter 4 and note 12).

28. Cf. the parallel account in 2 Chr 1.10–12—"Da mihi sapientiam et intelligentiam. . . . Petisti autem sapientiam et scientiam, ut iudicare possis populum meum. . . . Sapientia et scientia datae sunt tibi"—and Solomon's own prayer for sapientia in the Book of Wisdom (esp. 9.1–12).

29. In the original edition of the *Pantagruel* this function was made explicit from the beginning of the demonstration section, whose single chapter bore the title: "Comment Pantagruel equitablement jugea d'une controverse merveilleusement obscure et difficile, si justement que son jugement fut dit plus admirable que celluy de Salomon" (ed. Saulnier, 9 bis:55).

30. "Atque utinam saltem Christiani Principes omnes sapientissimum illum Regem imitentur, cui cum daretur optio, quicquid vellet ab eo qui nihil non praestare poterat, nihil aliud optavit quam sapientiam, et eam sapientiam, qua populum sibi commissum recte gubernaret" (*Adagia* 1.3.1 ["Aut regem, aut fatuum nasci oportere"], *Opera* 2:108f–09a).

This is a typical expression of a common theme in Erasmus. Cf. *Institutio principis christiani* 1: "Laudatur ab omnibus Solomon, qui cum integrum esset optare quidquid vellet, protinus accepturus quidquid petisset, non optarit opum vim, non totius orbis imperium, non exitium inimicorum, non insignem famae gloriam, non voluptates, sed sapientiam: neque quamvis sapientiam, sed eam, qua posset regnum sibi creditum cum laude administrare" (*Opera* 4.581e).

31. "Unum praeceptum Christus appellavit suum, nempe caritatis. Cum hac quid aeque pugnat atque bellum? . . . Christi typum habebat Solomon, quod Hebraeis pacificum sonat, ab hoc sibi templum exstrui voluit. David alioqui diversis virtutibus egregie clarum, tamen hoc elogio submovit ab exstructione templi, quod sanguinarius esset. . . . Nato Christo, non bellum, neque triumphos,

sed pacem canunt angeli. De nondum nato praecinuit vates ille mysticus: 'Et factus est in pace locus ejus'" (*Opera* 2.959d–f).

32. "David aliis virtutibus Deo fuit gratissimus, et tamen vetuit ab hoc sibi condi templum non ob aliud, nisi quod sanguinarius, hoc est, bellator esset. Solomonem pacificum in hoc delegit. Si haec acta sunt inter Judaeos, quid de nobis fiet Christianis? Illi Solomonis umbram habebant, nos verum Solomonem, pacificum illum Christum omnia conciliantem, quae in coelis sunt, et quae in terra" (*Opera* 4.610d).

33. "Quisquis Christum annunciat, pacem annunciat. Quisquis bellum praedicat, illum praedicat, qui Christi dissimillimus est. Age jam, quae res Dei Filium pellexit in terras, nisi ut mundum Patri reconciliaret? ut homines inter se mutua et indissolubili caritate conglutinaret? postremo, ut ipsum hominem sibi faceret amicum? Mea igitur gratia legatus erat, meum agebat negotium. Atque ob id Solomonem sui typum ferre voluit, qui nobis εἰρηνοποιός, id est, *pacificus,* dicitur. Quantumvis magnus erat David, tamen, quia bellator erat, quia sanguine fuerat inquinatus, non sinitur exstruere domum Domini, non meretur hac parte gerere typum Christi pacifici" (*Opera* 4.630b–c).

34. We find a similar mention of the convivium as a sign of reconciliation and fraternal communion after a protracted legal dispute in the story of Perrin Dendin, the great "apoincteur des procès," recounted by Judge Bridoye in the *Tiers Livre:* Dendin "estoit presque tous les jours de banquet, de festin, de nopces, de commeraige, de relevailles, et en la taverne, pour faire quelque apoinctement, entendez; car jamais n'apoinctoit les parties qu'il ne les feist boyre ensemble, par *symbole de reconciliation, d'accord perfaict et de nouvelle joye*" (*TL* 41:573, emphasis mine).

35. The phrase "sans accepter personne," which seems to have escaped the notice of Rabelais's commentators, is a biblical one transposed directly from the Vulgate's "personam accipere." Its appearance here is important because it alludes to a corollary to the New Law of caritas elaborated by the apostle James: "My [brothers], show no partiality [*personarum acceptio*] as you hold the faith of our Lord Jesus Christ. . . . If you really fulfil the royal law, according to the scripture, 'You shall love your neighbor as yourself,' you do well. But if you show partiality [*personas accipitis*], you commit sin, and are convicted by the law as transgressors" (Jas 2.1 and 8–9).

CHAPTER 4

PANURGE

1. See Schrader, *Panurge und Hermes;* Griffin, "The Devil and Panurge"; La Charité, *Recreation,* pp. 84–91; and Defaux, *Le curieux.*

2. For the most complete treatment of the meaning of Panurge's name in dictionaries and in Greek and Latin literature, see Schrader, *Panurge und Hermes,*

pp. 80–87. See also Defaux, *Le curieux,* pp. 134–35. The Suda, which is quoted by both Schrader (p. 81) and Defaux (p. 134), accurately reflects the ambivalence of the word πανοῦργος in antiquity, defining it negatively as a "worker of mischief in all things" and positively as a "prudent and experienced man." Dictionaries not quoted by Schrader or Defaux tend to favor the negative meaning. Jean Chéradame's Greek-Latin dictionary, for example, defines πανοῦργος ambivalently as "astutus, callidus" and πανουργία as "astutia, calliditas," but the verb πανουργέω negatively as "scelestus sum, malefacio, dolose ago." Budé in his *Commentarii linguae graecae* quotes Aristotle's definition of πανουργία as "solertia minime commendabilis" (p. 110), or "fraus, vafritia subdola et improba" (p. 682), and defines πανουργέω as κακουργέω, "to do evil." Jacques Toussain's *Lexicon graecolatinum* offers the fullest, and most negative, definition of πανοῦργος: "propriè eum significat qui omnibus in rebus versatus est, à πᾶν et ἔργον. . . . Verum quia huiusmodi callidi esse solent, factum est, ut accipiatur Atticis scriptoribus pro callido, fraudulento, doloso, astuto, vafro, versuto, versipelli, veteratore, improbo, fallaci, maleficioso, et qui versutia sua quidvis potest agere, etc." Toussain defines πανουργία similarly as "fraus, vafricia subdola et improba, astutia, calliditas, astus, versutia . . . solertia minimè commendabilis, . . . flagitium, malitia, . . . pro crimine et scelere."

3. Πανοῦργος appears with this sense thirteen times in Proverbs and four times in Sirach. Typical examples: "[Every] prudent man [πανοῦργος] acts with knowledge, but a fool flaunts his [wickedness]" (Prov 13.16); "The wisdom of [the prudent (πανούργων) will] discern [their ways], but the folly of fools [leads astray]" (Prov 14.8); "A fool despises his father's instruction, but he who heeds admonition is [more] prudent [πανουργότερος]" (Prov 15.5). See also Proverbs 12.16, 13.1, 14.15, 14.18, 14.24, 19.25, 21.11, 22.3, 27.12; and Sirach 6.32, 21.12, 21.20, 37.19.

As for the noun πανουργία, Solomon begins the Book of Proverbs by stating his desire to give "prudence [πανουργίαν] to the simple, knowledge and discretion to the youth" (Prov 1.4); and Wisdom begins her second prosopopeia similarly with the exhortation: "O simple ones, learn prudence [πανουργίαν]; O foolish men, pay attention" (Prov 8.5). In Sirach the noun is used both positively (Sir 34.10 [=31.10]) and negatively (19.25, 21.12).

4. See also 2 Cor 12.16, which contains the only occurrence of the adjective πανοῦργος in the entire New Testament. As I shall try to show in the following pages, 2 Cor 12.16, 1 Cor 3.19, and Lk 20.23 are crucial passages for a proper understanding of Panurge.

5. It should be pointed out, however, that the strong textual echoes linking the end of *P* 8 with the beginning of *P* 10 are themselves a good indication that the interruption of *P* 9 was intended, because such a striking similarity of diction would hardly be necessary if Pantagruel's defense of theses immediately followed Gargantua's admonition to defend theses.

6. ". . . à present viens de Turquie, où je fuz mené prisonnier . . . et voluntiers vous racompteroys mes fortunes, qui sont plus merveilleuses que celles de Ulysses,

mais, puis qu'il vous plaist me retenir avecques vous . . . nous aurons, en aultre temps plus commode, assez loysir d'en racompter, car pour ceste heure j'ay necessité bien urgente de repaistre" (*P* 9:269–70). "Mais or me dictes comment (dist Pantagruel) vous eschappastes leurs mains" (*P* 14:289).

7. In the original 1532 *Pantagruel* the sequence of (misnumbered) chapters was the following:

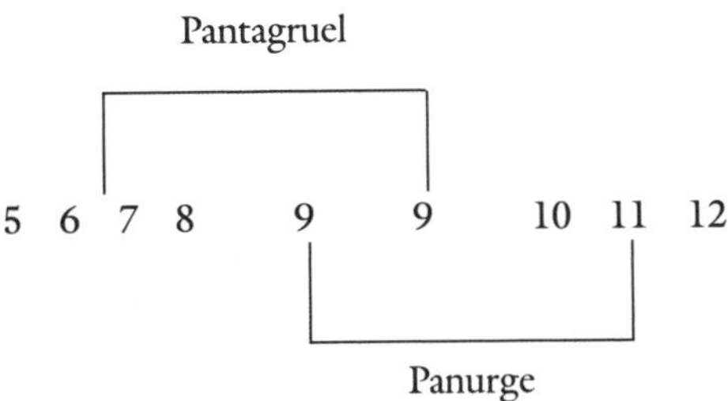

It is easy to see from this diagram why so many readers have been tempted to suppose that the printer, working hastily from a hastily written manuscript, might simply have reversed the order of two consecutive chapters, one of which he inadvertently misnumbered. The first chapter 9 does seem to belong with chapters 10–12, the second with chapters 5–8.

But as we noted in the preceding chapter (note 5), the fact that Rabelais later corrected the numbering of chapters but left their sequence unchanged is a compelling argument that the original order was the intended one and that Panurge appears where he does for a reason.

8. Analogous pairs in later works of the same tradition—especially Don Quijote and Sancho Panza in Cervantes's parodic epic romance and Hal and Falstaff in Shakespeare's *Henry the Fourth, Part 1*—can help the modern reader to understand the epic function of Panurge and his relationship to Pantagruel. This medieval, dialectical relationship between hero and companion was put to increasingly prominent use in seventeenth- and especially eighteenth-century literature, the best-known avatars being Dom Juan and Sganarelle, Robinson Crusoe and Friday, Pamino and Papageno, Candide and Pangloss, and Jacques le fataliste and his master. Having reached its fullest elaboration in the prose of the Enlightenment the convention of the epic *comes* virtually disappeared with the advent of the solitary Romantic hero, only to reappear virtually intact in the heroic narratives of the popular media in the twentieth century: radio and television westerns (Lone Ranger and Tonto), science fiction cartoon strips (Batman and Robin), and comedy duos (Hardy and Laurel, Dean Martin and Jerry Lewis).

9. In an interpolation of 1533 Epistemon remarks explicitly on the parallel between Panurge's languages and those of Pathelin: "Parlez vous christian, mon amy, ou langaige Patelinoys? Non, c'est langaige Lanternois" (*P* 9:266).

10. By 1542 the proportion of incomprehensible languages had increased dramatically, with the addition of four less familiar or nonexistent languages: Scots-English (1533), Basque (1542), "Lanternois" (1533), and Danish (1534).

11. Passages contained in brackets here did not figure in the original edition of the *Pantagruel* but were added in later editions beginning in 1533.

12. The function of these languages is thus almost identical to that of the galimatias spoken by Baisecul and Humevesne in *P* 10–13 (see above, chapter 3, note 27). In both episodes Rabelais's purpose is to force upon his reader the uncomfortable experience of incomprehension. The only difference is that in the trial our incomprehension is meant only to corroborate what the narrator has said about the difficulty of the case and show us that, unlike Pantagruel, we are not smarter than the greatest jurists of Europe. Here, on the contrary, our incomprehension is supposed to lead us to a higher order of comprehension, which is concerned with the spirit rather than the letter of what is being said.

13. Although Panurge is far too pungent a character to be considered an Everyman, there is nevertheless something universal and average about him. He will later be described as being of median height and age: "Panurge estoit de stature moyenne, ny trop grand, ny trop petit . . . et pour lors estoit de l'eage de trente et cinq ans ou environ" (*P* 16:300). This last detail establishes that Panurge is exactly middle-aged, like Dante's exemplary pilgrim who begins his epic journey "nel mezzo del cammin di nostra vita" (*Inferno* 1.1)—that is, at the age of thirty-five, according to the canonical scheme of the life of man.

14. This and all other direct references to "theologians" and the "Sorbonne" in these chapters are quoted from the first edition of the *Pantagruel*. They were expurgated or modified in 1542.

15. The strict parallelism between the two episodes is reinforced by conspicuous textual echoes. Just as Pantagruel "mist tous de cul" the representatives of the Faculty of Arts and "feist tous quinaulx" the representatives of the higher Faculties of the University, "nonobstant leurs ergotz et fallaces" (*P* 10:271), so Panurge claims to have "faictz quinaulx et mist de cul" the various devils with whom he has argued (*P* 18:317). Just as Pantagruel's earlier victory over scholastic learning qualified him to demonstrate his Solomonic wisdom in the case of Baisecul vs. Humevesne, so Panurge's earlier victories now qualify him to meet this new challenge to his master's Solomonic wisdom. A further parallel, which also points to a crucial difference between Pantagruel and Panurge, may be seen in the following passages, the first of which follows Pantagruel's victory over the Scholastics, and the second, Panurge's victory over Thaumaste: "Dont tout le monde commença à bruyre et parler de son sçavoir si merveilleux, jusques es *bonnes femmes,* lavandieres, courratieres, roustissieres, ganyvetieres et aultres, lesquelles, quand il passoit par les rues, disoient: 'C'est luy!' A quoy *il prenoit plaisir,* comme Demosthenes" (*P* 10:271–72, emphasis mine); and "Panurge commença estre en reputation en la ville de Paris par ceste disputation que il obtint contre l'Angloys, et faisoit des lors bien valoir sa braguette, et la feist au dessus esmoucheter de broderie à la Romanicque. Et le monde le louoit publicquement, et en feust faicte une chanson, dont les petitz enfans alloyent à la moustarde, et estoit bien venu en toutes compaignies de *dames et demoiselles,* en sorte qu'*il devint glorieux*" (*P* 21:326,

emphasis mine). Characteristically, Pantagruel takes "pleasure" in the recognition of the lowest of low-born women, Panurge "pride" in the recognition of the highest of high-born ladies.

16. These famous Oxonian adversaries in the dispute over universals are favorite targets of Rabelais's antischolastic satire throughout his works. The Scotists are lampooned in *Gargantua* (*G* 7:33) and again in the *Tiers Livre,* where Heraclitus "the obscure" (σκοτεινός) is called a "grand scotiste et tenebreux philosophe" (*TL* 17:471). Ockham also is ridiculed in *Gargantua* (*G* 8:35). More to the point here, both Duns and Ockham are represented in the library of Saint-Victor, in a passage added in 1533: "*Barbouilamenta Scoti* . . . Les Marmitons de Olcam, à simple tonsure" (*P* 7:252 and 253).

A typical humanist view of England's role in corrupting Dialectic is to be found in Leonardo Bruni's *Dialogus de tribus vatibus florentinis,* written over a century earlier: "Quid est . . . in dialectica quod non *britannicis sophismatibus* conturbatum sit? Quid quod non ab illa vetere et vera disputandi via separatum et ad ineptias levitatesque traductum?" (p. 60, emphasis mine).

See also the end of Erasmus's *Paraclesis,* where the authority of various doctors of Theology is compared with that of the Gospels and the Epistles: "Quid Alberto magno, quid Alexandro, quid Thomae, quid Aegidio, quid Ricardo, quid *Occam* alii velint tribuere, per me sane cuique liberum erit: nolim enim cujusdam imminuere gloriam, aut cum inveteratis jam hominum studiis dimicare. Sint illa quantumvis erudita . . . haec tamen certissima fateantur opertet. . . . Quid, quaeso, simile in *Scoto?* (nolim id contumeliae causa dictum videri), quid simile in Thoma?" (*Opera* 5.143a–b, d, emphasis mine).

17. Original text of 1532. The words in brackets, which obviously enhance the correspondence between the two passages juxtaposed here, were inexplicably omitted from later editions beginning in 1534. The words "de geomantie," which survive through all later editions, do not appear in Saulnier's edition but figure in the 1532 variant recorded by Lefranc.

18. In an important article on this episode M. A. Screech, while providing a great deal of invaluable background information on Thaumaste's enigmas, unaccountably mistakes Thaumaste's vainglorious and impious challenge based on illegitimate, forbidden sciences for a "humble and discreet quest" for the Truth and consequently misses the point of the whole episode. See "The Meaning of Thaumaste."

19. It is interesting to note that although Pantagruel, as a humanist, cannot accept Thaumaste's reasons for proposing to debate without words, caritas requires that he accept the proposal itself. This he does with characteristic modesty, alleging a more acceptable reason for doing so: "Et loue grandement la maniere d'arguer que as proposée . . . car, ce faisant, toy et moy nous entendrons, et serons hors de ces frapements de mains que font ces badaulx sophistes quand on argue, alors qu'on est au bon de l'argument" (*P* 18:315). This reasoning is as far from Thaumaste's ("car les matieres sont tant ardues que les parolles humaines ne

seroyent suffisantes à les expliquer à mon plaisir" [314]) as is the spirit in which it generously casts the Englishman's vainglorious challenge.

20. In its original version the debate began not with a question by Thaumaste but more aggressively with a particularly crude offensive by Panurge: "Adoncques, tout le monde assistant, et speculant en bonne silence, Panurge, sans mot dire, leva les mains et en feist ung tel signe" (*P* 19:319 and 321 var.; Saulnier *P* 13:109–10).

21. A second verbal outburst by Thaumaste contributes nicely to this comic effect but has been misunderstood by recent readers. In uttering the words "Ha, j'entens . . . mais quoy?" (*P* 19:323) the cleric is not confessing that he hears or perceives something but does not know what it means. On the contrary, *entendre* means "understand, conceive, apprehend" and *quoy* is an expression of surprise or astonishment meaning "what say you? how say you to this? what would you thinke of it, or doe with it?" (Cotgrave), so that properly construed Thaumaste's utterance means: "Ah, yes, but how can that be? If what you say is true then how do you explain *x*?" The Englishman is confidently proposing to defeat a proposition he thinks he has understood perfectly, by demonstrating that it entails indefensible consequences. He is completely and comically caught up in the logic of the sublime argument that he believes he is carrying on with Panurge.

In a passage added in 1542 the representatives of all three Faculties of the old University—that is, those spectators who are being defended by the English dialectician and stand to be vindicated by his victory—are made to participate in this comedy of misinterpretation by disagreeing about the meaning of one of Panurge's most unambiguously obscene signs: "Les theologiens, medicins et chirurgiens penserent que . . . Les conseilliers, legistes et decretistes pensoient que . . ." (*P* 19:320–31).

22. The same verb appears occasionally in Acts to describe reactions to the miracles performed by the Apostles as well—most notably to the Apostles' speaking in tongues at Pentecost (2.7) and Peter's cure of a lame man (3.12), for example—and in Revelation to describe reactions to John's visions (13.3 and 17.6–8).

23. If, in addition to its primary function of alluding to a specific biblical situation and episode, the English cleric's name is meant to suggest the name "Thomas," as many have thought, the Thomas to which it points can obviously not be the English humanist and friend of Erasmus surnamed More. Given Thaumaste's function as a scribe and a Pharisee, a tempter of Christ and would-be avenger of the old guard, the only Thomas that fits would be the gothic sophist and theologian called Aquinas, if not the doubting disciple who presumed to test for himself the identity, and hence the divinity, of the resurrected Christ (Jn 20.24–29).

24. This pattern was equally rational in the original edition of the *Pantagruel,* where the longer chapter divisions resulted in the following pattern of alternation and eventual coincidence:

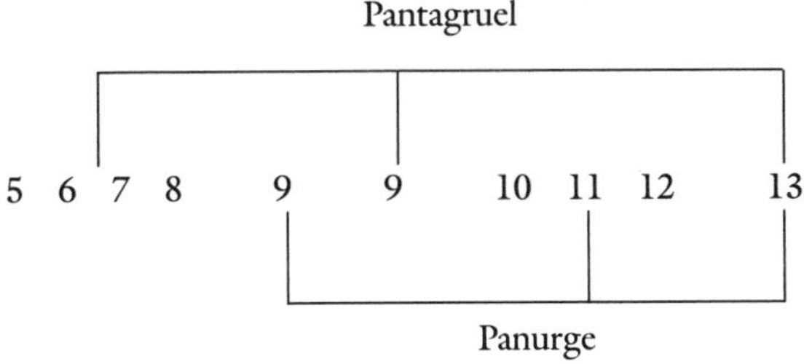

CHAPTER 5

ANARCHE IN UTOPIA

1. The specifically Utopian identity of Pantagruel's realm is maintained throughout the epic. The hero's mother is the "fille du roy des Amaurotes en Utopie" (*P* 2:228); Gargantua signs his letter to Pantagruel "De Utopie" (*P* 8:262); Pantagruel's native language is the "langaige de mon pays de Utopie" (*P* 9:269); the Dipsodes invade "le pays des Amaurotes" (*P* 23 title:335), lay waste "un grand pays de Utopie," and besiege "la grande ville des Amaurotes" (*P* 23:335); Pantagruel sails by the "royaulme de Achorie" to arrive at the port of "Utopie," which is a little over three leagues from "la ville des Amaurotes" (*P* 24:340); in his prayer before the duel with Loup Garou the hero mentions "toutes contrées tant de ce pays de Utopie que d'ailleurs, où je auray puissance et auctorité" (*P* 29:361); the victorious Pantagruel enters "la ville des Amaurotes" to liberate it (*P* 31 title:374); and Anarche becomes as fine a sauce-crier as was ever seen "en Utopie" (*P* 31:377).

In More's book the city of the Amauroti is the capital of Utopia, situated at the center of the island ("ea urbs . . . tanquam in umbilico terrae sita . . . prima, princepsque habetur," p. 112), and is the seat of the Utopian senate (pp. 112 and 116). An entire section of the *Utopia* is devoted to its description (2.2, pp. 116–122). The special significance of Achorie will be discussed at the end of this chapter.

All quotations from the *Utopia* in these pages are from volume 4 of *The Complete Works of St. Thomas More*, ed. Edward Surtz, S.J., and J. H. Hexter (New Haven: Yale University Press, 1965).

2. First among these is More's intimate friend Erasmus, who had dedicated his *Moriae encomium* to More. Others include Guillaume Budé, Jerome Busleiden, and Ulrich von Hutten. Letters of praise for the book and its author by Erasmus, Budé, and Busleiden are included among the parerga at the beginning of most early editions of the *Utopia*.

3. On these points see J. H. Hexter's introduction to the *Utopia*, pp. l–liv.

4. "Bellum utpote rem plane beluinam, nec ulli tamen beluarum formae in tam assiduo, atque homini est usu, summopere abominantur, contraque morem gen-

tium ferme omnium nihil aeque ducunt inglorium, atque petitam e bello gloriam. . . . Non temere capessunt [bellum] . . . nisi quo aut suos fines tueantur, aut amicorum terris, infusos hostes propulsent, aut populum quempiam tyrannide pressum, miserati (quod humanitatis gratia faciunt) suis viribus Tyranni iugo, et servitute liberent" (pp. 198–200).

5. Later textual evidence suggests that Rabelais knew this passage of the *Utopia* well. In the "parolles gelées" episode of the *Quart Livre,* the pilot Jamet Brayer mentions a "grosse et felonne bataille, entre les Arismapiens et les Nephelibates" (*QL* 56:206). This inscrutable allusion combines the antagonists of a war mentioned by Herodotus (between the *Arimaspians* and the griffins) and of a "bellum tam atrox" mentioned by Hythlodaeus (between the *Nephelogetae* and the Alaopolitae) a few lines below the passage quoted above (p. 200). See Berrong, "On the Possible Origin of the Name 'Nephelibates,'" pp. 93–94.

6. Page 132. See also p. 88, the "Achorii" (ἀ-χωρίον = without territory); p. 200, the "Alaopolitae" (ἀ-λαός πολίται = citizens of a city without people); and p. 116, the river "Anydrus" (ἀν-ὕδρος = without water).

7. This specifically political aspect of the *Pantagruel* will be promoted to the forefront of the *Gargantua* and rewritten in a more realistic mode. Thus in the later epic, Anarche, whose name identifies him as a purely symbolic antitype, is replaced by Picrochole, whose name suggests a psychological type, a "character" in the modern sense of the word, whose identity resides in his motivation rather than in his typological function. In keeping with this shift in focus the invasion, which is evoked only in the most schematic terms in the *Pantagruel,* is described in copious and realistic detail in the *Gargantua,* and its political moral is drawn by the characters themselves.

As a more explicit rewriting of the political dimension of the *Pantagruel,* the *Gargantua* provides an ideal gloss on many passages of its more oblique and allusive predecessor, as I shall occasionally point out in the following discussion.

8. "Quin hi quoque religioni Christianae, qui non assentiunt, neminem tamen absterrent, nullum oppugnant imbutum. . . . Utopus enim iam inde ab initio, quum accepisset incolas ante suum adventum de religionibus inter se assidue dimicasse . . . in primis sanxit, uti quam cuique religionem libeat sequi liceat, ut vero alios quoque in suam traducat, hactenus niti possit, uti placide, ac modeste suam rationibus astruat, non ut acerbe caeteras destruat, si suadendo non persuadeat, neque vim ullum adhibeat, et conviciis temperet, petulantius hac de re contendentem exilio, aut servitute mulctant. Haec Utopus instituit non respectu pacis modo quam assiduo certamine, atque inexpiabili odio funditus vidit everti, sed quod arbitratus est, uti sic decerneretur, ipsius etiam religionis interesse, de qua nihil est ausus temere definire, velut incertum habens, an varium ac multiplicem expetens cultum deus, aliud inspiret alii, certe vi ac minis exigere, ut quod tu verum credis idem omnibus videatur, hoc vero et insolens et ineptum censuit" (*Utopia,* "De religionibus Utopiensium," pp. 218–20).

9. "Ego nec in Turcas bellum temere suscipiendum esse censeo, primum illud

mecum reputans, Christi ditionem longe diversa via natam, propagatam, et constabilitam. Neque fortasse convenit aliis rationibus vindicari, quam quibus orta propagataque est. Et videmus hujusmodi bellorum praetextibus jam toties expilatam plebem Christianam, nec aliud quidquam actum. Jam si fidei negotium agitur, ea martyrum tolerantia, non militum copiis aucta illustrataque est: sin de imperio, de opibus, de possessionibus pugna est, etiam atque etiam videndum est nobis, ne res ea parum sapiat Christianismum. Quin ut nunc sunt fere, per quos hujusmodi bella geruntur, citius fiat, ut nos degeneremus in Turcas, quam illi per nos reddantur Christiani. Primum hoc agamus ut ipsi simus germane Christiani, deinde si visum erit, Turcas adoriamur" (*Opera* 4.610d–e).

10. This is a constantly recurring theme in Erasmus's moral works. See especially the long passage near the end of *Adagia* 4.1.1 ("Dulce bellum inexpertis") that begins: "Mihi sane ne hoc quidem adeo probandum videtur, quod subinde bellum molimur in Turcas" (*Opera* 2.966d–68c). This entire passage is little more than a detailed elaboration of the one quoted from the *Institutio* above. Cf. "si titulum crucisque tollas insigne, Turcae cum Turcis digladiamur" (966e); "In Turcas exspuimus, et ita nobis videmus pulchre Christiani, fortassis abominabiliores apud Deum, quam ipsi Turcae" (967a); "Minus mali est palam esse Turcam, aut Judaeum, quam hypocritam Christianum. . . . Malo Turcam ingenuum, quam fucatum Christianum" (968a); "Non haec dixerim, quod in totum damnem expeditionem in Turcas, si nos ultro impetant, sed ut bellum, cui Christum auctorem praeteximus, animis Christianis Christique praesidiis geramus" (968b). Cf. also, from the *Querela Pacis,* "Si cupimus Turcas ad Christi religionem adducere, prius ipsi simus Christiani" (*Opera* 4.640f); and from the epistle to Paul Volzius, which served in most sixteenth-century editions as a preface to the *Enchiridion:* "Quod si hic non adsit animus, citius futurum est, ut nos in Turcas degeneremus quam ut Turcas in nostras partes pertrahamus" (*Opera* 3^1.339a, and *Epistolae,* ed. Allen, #858, 3.365).

11. In direct opposition to the popes and princes who had never ceased, since the fall of Constantinople in 1453, to call for crusades against the Infidel, Erasmus continually used the Turks as an object lesson to Christians, calling on the latter to reform Christianity so as to attract the Turks to the Christian faith rather than using that faith as a pretext for unchristian warfare, and exhorting them to restore peace among Christian princes so as not to remain divided and therefore vulnerable. In deliberately replacing the Turks with Anarche's Dipsodes as the typological antagonist of the Christian prince, the *Pantagruel* is entirely Erasmian.

Given this fact it is interesting to note that the neighboring Dipsodes are nevertheless associated, occasionally and indirectly, with the typical epic Infidel. The lone survivor of the 660 attacking knights in chapter 25, for example, is "monté sur un cheval Turq" (*P* 25:344); Anarche's army includes "baschatz" (*P* 28:355; cf. *P* 14:290–91); and Loup Garou and his 300 giants utter typical pseudo-Islamic curses: "par Mahom" (*P* 29:360), "par Golfarin, nepveu de Mahon" (*P* 29:363), "Mahon! Mahon! Mahon!" (*P* 29:364; cf. *P* 14:291). It would seem that the conventions of medieval epic are so strong as to require these sure signs of typological opposition to Christianity, even in enemies who are not in fact infidels in the usual Crusaders' sense of the word.

12. Cf. Plutarch, *Apophthegmata laconica,* Agesilaus 29–30 (*Moralia* 210e–f), and Erasmus, *Apophthegmata* 1.30 (*Opera* 4.98d). This passage is a virtual translation of Erasmus's Latin version: "Rursus alii cuidam percontanti, quam ob causam Sparta non cingeretur moenibus? ostendit cives armatos, 'Hi,' inquiens, 'sunt Spartanae civitatis moenia': significans Respublicas nullo munimento tutiores esse, quam *virtute* civium" (emphasis mine). The only peculiarity of Rabelais's text as a translation (aside from the characteristic reduplication by which a single Latin term is rendered by two or more French equivalents) is the apparently gratuitous addition of the metaphor of a wall of bones: "Il n'est muraille que de os." This unauthorized metaphor is crucial, for it alone will provide Panurge with the pretext for his prolix response to "Agesilaus."

13. "Bellum utpote rem plane beluinam . . . summopere abominantur. . . . eoque licet assidue militari sese disciplina exerceant, neque id viri modo, sed foeminae quoque, statis diebus, ne ad bellum sint, quum exigat usus, inhabiles" (*Utopia,* pp. 198–200). It should be noted, however, that the cities of Utopia are also well fortified: "Murus altus, ac latus oppidum [Amaurotum] cingit, turribus, ac propugnaculis frequens, arida fossa, sed alta, lataque ac veprium sepibus impedita tribus ab lateribus circumdat moenia, quarto flumen ipsum pro fossa est" (*Utopia,* pp. 118–20).

14. Because *Il principe* was written in 1513 and was circulated widely in manuscript before its posthumous publication in 1532 it is possible (though by no means certain) that Rabelais knew the work before undertaking to write the *Pantagruel* and could rely on his readers to know it at least by reputation. This is a question that need not concern us here, however, because the most important point for our purposes is simply that Machiavelli's transvalorization of the lion and fox image seems to presuppose the reader's familiarity with its use in classical political literature, and thus to indicate that a lion and a fox together would indeed have been recognized in the sixteenth century as emblems of a *political* commonplace.

For later testimony to the currency of the image, see Shakespeare's *Coriolanus,* in which the title character derides the commoners' uselessness in war, snearing: "He that trusts to you, / Where he should find you lions, finds you hares; / Where foxes, geese" (1.1.165–67).

I am grateful to my colleague Timothy Hampton for alerting me to the ubiquity of the fox-lion topos in sixteenth-century political writing. See Hampton's penetrating analysis of the topos in chapter 2 of his *Writing from History: The Rhetoric of Exemplarity in Renaissance Literature.*

15. Plutarch, *Vita Lysandri* 7.3–4, quoted from the 1559 edition of Amyot's *Les vies des hommes illustres Grecs et Romains* 1.306b–c.

Lysander's famous quip was proverbial in the Renaissance, well known as such not only to the educated elite (see Erasmus, *Adagia* 3.5.81) but to the illiterate as well, thanks to a popular saying current in Rabelais's day: "coudre la peau du regnard à celle du lion," which meant, according to Cotgrave, "to proceed both craftily, and violently; both by stratagems and strength; or to attempt that by craft which he cannot obtain by force."

16. Erasmus, *Apophthegmata* 1.91 (*Opera* 4.129e). Cf. Plutarch, *Apophthegmata laconica,* Lysander 3 (*Moralia* 229b). See also the preceding apophthegma in which Lysander is identified as an "egregius simulandi artifex."

17. In the best discussion to date of this episode Raymond La Charité argues that Panurge's fable is emblematic of the whole work in that the relationship it establishes between the lion and the fox is exactly analogous to that between Pantagruel and Panurge throughout the rest of the *Pantagruel* (*Recreation,* chap. 5, pp. 93–115). The present discussion will, I hope, corroborate this important insight and reveal the full measure of its importance.

18. Cf. "Haud facile dictu est, astutiores instruendis insidijs, an cautiores ad vitandas sient. . . . Nam si nimium sese sentiunt, aut numero, aut loco premi, tunc aut noctu, agmine silente, castra movent, aut aliquo stratagemate eludunt" (p. 212).

19. This is yet another of the many aspects of the *Pantagruel* that will be spelled out more explicitly and more prosaically in the *Gargantua.* The letter by which Grandgousier summons his son back home from Paris to defend his realm against the invading armies of Picrochole ends with the following admonition: "L'exploict sera faict à moindre effusion de sang que sera possible, et, si possible est, par engins plus expediens, cauteles et ruzes de guerre, nous saulverons toutes les ames et les envoyerons joyeux à leurs domiciles" (*G* 29:116).

20. It is perhaps significant that at the height of the climactic battle of the *Pantagruel,* Alcofrybas alludes once again to the classical prototype of the epic hero, this time to describe not Pantagruel, but Pantagruel's imperialist enemies. Seeing the Dipsodes' army drowned, Anarche's giants save their king by carrying him out of the flooded camp on their shoulders "comme fist Enéas son pere Anchises de la conflagration de Troye" (*P* 29:359). This unexpected comparison serves, among other things, to draw attention to the crucial difference between the relatively bloodless, Utopian victory with which the *Pantagruel* climaxes and the slaughters that mark the end of the *Iliad* and the *Aeneid.*

21. As in the case of Pantagruel's genealogy in chapter 1, Abel Lefranc saw in this episode a destructive, rationalistic parody of Scripture and of the Christian faith (Lefranc, ed., *Oeuvres,* vol. 3, pp. xlvii–l, and *Rabelais,* pp. 186–91), while Lucien Febvre argued for the innocence of the episode by pointing out that the "resurrection" of Epistemon by Panurge is virtually identical to the resuscitation of Richard by Maugis in chapter 11 of *Les quatre fils Aymon* (*L'Incroyance,* pp. 196–203). Like the dispute over the genealogy, the dispute over the resurrection is framed in such a way as to conceal the real importance of the episode.

22. In its original form the catalog of some forty-four heroes began with the

same three names mentioned by Lucian in the passage of the *Menippus* referred to above, except that the cobbler Philip of Macedon is replaced by his son, Alexander: "Je veis: Alexandre le Grand qui repetassoit de vieilles chausses, et ainsi gaignoit sa pauvre vie. Xerces cryoit la moustarde. Darius estoit cureur de retraictz" (ed. Saulnier 20:160; cf. *Menippus* 17). In later editions this direct borrowing was obscured by the interpolation of eighteen new names between those of Xerxes and Darius, as well as the addition of twenty-three other names inserted at various points throughout the catalog.

23. Most of these names were added in 1534. Of the many Romans cited here, for example, only Romulus, Scipio, Pompey, Caesar, Octavian, and Nero are mentioned in the first edition of the *Pantagruel.*

24. Both Nicholas III and Boniface VIII had already been consigned to hell more than two centuries before Epistemon's visit by Dante, who placed them in the *bolgia* of the simoniacs (*Inferno* 19).

25. Many of these popes are condemned in various works of Erasmus, but none so frequently or so zealously as Julius II. See especially the dialogue *Julius exclusus e coelis,* commonly attributed to Erasmus by his contemporaries, in which Julius demands admission into heaven but is sent straight to hell by Peter, who is disgusted by his unworthy successor's account of endless military campaigns against the Christian princes of Europe. Near the end of his "apology" Julius brags that with "sexcentis litteris non absque ingenio scriptis tandem involui principes bello omnium gravissimo. . . . Hi igitur cum suo morem gererent animo, tamen honestissimum titulum acceperunt a nobis, ut quo maiorem cladem inferrent populo Christiano, hoc religiosius viderentur Ecclesiam Dei protegere. . . . Iam vero longum fuerit explicare sigillatim, quibus artibus eos principes ad tam periculosum bellum excitarim in Christianos, quos nullus unquam Pontifex vel in Turcas potuit excitare" (*Erasmi opuscula,* pp. 112 and 14). For a similar portrait of Julius in Rabelais, cf. *QL* 50:187–88.

26. As in Lucian the theme of political power is doubled by the theme of material wealth in this episode. Cf., for example, *Menippus* 12, where Minos is said to judge most harshly "those who were swollen with pride because of their wealth and power" ("τῶν ἐπὶ πλούτοις τε καὶ ἀρχαῖς τετυφωμένων"), and Epistemon's account of the fate of usurers in hell (*P* 30:373). But in Lucian politics is entirely subordinated to the theme of inequality of wealth and station. The injustices that concern Menippus are those done by the rich ("οἱ πλούσιοι") who "plunder, oppress, and thoroughly despise the poor" ("ἁρπάζοντες καὶ βιαζόμενοι καὶ πάντα τρόπον τῶν πενήτων καταφρονοῦντες" [*Menippus* 20]). The four "kings and satraps" he mentions by name are offered only as egregious examples of the economic inequity among mortals (*Menippus* 17). The same is true of Rabelais's other Lucianic source for the episode, *The Downward Journey.*

In adapting his sources to his own purposes Rabelais inverted this relation between the social and the political aspects of inequality. Epistemon mentions usurers only as an afterthought, and at the request of Pantagruel, while expanding Menippus's short list of kings and satraps into an overwhelming index of notorious imperialists who are damned not for their wealth per se but for their service to the cause of empire and their abuse of political power.

27. That the *Aeneid* is sometimes understood today as undermining the imperialist ideal it purports to glorify, and that the *Iliad,* with its sustained sympathy for the Trojans and moving conclusion describing the funeral rites for Hector, reads to a modern like a fictionalized diatribe against wars of aggression, need not concern us here. The important point for our purposes is the traditional view of epic as an apology for empire. According to this view, the *Aeneid* glorifies Augustus's Rome as unconditionally as the Carolingian epics of the Middle Ages glorify the Crusades and the triumph of Christendom.

28. "Achoriorum populi . . . qui quum olim bellum gessissent, ut regi suo aliud obtinerent regnum, quod affinitatis antiquae causa sibi contendebat haereditate deberi, consequuti tandem id, ubi viderunt nihilo sibi minus esse molestiae in retinendo, quam in quaerendo pertulerunt, verum assidua pullulare semina, vel internae rebellionis, vel externae incursionis, in deditos ita semper aut pro illis, aut contra pugnandum, nunquam dari facultatem dimittendi exercitus. . . . Cum viderent alioqui tantis malis nullum finem fore, inito tandem consilio, regi suo humanissime fecerunt optionem retinendi utrius regni vellet. . . . Proinde avitum regnum coleret, ornaret quantum posset, et faceret quam florentissimum. Amet suos et ametur a suis, cum his una vivat, imperetque suaviter, atque alia regna valere sinat, quando id quod nunc ei contigisset, satis amplum superque esset" (pp. 88–90).

As the particulars of Hythlodaeus's anecdote make plain, the king of the Achorii functions not only as an example to the king of France but as a thinly veiled figure of Charles VIII, Louis XII, and François I themselves. This identification is reinforced by the geographical situation of the kingdom of the Achorii, which lies opposite Utopia to the southeast ("Achoriorum populi, Utopiensium insulae ad Euronoton oppositi")—that is, in exactly the same relation to Utopia that France lies in relation to England.

29. Lefranc, *Rabelais,* pp. 361–72. Nicole Aronson's well-founded reservations concerning this thesis apropos of the *Gargantua* and the *Tiers Livre* apply equally well to the *Pantagruel.* See *Les idées politiques de Rabelais,* especially pp. 13–16, 131, and 139–41.

30. At about the same time that Rabelais first published the *Pantagruel* Erasmus was contriving to suggest something similar by dedicating each of his *Paraphrases* of the Gospels to one of the four great Christian princes of Europe. Having dedicated Matthew to Charles V in 1522, John to the Archduke Ferdinand of Austria and Luke to Henri VIII in 1533, he dedicated Mark to François I in 1533. His sole purpose in doing so, as he explains to François in his dedicatory letter, is to encourage peace among them. "Atque utinam," he exclaims, "quam congruenter nomina vestra jungit Codex Euangelicus, tam concorditer pectora vestra conglutinet spiritus Euangelicus!" (*Opera* 7.149–50). This entire epistle provides an interesting and pertinent gloss on the political dimension of the *Pantagruel.*

CHAPTER 6

THE NEW ORDER IN UTOPIA

1. This passage is sometimes misconstrued to mean that Pantagruel intends to exterminate the "papelars et faulx prophetes" as "abuseurs" (see, e.g., Screech, *Evangélisme,* 88–89). Nothing could be farther from the meaning of the text than such clumsy intimations of an Inquisition. Pantagruel specifically states that it is the "abus" that he will exterminate, not the "abuseurs." And since these abuses are all said to originate in "constitutions humaines et inventions depravées"—that is, in practices, institutions, and articles of faith not authorized by the Bible, which is the single authority in all matters of faith—then "extermination" will consist in nothing more drastic than making that single authority fully and completely known to all, which is precisely what Pantagruel states he will do: "Je feray prescher ton sainct Evangile purement, simplement et entierement, si que les abus . . . seront . . . exterminez." Far from exterminating, exiling, or even silencing the doctors of a corrupt Church, Pantagruel would simply correct their error by confuting it with the words of the sacred text they have chosen to ignore.

2. Eusebius, *De vita Constantini* 1.26–29, and *Historia Ecclesiastica* 9.9. Throughout the Middle Ages and Renaissance the *Historia* was a far more important source for the episode of the sign than was the *Vita,* in spite of the fact that the text of the *Historia* contains no direct reference to the sign. This is because the *Historia* was generally known not in Eusebius's original Greek text but in the extremely free Latin translation by Rufinus (345–410), whose version relates the episode of the sign in even greater detail than Eusebius does in the *Vita.* At the moment of the "miracle" (τὰ παράδοξα) of Maxentius's virtual self-defeat by drowning in the Tibur, which Eusebius goes on at laborious lengths to compare to that of Pharoah's drowning in the Red Sea (*Historia* 9.9.4–8), Rufinus interpolates the following passage, in which the more manifest miracle of the sign is compared to the one vouchsafed to Saul-Paul at the moment of his conversion: "Etenim cum religiosissimus Imperator Constantinus, Constantii aeque moderatissimi et egregii principis filius, adversum Maxentium urbis Romae tyrannum bellum pararet, atque exercitum duceret, erat quidem iam tunc Christianae religionis fautor, verique dei venerator, nondum tamen (ut est solemne nostris initiari) *signum dominicae passionis* acceperat. Cum igitur anxius, et multa secum de imminentis belli necessitate pervolens iter ageret, atque ad coelum saepius oculos elevaret, et inde sibi divinum deprecaretur auxilium, videt per soporem ad Orientis partem in coelo *signum crucis* igneo fulgore rutilare. Cumque tanto visu fuisset exterritus, ac novo perturbaretur aspectu, adstare sibi videt angelos, dicentes: 'Constantine ἐν τούτῳ νίκα,' id est: 'in hoc vince.' Tum vero laetus redditus, et de victoria iam securus, *signum crucis quod in coelo viderat,* in sua fronte designat et ita coelitus invitatus ad fidem, non mihi illo videtur inferior, cui de coelo similiter dictum est: 'Saule Saule quid me persequeris? ego sum Iesus Nazarenus' [Acts 9.4–5]: nisi quia hic non adhuc persequens, sed iam consequens invitatur. Exin *signum quod in coelo sibi fuerat demonstratum,* in militaria vexilla

transformat, ac Labarum quem dicunt, in *speciem dominicae crucis* exaptat, et ita armis vexillisque religionis instructus, adversum impiorum arma proficiscitur. Sed in dextera sua manu *signum* nihilominus *crucis* ex auro fabrefactum habuisse perhibetur" (ed. B. Rhenanus [1523], p. 207; ed. Schwartz-Mommsen, 2.827–29, emphasis mine).

3. Parallels with the *Historia* are particularly striking here. Constantine, like Pantagruel, is primarily concerned with avoiding bloodshed, ends the critical confrontation with the death of only the most guilty, is explicitly compared in his success to Moses crossing the Red Sea, and is received by the liberated citizens with unbounded joy: "Tum vero laeti omnes cum coniugibus ac liberis, Senatus Populusque Romanus ingenti peste liberati, et iugo tyrannicae immanitatis exempti, Constantinum velut salutis auctorem ac restitutorem libertatis excipiunt" (*Historia* 9.9.9, ed. Rhenanus [1523], p. 208; ed. Schwartz-Mommsen, 2.831–33). Cf. "Sortirent au devant de luy tous les habitans de la ville, en bon ordre, et en grande pompe triumphale, avecques une liesse divine, le conduirent en la ville: et furent faictz beaulx feuz de joye par toute la ville" (*P* 31:374).

4. Mark's version suggests this half-conversion even more strongly by having the scribe agree enthusiastically with Jesus' answer to his question. Jesus, seeing that the scribe has "answered wisely," then responds: "You are not far from the kingdom of God" (Mk 12.32–34).

5. At the beginning of the *Gargantua* Alcofrybas will allude again to the inevitable eschatological inversion of hierarchies that is so fundamental to the Christian idea of an afterlife, though in a far more comic and self-ironic way, as a consolation for his own obscurity and poverty in the present: "Et, pour vous donner à entendre de moy qui parle, je cuyde que soye descendu de quelque riche roy ou prince au temps jadis; car oncques ne veistes homme qui eust plus grande affection d'estre roy et riche que moy. . . . Mais en ce je me reconforte que en l'aultre monde je le seray, voyre plus grand que de present me l'auseroye soubhaitter" (*G* 1:12).

6. This much-discussed parallelism is signaled from the very start by a striking similarity in their opening paragraphs: "Quelque jour que Pantagruel se pourmenoit après soupper avecques ses compaignons, par la porte dont l'on va à Paris, il rencontra un escholier tout jolliet qui venoit par icelluy chemin, et après qu'ilz se furent saluez, luy demanda: 'Mon amy, d'ont viens tu à ceste heure?' " (*P* 6:244, var.; Saulnier *P* 6:31–32). Cf. "Un jour Pantagruel, se pourmenant hors la ville, vers l'abbaye Sainct Antoine, devisant et philosophant avecques ses gens et aulcuns escholiers, rencontra un homme beau de stature et elegant en tous lineamens du corps. . . . Et ainsi qu'il fut au droict d'entre eulx, il luy demanda: 'Mon amy, je vous prie que un peu veuillez icy arrester et me respondre à ce que vous demanderay. . . . Qui estes vous? Dont venez vous? Où allez vous?' " (*P* 9:263–64).

7. Another, corollary difference between the Limousin and Panurge is that whereas the sated and self-satisfied schoolboy vaunts his own holiness by presumptuously claiming to practice the Great Commandment (vaingloriously pindarized as "je dilige et redame mes proximes") in the process of justifying and even

boasting about his own uncharitable behavior, the starving and pathetic Panurge speaks only of his own wretchedness and evokes the Great Commandment (in foreign but legitimate, natural languages) only to implore Pantagruel to act on charity in this moment of extreme need.

8. Anarche's punishment at the hands of Panurge is often compared to that of Marquet, the "fouaciers," and Picrochole's advisers and generals, who at the conclusion of the *Gargantua* are similarly made to ply a more humble, honest, and useful trade. But the significance of Anarche's demotion is entirely different from theirs. Whereas the instigators of Picrochole's unjust invasion are simply made to serve the cause of enlightenment, which they had formerly hindered, by pulling the royal printing presses (*G* 51:186–87), Anarche is deliberately made to signify, and to anticipate, the inverted order of the kingdom of God. Even in their points of greatest similarity the *Gargantua* remains characteristically realistic and exemplary, the *Pantagruel* characteristically symbolic and emblematic.

9. "Secularized" in the strict sense that Pantagruel's city of God is founded on the *second* article of the Great Commandment and is therefore concerned primarily with an evangelical community of redeemed men *in this world,* whereas the city of God imagined by Augustine, being founded on the *first* article of the Great Commandment, is principally concerned with the ultimate reconciliation of man and God *in heaven.* This difference is entirely consistent with the typological design of the *Pantagruel,* as opposed to that of *De civitate dei.* Whereas Rabelais's epic turns on the opposition between hatred and love between brothers, Augustine's treatise turns on the opposition between self-love and the love of God: "Fecerunt itaque civitates duas amores duo, terrenam scilicet amor sui usque ad contemptum Dei, caelestem vero amor Dei usque ad contemptum sui" (see *De civ. dei* 14.28).

10. Chapters 32 and 33 must be viewed as the concluding chapters of the epic in spite of the presence of a subsequent chapter 34, because the latter is clearly set apart from the narrative proper as an epilogue in which the narrator returns to the situation and the tone of the prologue: "Or, Messieurs, vous avez ouy un commencement de l'Histoire horrificque de mon maistre et seigneur Pantagruel. Icy je feray fin à ce premier livre" (*P* 34:385). In the original edition of the *Pantagruel* this epilogue was much shorter and did not constitute a separate chapter but was merely appended to the final chapter of the narrative (numbered 23). In the definitive edition the expanded, detached epilogue works together with the prologue to frame the entire epic that begins in chapter 1 with Pantagruel's origin and genealogy and ends in chapter 33 with his disease and cure.

11. Bakhtin, *Rabelais and His World,* chaps. 5 and 6. For a powerful confutation of Bakhtin's totally undocumented claims concerning the popular body, see Stephens, *Giants,* chapter 1 ("Giants and the Representation of Culture: The Modern Myth of Rabelais's Folklore"). A somewhat more useful approach than Bakhtin's to the "popular" motif of the world inside a giant's (Gargantua's) mouth is found in Antonioli, "Le motif de l'avalage."

12. For a full treatment of these ideas see Kantorowicz, *The King's Two Bodies,*

chap. 5 (esp. pp. 207–32), and Hale, *The Body Politic,* chap. 2. Quotations from Seneca, Gratian, Lucas de Penna, and Matthaeus de Afflictis are cited from Kantorowicz, pp. 214–16, nn. 60, 65–66, and pp. 439–40, n. 403.

13. See Lubac, *Corpus mysticum;* Kantorowicz, pp. 194–206; and Hale, pp. 32–39. As Kantorowicz shows throughout his study, there was a constant and powerful mutual influence between the ecclesiological and political representations of a mystical body, such that the pope eventually adopted all the symbols of imperial power and the emperor all those of the papacy.

14. "Caro mea est, frater est in Christo. Quod in membrum confertur, nonne in universum corpus redundat, atque inde in caput? Omnes sumus invicem membra" (*Opera* 5:45c).

"Parricidium vocatur, si frater occidat fratrem. At Christianus conjunctior Christiano, quam ullus germanus germano. . . . Quam absurdum est, eos pene continenter inter se belligerari, quos una domus habet Ecclesia, qui ejusdem corporis membra communi capite gloriantur, nempe Christo. . . . Unum praeceptum Christus appellavit suum, nempe caritatis" (*Opera* 2.959c–d).

15. A third use of the corporate metaphor is relevant here. In Xenophon's *Memorabilia* Socrates attempts to reconcile two feuding brothers by enjoining the younger of the two to challenge his older brother in a contest of kind words and deeds. His clinching argument is the following: "You two are in the same situation as a pair of hands which, though the god made them for assisting one another, were freed from their duty and turned to hindering one another, or a pair of feet which, though made by divine providence for cooperating with one another, neglected their duty and began tripping each other up. Would it not be stupid and disastrous to use for harm things made for help? Now it seems to me that the god made brothers for greater mutual aid than hands or feet or eyes or anything else he fashioned in pairs for men. For if it should be necessary for hands to work simultaneously on things more than a span apart, they could not do it; feet could not arrive in one stride at things even a span away; eyes, though they may seem to reach the most distant things, cannot simultaneously see even closer things if one is in front and one behind. But a pair of brothers who are friends, even when they are very far apart, act simultaneously for the mutual aid of one another" (2.3.18–19).

16. An earlier episode has already alluded to the fact that Pantagruel's subjects are by definition members of his body politic. On first arriving in Utopie, just before taking up arms against the enemy, Pantagruel asks his companions: "Estez vous deliberez de vivre et mourir avecques moy?" to which they reply, "Seigneur, ouy, . . . tenez vous asseuré de nous comme de vos doigtz propres" (*P* 24:341).

17. As the symbol of the intelligible (as opposed to the visible), the sun is the most important element in Plato's image of the cave. It alone distinguishes the world outside the cave from the world inside. From the peasant's account of the worlds inside and outside Pantagruel's mouth it appears that the only essential difference between them is, similarly, such "belles besoignes" as the sun and the moon.

The word *sun* (ἥλιος) occurs four times in the brief exposition at the beginning of book 7 of the *Republic* (515e, 516b [twice], 516e). The moon is mentioned once (516b).

18. According to the same metaphor, "surgery"—that is, the excision of an entire group or class of citizens—was considered only as a last resort. See the passage from d'Aubigné's *Les tragiques* quoted earlier in this chapter.

Although the metaphor of disease was far less common in an ecclesiological context, Augustine could nevertheless distinguish between the perfection of Christ and the imperfection of his Church by stating that while the members of the body of Christ frequently need human correction, the head never does: "Non enim Christi ipsius, quod est caput ecclesiae, possent inveniri ulla peccata, quae opus esset humanis correptionibus servata misericordia divinitus coherceri; sed in eius corpore ac membris, quod populus eius est" (*De civ. dei* 17.9).

19. The episode of Pantagruel's illness is actually a kind of comical inversion of the fable told by Menenius Agrippa. In Menenius's version the members refuse to provide food and drink for the stomach, with the result that the stomach cannot perform its services for the other members. In Alcofrybas's version it is the stomach that fails to function, with the result that the other members cannot perform their services for it (Pantagruel can neither eat nor drink). Either way, the whole suffers the consequences of a failure in the parts.

Toward the end of the sixteenth century Agrippa d'Aubigné continued to follow the Menenius Agrippa tradition closely by identifying the "financiers" and "justiciers" of France as the swollen stomach of a melancholic, hydropic giant (*Les tragiques* 1.131–70). For another, more original treatment of the stomach as an antisocial organ in Rabelais, see the episode of "messere Gaster" in the *Quart Livre* (*QL* 57–62).

20. In the "louange des presteurs et debteurs" of the *Tiers Livre* Panurge will develop this same metaphor at far greater length as he describes in detail the pernicious effects of sabotage, as opposed to the beneficial effects of mutual aid, among the members of bodies both individual and politic (*TL* 3:419–20 and 4:421–24).

EPILOGUE

1. See "La Musagnoeomachie" (1550), lines 205–19, in Du Bellay, *Recueils lyriques de 1550 à 1553,* pp. 12–13, and especially the first six lines of the "Discours sur la louange de la vertu et sur les divers erreurs des hommes, à Salmon Macrin" (1552): "Bien que ma Muse petite / Ce *doulx-utile* n'immite / Qui si *doctement* escrit, / Ayant premier en la France / Contre la saige ignorance / Faict renaistre Democrit . . ." (*Recueils lyriques,* p. 145, emphasis mine). Horace's original formulation of the ideal is the following: "Aut *prodesse* volunt aut *delectare* poetae / Aut simul et *iucunda* et *idonea* dicere *vitae.* / . . . Centuriae seniorum agitant expertia frugis, / Celsi praetereunt austera poemata Ramnes: / Omne tulit

punctum qui miscuit *utile dulci,* / Lectorem *delectando* pariterque *monendo*" (*AP* 333–34 and 341–44, emphasis mine).

2. In stating this fundamental fact of Renaissance life Richard Berrong, following Peter Burke, has spoken pertinently of the "biculturalism" of Renaissance humanists (*Rabelais and Bakhtin,* pp. 13–16). The phrase is apt provided we understand it correctly. As Burke and Berrong make clear, humanists became "bicultural" not by learning two foreign cultures—one humanist and one popular—but by adding a foreign culture (classical or biblical) to their native, common culture, much in the same way that a person becomes bilingual not by learning two languages but by adding a foreign language to his native tongue.

3. As the first reader to take the popular elements in Rabelais seriously and to build a coherent interpretation around them, Mikhail Bakhtin rendered an inestimable service to Rabelais studies. What makes his influential reading so misleading and ultimately harmful, however, is that although he accurately describes certain functions of so-called popular culture in the *Pantagruel,* he steadfastly refuses to consider those functions (or perhaps was prevented by Stalinist orthodoxy from considering them) in terms of the particular historical and cultural milieu in which they were designed to be understood, and consequently misinterprets them completely. "Carnival" and "popular culture" are indeed the positive and revolutionary forces that Bakhtin claims they are, but not for the anachronistic (and entirely undocumented) reasons he asserts. They exalt the people and overturn "official culture" not in the spirit of some romantic, nineteenth-century notion of class struggle but in the specifically messianic, anti-Pharisaical spirit that Karl Marx's forebears—Moses, Isaiah, Jesus, and Paul—had spelled out in texts that formed the very core of sixteenth-century official culture. By situating Rabelais's books in the wrong cultural context (and in an ahistorical, purely imaginary context at that) Bakhtin makes his truest and potentially most useful observations even more misleading than false ones would have been.

4. "Itaque miser ego lecturus Tullium ieiunabam. . . . Si quando in memet reversus prophetam legere coepissem, sermo horrebat incultus et, quia lumen caecis oculis non videbam, non oculorum putabam culpam esse, sed solis. . . . Subito raptus in spiritu ad tribunal iudicis pertrahor. . . . Interrogatus condicionem Christianum me esse respondi: et ille, qui residebat: 'Mentiris,' ait, 'Ciceronianus es, non Christianus; "ubi thesaurus tuus, ibi et cor tuum'" [Mt 6.21]. Ilico obmutui et inter verbera—nam caedi me iusserat—conscientiae magis igne torquebar" (*Epistulae* 22.30.1–4, vol. 1, pp. 189–90).

5. "Visa est mihi indigna, quam Tullianae dignitati compararem. Tumor enim meus refugiebat modum eius, et acies mea non penetrabat interiora eius" (*Confessions* 3.5). "Iam ergo abs te didiceram, nec eo debere videri aliquid verum dici, quia eloquenter dicitur, nec eo falsum, quia incomposite sonant signa labiorum" (*Confessions* 5.6).

But Augustine goes on to say that inelegant expression does not necessarily guarantee the truth of a proposition either, nor elegant expression its falseness:

"Rursus nec ideo verum, quia inpolite enuntiatur, nec ideo falsum, quia splendidus sermo est." His point is that there is no connection between eloquence and truth, either positive or negative: "Sed perinde esse sapientiam et stultitiam, sicut sunt cibi utiles et inutiles; verbis autem ornatis et inornatis, sicut vasis urbanis et rusticanis utrosque cibos posse ministrari."

6. Rabelais was capable of writing both eloquent Ciceronian Latin and elegant, elevated French (not to mention good Demosthenian Greek). His Latin and French correspondence shows that he did so naturally when writing in his own name and voice. The adoption of an uncharacteristically low, vulgar style in the narration of his epics was therefore a deliberate decision based on the nature of what he had to say.

7. "Verbis apertissimis et humillimo genere loquendi se cunctis praebens, et exercens intentionem eorum, qui non sunt leves corde; ut exciperet omnes populari sinu, et per angusta foramina paucos ad te traiceret" (*Confessions* 6.5).

The appropriateness of a low, vulgar style to the message of the Bible and particularly of the New Testament was a commonplace in the sixteenth century. Typical formulations are the following: "Pleraque sunt in Euangelicis Litteris à vulgo sumta. Nec id indignum Christo, quin potius vel maxime congruebat, ut quemadmodum assumto corpore, velut unus quilibet è nobis esse voluit, ita sermonibus quam maxime familiaribus uteretur, quo nostram humilitatem modis omnibus ad suam proveheret sublimitatem" (Erasmus, *Adagia* 3.10.91 ["Culicem colant"], *Opera* 2.948a–b); "Quinetiam videmus Euangelii arcana nobis tradita esse verbis impolitis, et è media indoctorum plebe desumptis, ne quid inde hominum eloquentiae tribueretur" (Sebastianus Castalio, "Praefatio" to his Latin translation of the Bible, fol. a2); "Cela n'a point esté faict sans une grande providence de Dieu, que les hauts secretz du royaulme céleste nous ayent esté baillés soubz paroles contemtibles sans grand'éloquence; de peur que s'ilz eussent esté fondez et enrichiz d'éloquence, les iniques eussent calumnié qu'en icelle toute sa vertu eust esté colloquée. Or maintenant, puis que telle simplicité rude et quasi agreste nous esmeut en plus grande reverence, que toute la faconde des Rhetoriciens du monde, que pouvons nous estimer, sinon que l'Escriture contient en soy telle vertu de verité qu'elle n'a aucun besoing d'artifice de paroles?" (Calvin, *Institution de la religion chrestienne,* chap. 1, "De la congnoissance de Dieu," vol. 1, pp. 68–69).

8. For a fuller demonstration of the point that the prologue to the *Gargantua* functions as an evangelical *captatio benevolentiae* that proposes caritas rather than simple *allegoresis* as a fundamental principle of interpretation, see Duval, "Interpretation and the 'Doctrine Absconce.'"

9. By a similar paradox today's stylists, for whom the language and tone of the *Pantagruel* are more essential than any ideological content, frequently come closer to the most profound meaning of the work than do the Rabelaisants, for whom popular humor is essentially irrelevant to its serious meanings. But as I hope to have suggested, neither stylists nor Rabelaisants can be considered completely adequate readers of the *Pantagruel,* because both accept the validity of distinctions

that the work itself rejects and condemns. The only truly valid reading is one in which distinctions between style and content, medium and message, humor and seriousness, humanistic erudition and popular culture, are irrelevant, being subsumed by the all-encompassing design of this remarkably coherent, self-consistent work.

10. "An non mirificus quidam Silenus fuit Christus? . . . Si summam Sileni faciem intuearis, quid juxta popularem aestimationem abjectius, aut contemptius? Tenues et obscuri parentes, domus humilis: ipse pauper et pauculos, et pauperculos habuit discipulos: non è Magnatum palatiis, non è Pharisaeorum cathedris, non è Philosophorum scholis, sed à telonio et retibus ascitos. Tum vita, quam à voluptatibus omnibus aliena, per famem, per lassitudinem, per convicia, per ludibria, ad crucem denique pervenit. . . . Hujusmodi Sileni fuerunt Apostoli, pauperes, inculti, illitterati, ignobiles, imbecilles, abjecti, omnibus omnium contumeliis expositi, irrisi, invisi, execrabiles, ac pene publicum orbis simul et odium et ludibrium" (*Opera* 2.771d–e, 772b).

11. "Jam habent et suos Silenos arcanae Litterae. . . . Euangelicas parabolas, si primum aestimes corticem, quis non judicet hominis esse idiotae? si nucem frangas, nimirum reperies arcanam illam, ac vere divinam sapientiam, planeque quiddam ipsi Christo simillimum" (*Opera* 2.773c–e).

REFERENCES

Allen, Don Cameron. *Mysteriously Meant: The Rediscovery of Pagan Symbolism and Allegorical Interpretation in the Renaissance.* Baltimore: Johns Hopkins University Press, 1970.

Allen, Judson Boyce. *The Friar as Critic: Literary Attitudes in the Late Middle Ages.* Nashville, Tenn.: Vanderbilt University Press, 1971.

Antonioli, Roland. "Le motif de l'avalage dans les chroniques gargantuines." In *Etudes seiziémistes offertes à V. L. Saulnier.* THR, 177. Geneva: Droz, 1980. Pp. 77–85.

———. *Rabelais et la médecine.* THR, 143. *ER* 12. Geneva: Droz, 1976.

Apollodorus. *The Library.* With an English translation by Sir James George Frazer. Loeb Classical Library. 2 vols. London: W. Heinemann, and New York: G. P. Putnam, 1921.

Aristotle. *Poetics,* with an English translation by W. Hamilton Fyfe. In *Aristotle, The Poetics. "Longinus," On the Sublime. Demetrius, On Style.* Rev. ed. Loeb Classical Library. Cambridge: Harvard University Press, 1932. Pp. 4–118.

Aronson, Nicole. *Les idées politiques de Rabelais.* Paris: Nizet, 1973.

Aubigné, Agrippa d'. *Les tragiques.* Ed. A. Garnier and J. Plattard. 4 vols. STFM. Paris: Didier, 1932–33.

Auerbach, Erich. *Mimesis: The Representation of Reality in Western Literature.* Trans. Willard R. Trask. Princeton: Princeton University Press, 1953.

Augustine [Aurelius Augustinus]. *The City of God Against the Pagans.* With an English translation by George E. McCracken, William M. Green, David S. Wiesen, Philip Levine, Eva Matthews Sanford, and William Chase Greene. Loeb Classical Library. 7 vols. London: W. Heinemann, and Cambridge: Harvard University Press, 1957–72.

———. *Saint Augustine's Confessions.* With an English translation by William Watts. Loeb Classical Library. 2 vols. London: W. Heinemann, and Cambridge: Harvard University Press, 1931.

Bakhtin, Mikhail. *L'Oeuvre de François Rabelais et la culture populaire au Moyen Age et sous la Renaissance.* Trans. Andrée Robel. Paris: Gallimard, 1970.

———. *Rabelais and His World.* Trans. Helene Iswolsky. Cambridge: MIT Press, 1968.

Bastiaensen, Michel. "La rencontre de Panurge." *Revue Belge de Philologie et d'Histoire* 52 (1974): 544–65.

Béné, Charles A. "Erasme et le chapitre VIII du premier Pantagruel (novembre 1532)." *Paedagogica Historica. International Journal of the History of Education* 1 (1961): 39–66.

Berrong, Richard M. "On the Possible Origin of the Name 'Nephelibates' (*Quart Livre,* Ch. 56)." *ER* 17 (1983): 93–94.

———. *Rabelais and Bakhtin: Popular Culture in* Gargantua and Pantagruel. Lincoln: University of Nebraska Press, 1986.

Bersuire, Pierre [Petrus Berchorius]. *Metamorphosis Ovidiana moraliter a Magistro Thoma Walleys Anglico . . . explanata.* Facsim. ed. Ed. Stephen Orgel. The Philosophy of Images, 1. 1509; rpt. New York: Garland, 1979.

Bible. *Biblia Hebraica Stuttgartensia.* Ed. K. Elliger, W. Rudolph et al. 2d ed. Stuttgart: Deutsche Bibelgesellschaft, 1984.

———. *Biblia, interprete Sebastiano Castalione, una cum eiusdem annotationibus.* Basel: J. Oporinus, 1551.

———. *Biblia sacra iuxta Vulgatam Clementinam.* Ed. A. Colunga and L. Turrado. 4th ed. Madrid: Biblioteca de Autores Cristianos, 1965.

———. *The New Oxford Annotated Bible with the Apocrypha.* Revised Standard Version. Ed. Herbert G. May and Bruce M. Metzger. Expanded ed. New York: Oxford University Press, 1977.

———. *Novum Testamentum Graece.* Ed. Alexander Souter. 2d ed. Oxford: Clarendon, 1947.

———. *The Septuagint with Apocrypha: Greek and English.* Ed. Sir Lancelot C. L. Brenton. 1851; rpt. Grand Rapids, Mich.: Zondervan, 1982.

———. *Textus Bibliae cum glossa ordinaria, Nicolai de Lyra postilla, moralitatibus eiusdem. . . .* 6 vols. Paris: Jacob Mareschal, 1528–29.

Boccaccio, Giovanni. *Genealogia deorum gentilium.* Ed. Vincenzo Romano. 2 vols. Bari: Laterza, 1951.

Brault, Gerard. "'Ung abysme de science': On the Interpretation of Gargantua's Letter to Pantagruel." *BHR* 28 (1966): 615–32.

Bruni, Leonardo. *Dialogus de tribus vatibus florentinis.* In *Prosatori latini del quattrocento,* ed. Eugenio Garin. La Letteratura Italiana, Storia e Testi, 13. Milan: Ricciardi, 1952. Pp. 44–99.

Budé, Guillaume. *Commentarii linguae graecae.* Paris: Jodocus Badius, 1529.

Burke, Peter. *Popular Culture in Early Modern Europe.* New York: New York University Press, 1978.

Calvin, Jean. *Institution de la religion chrestienne.* Ed. Jacques Pannier. 2d ed. 4 vols. Paris: Les Belles Lettres, 1961.

Cave, Terence. *The Cornucopian Text: Problems of Writing in the French Renaissance.* Oxford: Clarendon, 1979.

Chaeradamus, Joannes [Jean Chéradame]. *Lexicon graecum.* Paris: 1523.

Cicero [Marcus Tullius Cicero]. *De officiis.* With an English translation by Walter Miller. Loeb Classical Library. London: W. Heinemann, and New York: G. P. Putnam, 1913.

Coleman, Dorothy. *Rabelais: A Critical Study in Prose Fiction.* Cambridge: Cambridge University Press, 1971.

Comes, Natalis [Natale Conti]. *Mythologiae.* The Renaissance and the Gods. 1567; rpt. New York: Garland, 1976.

Concordance to the Novum Testamentum Graece. 3d ed. Institute for New Testament Textual Research and the Computer Center of Münster University. Berlin: Walter de Gruyter, 1987.

A Concordance to the Septuagint and the Other Greek Versions of the Old Testament. Ed. Edwin Hatch, Henry A. Redpath et al. 2 vols. and supplements. Oxford: Clarendon, 1897–1906.

Cotgrave, Randle. *A Dictionarie of the French and English Tongues*. Facsim. ed. Ed. William S. Woods. 1611; rpt. Columbia, S.C.: University of South Carolina Press, 1950.

Cranz, Ferdinand Edward. *A Bibliography of Aristotle Editions, 1501–1600*. 2d ed. revised by Charles B. Schmitt. Bibliotheca Bibliographica Aureliana, 38. Baden-Baden: Koerner, 1984.

Dante Alighieri. *La divina commedia*. Ed. Charles H. Grandgent. Rev. ed. Boston: D.C. Heath, 1933.

Defaux, Gérard. "Au coeur du *Pantagruel:* Les deux chapitres IX de l'édition Nourry." *Kentucky Romance Quarterly* 21 (1974): 59–96.

———. *Le curieux, le glorieux et la sagesse du monde dans la première moitié du seizième siècle: L'Exemple de Panurge (Ulysse, Demosthène, Empédocle)*. French Forum Monographs, 34. Lexington, Ky.: French Forum, 1982.

———. *Pantagruel et les sophistes: Contribution à l'histoire de l'humanisme chrétien au seizième siècle*. Archives Internationales d'Histoire des Idées, 63. The Hague: Nijhoff, 1973.

Dio [Cassius Dio Cocceianus]. *Dio's Roman History*. With an English translation by Earnest Cary. Loeb Classical Library. 9 vols. London: W. Heinemann, and New York: Macmillan, 1914–27.

Dionysius of Halicarnassus. *The Roman Antiquities*. With an English translation by Earnest Cary. Loeb Classical Library. 7 vols. Cambridge: Harvard University Press and London: W. Heinemann, 1937–50.

Du Bellay, Joachim. *Recueils lyriques de 1550 à 1553*. Vol. 4 of *Oeuvres poétiques,* ed. Henri Chamard. STFM. 1919; rpt. Paris: Nizet, 1983.

Duval, Edwin M. "Interpretation and the 'Doctrine Absconce' of Rabelais's Prologue to *Gargantua*." *ER* 18 (1985): 1–17.

———. "The Medieval Curriculum, the Scholastic University, and Gargantua's Program of Studies (*Pantagruel,* 8)." In *Rabelais's Incomparable Book: Essays on His Art,* ed. Raymond C. La Charité. French Forum Monographs, 62. Lexington, Ky.: French Forum, 1986. Pp. 30–44.

Erasmus, Desiderius. *Desiderii Erasmi opera omnia*. Ed. J. Clericus. 10 vols. in 11. 1703–06; rpt. Hildesheim: Georg Olms, 1961–62.

———. *Erasmi opuscula: A Supplement to the Opera Omnia*. Ed. Wallace K. Ferguson. The Hague: Nijhoff, 1933.

———. *Opus epistolarum Des. Erasmi Roterodami*. Ed. P. S. Allen. 12 vols. Oxford: Clarendon, 1906–65.

Eskin, Stanley G. "Mythic Unity in Rabelais." *PMLA* 79 (1964): 548–53.

Estienne, Robert. *Dictionarium poeticum, quod vulgo inscribitur Elucidarius carminum.* Paris: R. Stephanus, 1535.

Eusebius. *Die Kirchengeschichte . . . Die Lateinische Uebersetzung des Rufinus.* Eds. Eduard Schwartz and Theodor Mommsen. 3 vols. (vols. 2:1–3 of *Eusebius Werke*). Die Griechischen Christlichen Schriftsteller der ersten drei Jahrhundert. Leipzig: Hinrichs, 1903–09.

———. *Historia ecclesiastica.* Trans. Rufinus. In *Autores historiae ecclesiasticae,* ed. Beatus Rhenanus. Basel: Froben, 1523.

Febvre, Lucien. *Le problème de l'incroyance au seizième siècle: La religion de Rabelais.* 1942; rpt. Paris: Albin Michel, 1968.

Fowler, Alastair. *Kinds of Literature: An Introduction to the Theory of Genres and Modes.* Cambridge: Harvard University Press, 1982.

Françon, Marcel. *Autour de la lettre de Gargantua à son fils (Pantagruel, 8).* 2d ed. Cambridge: Harvard University Press, 1964.

Fumaroli, Marc. "Jacques Amyot and the Clerical Polemic Against the Chivalric Novel." *RQ* 38 (1985): 22–40.

Giraldi, Lilio Gregorio. *De deis gentium.* The Renaissance and the Gods. 1548; rpt. New York: Garland, 1976.

Gregory of Tours. *Historia Francorum.* Paris: Jodocus Badius, 1512.

———. *Historia Francorum.* Vol. 1:1 of *Gregorii Turonensis Opera,* ed. W. Arndt and Br. Krush. Monumenta Germaniae Historicae. Scriptores Rerum Merovingicarum, 1. Hanover, 1885.

———. *The History of the Franks.* Trans. Lewis Thorpe. New York: Penguin, 1974.

Griffin, Robert. "The Devil and Panurge." *Studi francesi* 47–48 (1972): 329–36.

Hale, David George. *The Body Politic: A Political Metaphor in Renaissance English Literature.* The Hague: Mouton, 1971.

Hampton, Timothy. *Writing from History: The Rhetoric of Exemplarity in Renaissance Literature.* Ithaca: Cornell University Press, 1990.

Horace [Quintus Horatius Flaccus]. *De arte poetica (Epistola ad Pisones).* In *Satires, Epistles, Ars Poetica,* with an English translation by H. Rushton Fairclough. Rev. ed. Loeb Classical Library. London: W. Heinemann, and Cambridge: Harvard University Press, 1929. Pp. 450–89.

———. *The Odes and Epodes.* With an English translation by C. E. Bennett. Rev. ed. Loeb Classical Library. London: W. Heinemann, and Cambridge: Harvard University Press, 1927.

Hugh of Saint Victor. *Allegoriae in vetus testamentum.* In vol. 175 of *Patrologiae cursus completus [Patrologia Latina],* ed. J.-P. Migne. Paris: Migne, 1854. Pp. 635–924.

———. *De bestiis et aliis rebus libri quatuor.* In vol. 177 of *Patrologiae cursus completus [Patrologia Latina],* ed. J.-P. Migne. Paris: Migne, 1854. Pp. 15–164.

Huguet, Edmond. *Dictionnaire de la langue française du seizième siècle.* 7 vols. Paris: Champion, 1927–33, and Didier, 1950–67.

Hyginus. *Fabulae.* Ed. H. I. Rose. 3d ed. Leiden: Sijthoff, 1967.

Isidore of Seville. *Etymologiarum sive Originum libri XX*. Ed. W. M. Lindsay. 2 vols. Oxford: Clarendon, 1911.

Jeanneret, Michel. *Des mets et des mots: Banquets et propos de table à la Renaissance*. Paris: José Corti, 1987.

Jerome [Eusebius Hieronymus]. *Sancti Eusebii Hieronymi Epistulae*. Ed. Isidorus Hilberg. Corpus Scriptorum Ecclesiasticorum Latinorum, 54–56. 3 vols. Vienna: Tempsky, 1910–18.

———. *Select Letters of Saint Jerome*. With an English translation by F. A. Wright. Loeb Classical Library. 1933; rpt. Cambridge: Harvard University Press, and London: W. Heinemann, 1963.

Kaiser, Walter. *Praisers of Folly: Erasmus, Rabelais, Shakespeare*. Cambridge: Harvard University Press, 1963.

Kantorowicz, Ernst H. *The King's Two Bodies: A Study in Medieval Political Theology*. Princeton: Princeton University Press, 1957.

La Charité, Raymond C. "Gargantua's Letter and *Pantagruel* as Novel." *L'Esprit Créateur* ("A Rabelais Symposium," ed. Jerry C. Nash) 21 (1981): 26–39.

———. *Recreation, Reflection and Re-creation: Perspectives on Rabelais's* Pantagruel. French Forum Monographs, 19. Lexington, Ky.: French Forum, 1980.

Lampe, G. W. H. *A Patristic Greek Lexicon*. Oxford: Clarendon, 1961.

Lefèvre d'Etaples, Jacques. *Commentarii in quatuor evangelia*. Basel: Andrea Cratander, 1523.

———. *Quincuplex psalterium. Fac-similé de l'édition de 1513*. THR, 170. Geneva: Droz, 1979.

Lefranc, Abel. *Rabelais: Etudes sur Gargantua, Pantagruel, le Tiers Livre*. Paris: Albin Michel, 1953.

Livy [Titus Livius]. *Livy*. With an English translation by B. O. Foster, Frank Gardner Moore, Evan T. Sage, and Alfred C. Schlesinger. Loeb Classical Library. 14 vols. London: W. Heinemann, and New York: G. P. Putnam, 1922–59.

Lubac, Henri de. *Corpus mysticum: L'Eucharistie et l'église au Moyen Age. Etude historique*. Paris: Aubier, 1944.

Lucan [Marcus Annaeus Lucanus]. *The Civil War (Pharsalia)*. With an English translation by J. D. Duff. Loeb Classical Library. London: W. Heinemann, and New York: G. P. Putnam, 1928.

Lucian. *The Downward Journey, or the Tyrant*. In vol. 2 of *Lucian*, with an English translation by A. M. Harmon. Loeb Classical Library. London: W. Heinemann, and New York: Macmillan, 1915. Pp. 1–57.

———. *Menippus*. In vol. 4 of *Lucian*, with an English translation by A. M. Harmon. Loeb Classical Library. London: W. Heinemann, and New York: G. P. Putnam, 1925. Pp. 71–109.

Machiavelli, Niccolò. *Il principe*. In *Opere*, ed. Ezio Raimondi. Milan: Mursia, 1969. Pp. 3–68.

Marliani, Joannes Bartholomaeus. *Topographia antiquae Romae*. Ed. François Rabelais. Lyon: Gryphius, 1534.

Marot, Clément. *L'Enfer.* In *Oeuvres satiriques,* ed. C. A. Mayer. London: Athlone, 1962. Pp. 53–73.

———. *Psaumes.* In *Les traductions.* Vol. 6 of *Oeuvres complètes,* ed. C. A. Mayer. Geneva: Slatkine, 1980. Pp. 317–472.

Masuccio Salernitano. *Il novellino.* Ed. Giorgio Petrocchi. I Classici Italiani. Florence: Sansoni, 1957.

More, Thomas. *Epigrammata.* In *Latin Poems,* ed. Clarence H. Miller, Leicester Bradner, Charles A. Lynch, and Revilo P. Oliver. Vol. 3:2 of *The Complete Works of St. Thomas More.* New Haven: Yale University Press, 1984.

———. *Utopia.* Ed. Edward Surtz, S.J., and J. H. Hexter. Vol. 4 of *The Complete Works of St. Thomas More.* New Haven: Yale University Press, 1965.

Moss, Ann. *Ovid in Renaissance France: A Survey of the Latin Editions of Ovid and Commentaries Printed in France before 1600.* Warburg Institute Surveys, 8. London: University of London, 1982.

A New Concordance of the Bible. Thesaurus of the Language of the Bible: Hebrew and Aramaic Roots, Words, Proper Names, Phrases and Synonyms. Ed. Abraham Even-Shoshan. Jerusalem: Kiryat Sefer, 1987.

Ovid [Publius Ovidius Naso]. *Metamorphoses.* With an English translation by Frank Justus Miller. 3d ed. revised by G. P. Goold. Loeb Classical Library. 2 vols. Cambridge: Harvard University Press, and London: W. Heinemann, 1976–77.

———. *P. Ovidii Nasonis Metamorphoseos libri moralizati cum pucherrimis fabularum principalium figuris.* Ed. Raphael Regius. With commentaries by Lactantius Firmianus, Petrus Lavinius, Philippus Beroaldus, Ludovicus Coelius Rhodoginus, and Iacobus Bononiensis. Lyon: Huguetan, 1518. Facsim. ed. The Renaissance and the Gods, 3. New York: Garland, 1976.

Ovide moralisé: Poème du commencement du quartorzième siècle. Ed. C. de Boer. 5 vols. 1915; rpt. Wiesbaden: Martin Sändig, 1966–68.

Pausanias. *Description of Greece.* With an English translation by W. H. S. Jones. Loeb Classical Library. 5 vols. London: W. Heinemann, and New York: G. P. Putnam, 1918–35.

Perottus, Nicolas. *Cornucopiae, sive linguae latinae commentarii.* Venice: Aldus, 1513.

Pierre de Beauvais. *Le bestiaire de Pierre de Beauvais (version courte).* Ed. Guy R. Mermier. Paris: Nizet, 1977.

Plato. *The Republic.* With an English translation by Paul Shorey. Loeb Classical Library. 2 vols. London: W. Heinemann, and Cambridge: Harvard University Press, 1935–37.

Plattard, Jean. *L'Oeuvre de Rabelais: Sources, invention et composition.* 1910; rpt. Paris: Champion, 1967.

Pliny [Gaius Plinius Secundus]. *Natural History.* With an English translation by H. Rackham. Loeb Classical Library. 10 vols. Cambridge: Harvard University Press, and London: W. Heinemann, 1938–63.

Plutarch. *Plutarch's Lives.* With an English translation by Bernadotte Perrin. Loeb

Classical Library. 11 vols. London: W. Heinemann, and New York: Macmillan, 1914–26.

———. *Apophthegmata laconica.* In vol. 3 of *Moralia,* with an English translation by F. C. Babbitt. Loeb Classical Library. London: W. Heinemann, and New York: G. P. Putnam, 1931.

———. *Les Vies des hommes illustres Grecs et Romains, comparées l'une avec l'autre par Plutarque de Chaeronaee, translatées de Grec en François.* Trans. Jacques Amyot. 2 vols. Paris: Michel de Vascosan, 1559.

———. *Vitae Graecorum Romanorumque illustrium, autore Plutarcho.* Ed. Simon Grynaeus. Basel: Iohann Bebel, 1531.

———. *Vitae Plutarchi Cheronei novissime post Jodocum Badium Ascensium longe diligentius repositae maioreque diligentia castigatae . . . necnon cum Aemilii Probi vitis.* Venice: Melchior Sessa and Petrus de Ravanis, 1516.

Quint, David. *Origin and Originality in Renaissance Literature: Versions of the Source.* New Haven: Yale University Press, 1983.

Rabelais, François. *Gargantua: Première édition critique faite sur l'editio princeps.* Ed. M. A. Screech and Ruth Calder. TLF, 163. Geneva: Droz, 1970.

———. *Oeuvres complètes.* Ed. Pierre Jourda. 2 vols. Paris: Garnier, 1962.

———. *Oeuvres de François Rabelais.* Ed. Abel Lefranc, Jacques Boulenger, Henri Clouzot, Paul Dorveaux, Jean Plattard, and Lazare Sainéan. 6 vols. Paris: Champion, 1913–31, and Geneva: Droz, 1955.

———. *Pantagruel: Première publication critique sur le texte original.* Ed. V. L. Saulnier. 2d ed. TLF, 2. 1946; Geneva: Droz, 1965.

———. *Pantagrueline prognostication pour l'an 1533. Les almanachs pour les ans 1533, 1535 et 1541. La grande et vraye pronostication nouvelle de 1544.* Ed. M. A. Screech, Gwyneth Tootill, Anne Reeve, Martine Morin, Sally North, and Stephen Bamforth. TLF, 215. Geneva: Droz, 1974.

———. *Le Quart Livre.* Ed. Robert Marichal. TLF, 10. Geneva: Droz, 1947.

———. *Le Tiers Livre.* Ed. M. A. Screech. TLF, 102. Geneva: Droz, 1964.

Rigolot, François. *Les langages de Rabelais.* THR, 121. *ER* 10. Geneva: Droz, 1972.

Robert, Paul. *Le Petit Robert: Dictionnaire alphabétique et analogique de la langue française.* Paris: Société du Nouveau Littré, 1972.

Sainéan, Lazare. *La langue de Rabelais.* 2 vols. 1922–23; rpt. Geneva: Slatkine, 1976.

Saulnier, V. L. *Le dessein de Rabelais.* Paris: Société d'Edition d'Enseignement Supérieur, 1957.

———. *Rabelais. I: Rabelais dans son enquête.* Paris: Société d'Edition d'Enseignement Supérieur, 1983.

Scève, Maurice. *Delie: Object de plus haulte vertu.* Ed. I. D. McFarlane. Cambridge: Cambridge University Press, 1966.

Schrader, Ludwig. *Panurge und Hermes: Zum Ursprung eines Charakters bei Rabelais.* Romanistische Versuche und Vorarbeiten, 3. Bonn: Romanisches Seminar der Universität Bonn, 1958.

Screech, Michael A. *L'Evangélisme de Rabelais: Aspects de la satire religieuse au seizième siècle*. THR, 32. *ER* 2. Geneva: Droz, 1959.

———. "The Meaning of Thaumaste (A Double-Edged Satire of the Sorbonne and of the *Prisca Theologia* of Cabbalistic Humanists)." *BHR* 22 (1960): 62–72.

———. *Rabelais*. Ithaca: Cornell University Press, 1979.

———. *The Rabelaisian Marriage: Aspects of Rabelais's Religion, Ethics and Comic Philosophy*. London: Edward Arnold, 1958.

Seneca [Lucius Annaeus Seneca]. *De ira*. Vol. 1 of *Moral Essays*, with an English translation by John W. Basore. Loeb Classical Library. London: W. Heinemann, and New York: G. P. Putnam, 1928. Pp. 106–355.

Seyssel, Claude de. *La monarchie de France et deux autres fragments politiques*. Ed. Jacques Poujol. Paris: d'Argences, 1961.

Stephens, Walter. *Giants in Those Days: Folklore, Ancient History, and Nationalism*. Lincoln, Nebraska: University of Nebraska Press, 1989.

Suidas [The Suda]. *Suidae Lexicon*. Ed. Ada Adler. Lexicographi Graeci, 1. 5 vols. 1928–38; rpt. Stuttgart: Teubner, 1967–71.

Textor, Joannes Ravisius [Jean Tixier]. *Officina*. Venice: Zalterius, 1588.

Tobler, Adolf, and Erhard Lommatzsch. *Altfranzösisches Wörterbuch*. 10 vols. in 11. Berlin: Weidmannsche Buchhandlung, 1925–36, and Wiesbaden: Franz Steine, 1954–76.

Torrentinus, Herman. *Elucidarius poeticus continens historias poeticas, fabulas, insulas, regiones, urbes*. . . . Basel: Keller, 1601.

Toussain, Jacques. *Lexicon graecolatinum*. Paris: C. Guillard, 1552.

Vergil [Publius Vergilius Maro]. *Virgil*. With an English translation by H. Rushton Fairclough. Rev. ed. Loeb Classical Library. 2 vols. Cambridge: Harvard University Press, and London: W. Heinemann, 1934–37.

Vida, Marco Girolamo. *The "De Arte Poetica."* Ed. and trans. Ralph G. Williams. New York: Columbia University Press, 1976.

Villon, François. *Oeuvres*. Ed. Auguste Longnon. 4th ed. rev. by Lucien Foulet. Les Classiques Français du Moyen Age. Paris: Champion, 1967.

Vincent de Beauvais. *Speculi maioris Vincentii Burgundi praesulis Belvacensis . . . tomi quattuor*. Venice: Dominicus Nicolinus, 1591.

Vives, Juan Luis. *De tradendis disciplinis, seu de institutione christiana*. Antwerp: Hillenius, 1531.

Weinberg, Bernard. *A History of Literary Criticism in the Italian Renaissance*. 2 vols. Chicago: University of Chicago Press, 1961.

Weinberg, Florence M. *The Wine and the Will: Rabelais's Bacchic Christianity*. Detroit: Wayne State University Press, 1972.

Xenophon. *Memorabilia and Oeconomicus*. With an English translation by E. C. Marchant. Loeb Classical Library. London: W. Heinemann, and New York: G. P. Putnam, 1923.

INDEX